TRADE UNIONS AND DEMOCRATIC PARTICIPATION IN EUROPE

Trade Unions and Democratic Participation in Europe

A scenario for the 21st century

Edited by
GERARD KESTER
HENRI PINAUD

Avebury

Aldershot • Brookfield USA • Hong Kong • Singapore • Sydney

Published by
Avebury
Ashgate Publishing Limited
Gower House
Croft Road
Aldershot
Hants GU11 3HR
England

Ashgate Publishing Company
Old Post Road
Brookfield
Vermont 05036
USA

British Library Cataloguing in Publication Data

Trade Unions and Democratic Participation
in Europe
     I. Kester, Gerard II. Pinaud, Henri
     331.0112094

     ISBN 1 85972 302 0

Library of Congress Catalog Card Number: 95-95-83296

Printed in Great Britain by
Antony Rowe Ltd, Chippenham, Wiltshire

Contents

Part II: analysis of experience

Part III: trade union - university cooperation on democratic participation

List of contributors

Janine Goetschy
Centre National de la Recherche Scientifique, Travail et Mobilités, University of Nanterres, France

Michael Gold
University of Westminster, London Management Centre, United Kingdom

Fausta Guarriello
University of Rome, Italy

John Holford
University of Hong Kong

Gérard Kester
African Workers' Participation Development Programme, Institute of Social Studies, The Hague, The Netherlands

Peter Leisink
University of Utrecht, The Netherlands

Jacques Monat
Consultant to the International Labour Organisation and the Institute of Social Studies, Geneva, Switzerland

Henri Pinaud
Centre National de la Recherche Scientifique, Laboratoire Georges Friedman, Conservatoire National des Arts et Métiers, France

Thoralf Ulrik Qvale
Labour Research Institute, Oslo, Norway

Åke Sandberg
The Centre for Work Environment Studies, Stockholm, Sweden

György Széll
University of Osnabrück, Germany

Daniel Vaughan-Whitehead
The International Labour Organisation, Central and Eastern European Team

Edward Zammit
Workers' Participation Development Centre, University of Malta

Acknowledgements

We would like to express our sincere thanks to all those who have worked on the publication of this book.

In Brussels:

The DGV of the European Commission, for its generous financial assistance.

In The Hague:

Antoinette Otto, APADEP Project Officer at the Institute of Social Studies, for the lay-out and type-setting of the book.

Raoul Galarraga, APADEP Research Assistant at the Institute of Social Studies, for preparing the bibliography.

In Paris:

Marcus Broadbent, for the translation of many chapters from French to English.

Preface
Trade unions: breaking new ground in democratic participation on Europe's new frontiers

Alain Benlezar

The European Union has only just come into effect and it is already at a crossroads. Shaken by a triple crisis - of identity, confidence and motivation, the EU has found itself incapable of responding to the concerns expressed by the Union's citizens and employees. The message that the latter have sent to the Union leaders has been poorly understood. And yet these messages came through loud and clear during the European debate on the ratification of the Maastricht Treaty. That message clearly underlined the two chronic failings that threaten the stability of the Community, namely, an ailing social situation and the prospect of an almost exclusively representative form of institutional democracy, which ignores the participation of the community's citizens.

But in order to rise to the challenges of an integrated Europe, stop endemic unemployment and social exclusion, create a Europe of justice, solidarity, social and economic cohesion, and to encourage the citizens of Europe to challenge international competition, the participation of everyone is essential. Participation must begin between workers and their trade unions.

Trade unions are already fully committed to solving today's social issues. But they have chosen to ignore the subject of participation. As a result, employers have wasted no time in claiming the issue for themselves, developing forms of managerial and financial participation which originally hails from Japan. These are simply the most recent and "fashionable" forms of participation. They are not an alibi for the absence of more meaningful forms of participation.

Today the trade unions are waking up. They want to be leading players in a new and profound reexamination of the role that workers and trade unions can play in strengthening democracy and encouraging economic and social development. And it is not a moment too soon!

Today the time is ripe for the ETUC to commit itself to rehabilitating democratic participation. The CFDT shares this conviction and believes that trade unions will succeed in becoming the driving force behind forms of direct or indirect participation at all levels of the economy, from company and regional level all the way up to national, European and international level. Confronted with these high social stakes, trade unions must assume a leading role in drawing up a negotiated and sufficiently audacious employment policy which will bring together and mobilise as large a group of players as possible, incorporating new elements beyond the scope of the traditional social actors of the past.

These convictions are based on an analysis of the present situation, which is characterised by the following major trends:

- renewed debate on the concept of democracy and its intrinsic values both in the West and in Eastern Europe where, since the disappearance of the Berlin Wall, economic systems have imploded and the Soviet Empire has collapsed.

- tremendous pressure from a new ultra-liberalism in politics and economics which, in the name of liberating economic relations, has been systematically dismantling any obstacles that stand in the way of investments or the movement of capital. Trade unions and the collective agreements which they have drawn up are being branded as hindrances to company competitiveness. This approach, based on greed and Manicheism, is being encouraged by dogmatic theoreticians who are categorically opposed to a trade union role as a social regulator, preferring instead the Reagan-Thatcherite credo of "union busting".

- pressure from another quarter, (Japanese in origin), based on the notions of competitiveness and productivity. This has led many managers to introduce participation schemes which bypass trade unions and others to reject a form of participation which involves a legitimate trade union partner.

- a weakening in the trade union movement and increased difficulties for unions in establishing themselves in the service industry, a sector that is often extremely splintered and comprised mostly of small and medium-sized enterprises. Furthermore, traditional forms of unionism and its methods are being seriously questioned. This demands a reexamination of the triangular relationship between trade unions, representative bodies and employees.

- a limit to the capacity of the welfare state which was based on the importance of social policies and was financed by considerable transfers. Keynesian interventionism has reached its limit, a situation exasperated by a radical change in company models.

- the relative failure of ultra-liberal capitalist policies which led to a confrontation between the individual, stripped of any protection, and the forces of a destructive and deregulative market.

- a change in the expression of solidarity with a move away from the collective to the individual and from a global defence of workers' interests to company corporatism.

- a growing social rift with, on the one hand, the socially-integrated, gainfully employed, earning a salary and, on the other hand, the socially excluded. This rift is leading to the disappearance of traditional social-professional groups while one factor - work - remains constant, as the main point of reference for societies in Western Europe and the rest of the world.

- a transition from an industrial era to a service-dominated era with reduced working hours and different way of organising time (work time, study time and free time).

- a more optimistic outlook for Union legislation on information and consultation, after decades of stalemate. This positive outlook is mainly due to the creation of European works councils, to bargaining and to the important pilot schemes that these have generated.

Any sudden spread of participation will not miraculously solve all the problems confronting workers and trade unions today. But it is an essential prerequisite for achieving negotiated solutions to our problems. Participation is also a prerequisite to any responsible choice to be made between the two strategies which will characterise social relations in the 21st century. That choice is between a cooperative and a conflict strategy, between dialogue and antagonism.

Should trade unions introduce participative principles and policies in Western Europe, such a move will have a considerable influence on developments in Central and Eastern Europe and the Third World. These countries are being tempted to adopt destructive models of liberalism that will rend asunder their social fabric, their culture and their environment. Witness the British or North American models, or, worse still, models imposed by authoritarian regimes bent on liberticide.

We realise that participation must go beyond workers' issues. It must spread beyond these limits to social issues that it has ignored until now. Participation is without doubt a formidable democratic tool. It will doubtless also prove to be the dynamic force behind a renewal of trade unionism.

In the social sector, the most important of all, there must be no limit to the trade unions' aspirations in terms of participation. Therefore we opt for Scenario 21, presented by the researchers. The democratic principles and values which define it require an unconditional commitment to all forms of participation. However, our goal is not to impose a transferable model of participation that can simply be imposed on any society or situation.

To enrich debate, close, long-term collaboration with universities and academics is called for. We need such collaboration in order to gain understanding about the situation today and to evaluate developments and various experiments already under way. This kind of collaboration will provide us with the means to better understand the ever-changing realities of the situation and find alternative solutions to the strategies put forward by employers designed to bypass the trade unions.

It is for these reasons that we have launched the present project which culminated in the ETUC colloquium entitled "Trade Unions and Democratic Participation" held in Paris between 2 and 4 March 1994. This colloquium was not an end in itself. It should be seen as the first in the trade union movement's steps to claim back democratic participation.

At this point I would like to extend my warmest thanks to the European Commission, especially the DGV for its commitment and help, without which this project would never have got off the ground. It has helped us begin to break new ground in democratic participation on Europe's new frontiers.

Alain Benlezar is an official of the International Department of the Confédération Française Démocratique du Travail (CFDT)

Part I
POLICIES AND STRATEGIES

Introduction
Democratic participation: A challenge for democracy

Gérard Kester and Henri Pinaud

However unfashionable the subject may be today, it is essential that a renewed, fundamental debate be launched on one of the essential elements of democracy - worker participation. There is an underlying no-nonsense attitude in the current approach to neo-liberalism, privatisation and structural adjustments. Participation is conspicuously absent in this approach. In the years after the fall of the Berlin Wall, worker participation was associated with the failed socialist or Marxist systems of Eastern Europe and the Third World. When employers and more conservative forces are not being openly hostile to participation, they simply block any further infringements of managerial prerogatives and attempt to transform participatory structures into tools for management. Those forces which promote participation have been driven apart, misled or defeated by privatisation, by employers' initiatives to introduce capital-oriented forms of participation and by Thatcherism. These forces must now regroup.

Re-opening the debate on democratic participation is not a sign of nostalgia for utopian ideals. The defence and development of worker participation are essential if democracy itself is to be defended and is to grow. Only by strengthening democracy can we hope to respond to the unprecedented challenges thrown up by the new world of turbulent change in which we live. Worker participation, we believe, must be a priority in the defence of democracy in general.

The more immediate aim of the debate proposed here is to carry out a thorough analysis of developments in worker participation and industrial relations over the last twenty years and to consider short and long-term policy options, both in Europe and worldwide. The long-term aim of this debate is to create a lasting framework for more purposeful and consistent cooperation in participation policy-making, policy implementation, education and research.

To this end, we seek to re-establish committed links and cooperation between trade union and universities. Thus, in this book, we present a compilation of many years of research results for trade union consideration and evaluation.

Worker participation in Western Europe

Worker participation was a dynamic and growing phenomenon in many Western European countries in the 1960s and 1970s. By the end of the 1960s, most countries in Western Europe had experienced numerous social uprisings, protests against bad working conditions and a form of work organisation which condemned workers to humiliating tasks which offered no future and no interest. These social movements were decisive in provoking increased union demands for improvements to the quality of the work environment and the development of various direct and indirect forms of worker participation. The unrest also played an important role in prompting a search for and experimentation with new forms of work organisation, proposed by management and employers. Expressions of anger gradually diminished with the rise of unemployment and the weakening of the trade union movement and as employers at least partially heeded the demands of the 1970s. But workers' concerns about working conditions did not diminish, as is illustrated in many studies (see Chapter I). Furthermore, several research projects on worker participation showed that wherever conditions made this possible, there was a latent need for participation on the part of workers (see Chapter 3).

In the 1980s unemployment, working hours, wages and deregulation became the immediate worries of the workers, and trade unions returned to their traditional strategies of bargaining, industrial action and indirect representative participation within and beyond the workplace.

Although the initial main thrust towards democratic participation came from the workers and their trade unions, it is clear that governments have, in cooperation with or at the instigation of trade unions, also played an important role in the development of various direct and indirect forms of worker participation. This has been achieved constitutionally as in Italy, or by legislation passed by Labour, Socialist or Social-Democratic governments in Malta, the Netherlands, France, Germany and other countries. These governments have also offered financial support and facilitated participation schemes in the public sector and nationalised companies. Funding for education, training and academic research into worker participation has considerably helped spread and legitimate worker participation.

In terms of worker participation, the 1980s was a decade of stagnation but during those same years some existing forms of participation were enshrined in legal form while educational and advice services were also introduced. The 1980s saw a rapid rise in management and employer-initiated forms of participation. Conservative governments launched "people's capitalism" schemes, such as profit-sharing and employee-ownership. Thus, progress in worker participation veered off-course. This was participation as an ingredient of capitalism. In the United Kingdom, where both profit-sharing and employee share-ownership schemes were widely introduced in the 1980s, a major study showed that these schemes have tended to reduce the influence of workers in decision-making (Baddon et al, 1989).

2

It is ironic that employee and management organisations are now rapidly setting up national and international structures to defend their own forms of worker participation while trade unions, when not rejecting participation outright, remain totally divided over its aims, principles and forms (Chapter 1).

In the forthcoming elaboration of the EU social policy, it is to be feared that a tug-of-war between trade unions and employer organisations may lead to an ugly compromise. Doubtless, employers will claim that information and consultation at low management levels represent an area in which participation should be developed. Employers will stick to the long-established ILO principles of negotiation and bargaining and will agree to explore further forms of financial participation but will veto any further infringements of their decision-making prerogatives. If this proves to be the case, it will mean that a long-term trend towards increased democratic participation will be halted. Not only will development cease at national level, it will also stop at the intra-national level. Previously, a handful of countries in Europe were leaders in democratic participation, while other countries followed suit. Today this trend has ceased. The momentum has been lost.

But at the same time participation at the lowest managerial levels and financial participation (initiated by employers and managers) are on the increase. The emphasis is on "human resource development" and not on "labour development". Worker participation is becoming an expression of capital, a thirst for gold (Baddon et al, 1989) rather than a thirst for democracy.

Beyond Western Europe

The immediate concern of this book is developments in EU countries. Here, renewed enthusiasm for democratic participation is urgently needed to provide a new boost to the European social policy. The debate on the European works councils, European guidelines on information, consultation, education and training and the development of EU directives all add to the urgency of the matter. The ETUC is already engaged in this debate and has embraced this project as an opportunity for deepening and strengthening the impact of its policies on democracy at work and democracy in the economy, within the EU.

But is it acceptable to think in terms of an EU social policy alone? We may be totally absorbed by problems of European integration, but the rest of Europe is falling apart around us. Can we afford to adopt a trade union policy for the EU alone and simply wait and see if, how, when other European countries will eventually join the Union? And what about the Third World? Poor and exploited already, it is heading for an unprecedented disaster, especially in Africa.

An EU policy which does not take these wider challenges into account is a policy of shame. Remarkably, labour relations represent an area of great importance in these future global developments. This means that trade unions, with their tradition of international solidarity, have a special responsibility.

Today the reactions of the countries of Central and Eastern Europe and the Republics of the former Soviet Union reflect exactly the type of EU policy that employers would like to see formulated. These countries are developing unfettered market economies and the odds are very much against democratic participation. Workers, trade unions and the general public are suspicious of participation with its associations with the old political ideologies and systems. Behind the smokescreen of "democratic privatisation", foreign (i.e. Western European and American) capital is buying up the better parts of what used to be called "the means of production".

For trade unions at European level, the developments in Central and Eastern Europe are of immediate concern. The ETUC includes trade union federations from several Central and Eastern European countries and affiliations with trade unions from non-EU countries can be expected to grow in the near future. So an ETUC policy must embrace more than the EU. The need for a vigorous trade union response to employer and management-inspired definitions of labour relations is no less important in Central and Eastern Europe than it is in the EU (see Chapter 15).

Africa also has considerable experience with worker participation. By and large experiments in Africa have floundered, drifting from utopia to dogma, from dogma to slogans, slogans to repression, repression to dictatorship and from dictatorship to military regimes. Participation has echoed this downward spiral, moving from economic and social liberation to manipulation and from there to exploitation. Africa has now entered a period of turbulent political, economic and social transition. Structural adjustments are improving the economy for the few, while the many are being marginalised. While multi-party democracy is rapidly spreading, democracy at work and in labour relations is being reduced.

In Asia, Japan has increasingly become a point of reference in terms of labour relations, in particular because of its styles of management. Japan remains an important and fertile area from which to learn about participation. But the country's own institutions are undergoing considerable changes as they become less and less part and parcel of Japanese socio-cultural traditions (see Chapter 16).

At the risk of oversimplifying the argument, one could say that 19th century capitalism now has free play in Eastern Europe and Africa. There was at least a "social dimension" to be found in the countries of Eastern Europe and Africa during the period of the planned economies. Does such a dimension still exist today in the liberal market economies of these same countries? The shift from the public to the private sector is remorseless. Decisions are now rapidly being taken which are fundamentally transforming the economic, social and political landscape, without the workers' voices being heard in any effective way.

The internationalisation and the globalization of the economy means that we can no longer think in terms of Europe alone. The challenge that democratic participation represents is not unique to the EU or to Europe. This is a global challenge. The EU is committed to the socio-economic development of Central and Eastern Europe and the Third World. EU social policy and indeed EU participation policy might prove to be points of reference for other countries and continents.

Beyond the year 2000

In discussing distant future, George Orwell's "1984" has long been taken as a benchmark date. More recently, the year 2000 has supplanted it. But the closer 2000 comes, the more we are forced to look beyond and into the 21st century. Western Europe needs a long-term, global vision of the future and this is also true for other parts of the world where increasing social disintegration can be expected as conservatism, ethno-centrism and nationalism continue to spread.

The globalization of the world economy is taking place following the principles of the free market economy. The "new world order" which was supposed to pay us the so-called "peace dividend" is now being shaped by a triumphant capitalism, whose social policy is yet to be defined.

Important long-term changes in industrial relations are becoming increasingly clear. The labour market is not only heading towards lasting, structural unemployment but also to increasing part-time work, lean production, teleproduction, short-term employment contracts and hence, higher turnover. Migration adds to the unrest in the labour market and provokes serious problems of ethnic conflict and racism. Women, unemployed youngsters and, in a number of countries, early pensioners are some of the special "problem groups" within the workforce. The power structure of capital ownership is becoming increasingly elusive as capital is displaced as a result of decentralisation, relocation, privatisation and internationalisation. With this come shifting seats of power and accountability. Individualism is on the increase as are stress, violence and criminality. These worrying tendencies must be seen against a backdrop of population growth, migration, environmental pollution and increasing inequalities within and between countries and continents.

Faced with these fundamental changes in the societies of Western, Central, Eastern Europe and the Third World, it is imperative that we reexamine the internal problems of the market economy. In the light of the development of unfettered liberalism, democratic participation appears to be of strategic value both as an approach and as an ultimate objective.

A new elan for democratic participation

Since the advent of industrialisation, workers have been fighting to win a more democratic basis to their labour. In Chapter 3 of Part I, a debate on the intrinsic values and aspects of worker participation will be developed. It will be argued that participation is a basic human right and that ultimately, political democracy cannot flourish without social and economic democracy. The right of workers and their representatives to have access to decision-making on all matters directly or indirectly affecting their social and economic status is based on the fact that workers are partners in the production process.

The development of democratic worker participation in Western Europe is stagnating and in many other parts of the world it is on the wane. Worker participation is no longer a popular subject for political or trade union platforms. Organised employers, either by intuition or by design, urged on by the increasing popularity of capitalism, have done their utmost to link worker participation to capital. It is here that the strongest lines of defence must be erected, both in Western Europe, Eastern Europe and elsewhere in the world.

A new dynamism is needed. Innovation and creativity are required. We do not need more of the same or the transplantation of "models" and "systems", we need a new response to new realities. Within the institutionalised patterns of industrial relations over the last fifty years, a number of classic forms of participation have been established and developed in various countries. These include works councils, "*droit d'expression*", worker involvement, "*Mitbestimmung*", etc. These forms of participation, while still valid as democratic instruments in work organisations, do not provide democratic answers to the new problems thrown up by the social market economy, such as deregulation, different forms of employment and many of the problems mentioned in the earlier sections of this introduction ("Beyond Western Europe", "Beyond the year 2000"). A new, long-term vision of the future is required.

To achieve this it is necessary to differentiate between the different levels of development in democratic participation. The work organisation level remains very important but in order to achieve really democratic participation and tackle problems at sectoral, regional and national levels, new initiatives are needed. The rapid internationalisation and globalization of the economy have prompted a need for a form of democratic control at this level. Different strategies are required for these different levels. It is now clear that "European models" are unlikely to prove successful. The seemingly interminable "Vredeling directives" are a good illustration of this (see contribution by Janine Goetschy in Part I, Chapter 2, and in Part II, Chapter 13). National strategies will be required in order to develop democracy within the context of the social, economic, political and legal traditions of a specific country. Transplanting forms of democratic participation from one country to another may create insurmountable problems (see Gold on worker directors in the United Kingdom, Chapter 9).

A European strategy would address democratic regulation of supranational issues (e.g. the European works councils) or the development of general policies, to be worked out in detail later by each country as it sees fit. European integration is now a goal to which we are committed and participative democracy can provide a trade union response to the increasing problems of nationalism in Europe. The new Europe now emerging is presently characterised not by subsidiarity but by regional divorce.

A new dynamism thus implies new vision and renewed commitment. Recently, the concept of citizenship has been revived (Coenen and Leisink, 1993). For many years the word had "bourgeois" connotations but with growing awareness that, in addition to civil, political and social rights, citizens also have democratic rights that must be claimed, exercised and defended. The term is now far more often understood as a part of participative democracy. The economic rights of citizens include the right to form trade unions (still not respected in some countries), the right to negotiate, the right to information and the right to consultation and co-determination. The advantage of adopting the notion of citizenship is that it places democratic participation in a broader context and as a result is more directly linked to political democracy. The challenge is to apply the concept of participation to the world of work and workers and not limit it to work organisation alone.

The role of universities

This challenge is not only confined to trade unions. The lack of interest in worker participation is a general social phenomenon and has affected supporting institutions outside the trade unions. One report shows that the amount of academic research into worker participation is substantially lower today that it was in the 1970s. The report continues "both policy makers and researchers...are increasingly inclined to view participation as a luxury that their country cannot currently afford" (Report Research Committee X of the International Sociological Association, 1992).

Universities are now becoming training grounds where students are prepared for employment in the economy. Austerity has hit universities and education budgets throughout Europe and employers have successfully lobbied to ensure that education is geared to more practical ends, tailored to their needs. But universities and research institutes should serve trade unions as much as the other social partners, such as employers.

Universities must once again assume the important role they can play in supporting trade unions to develop policies on democratic participation. They can do so by conducting permanent research in the area. In the long-term, a permanent supporting structure should be envisaged to coordinate trade union - university cooperation. These arguments will be developed in Part III.

A challenge for the trade union movement

Today, the trade union movement is in a strategic position to reinforce democratic participation at all levels from the workplace to national and international level, within Europe and beyond. The unions must choose between two major policy options:

7

either

(a)   the trade unions continue their action through negotiations and bargaining and, when deemed necessary, resort to the "strike" weapon. Trade unionism characterised by claims, bargaining and strikes is essential in a capitalist system and must be defended and developed. But there is a danger that all union energy may be directed at issues surrounding the employment contract such as wages and the work environment. This would leave economic and social policy within and beyond company level, beyond the reach of democratic control.

or

(b)   the trade unions continue to develop a participation policy in parallel with and not in place of bargaining. The unions could focus much of their energies into seeking ways of taking an active part in decision-making processes at all levels of the economy. Thus trade unionism would be characterised not only by claims but also by proposals (*"syndicalisme de proposition"*) in the workplace and beyond: proactive trade unionism.

There are many compelling reasons for choosing the second option. For if the unions do not make it clear that *they* are staunch defenders of worker participation, then employers will. Indeed employers have already done so in recent years. Today employers have the initiative in participation which the trade unions could have had themselves. Managers make use of participation as a stopgap device for collective bargaining. In doing so they transform worker participation into a tool of human resource management rather than a tool of democratic control over capital. Once employers have established their own participation schemes, these schemes are encouraged as a forum in which to take up wage-contract issues. Thus at the very least this can produce a dual system of representation of the interests of workers, with obvious advantages to the employers. At the very worst such schemes can threaten the very existence of trade unions.

The second compelling reason why the trade unions should choose the second option is that if they do not, they could very easily come to be regarded as mere troublemakers, both by the general public and by workers. Employers may push the unions increasingly towards conflictual action, preserving for themselves the "democratic forum" and thereby casting themselves as responsible partners in comparison to union troublemakers.

These two arguments can prove very useful when examining what is widely referred to today as "the trade union crisis". Renewed interest in democratic participation on the part of the trade unions could be of immense value. It would help bolster existing forms of participation and make participation a prominent feature of the process of democratisation. This can be achieved by making employer and management-initiated forms of participation more democratic and by bringing a much wider range of labour and socioeconomic issues under democratic control. The effectiveness of existing forms of participation could be improved by placing greater emphasis on the structure or restructuring of work organisation and organisational policies rather than adopting a defensive attitude and concentrating solely on the very limited sphere of employment conditions. Clearly, this new dynamism to promote participation will require considerable new investments and this will have consequences for trade union orientation, organisation, education and training.

In the final chapter of Part I three possible scenarios will be presented for discussion:

- the "Bread and Butter" or "Wage Packet" Scenario
- the "Consolidation" Scenario
- the "Growth of Democratic Participation" Scenario, or "Scenario 21"

1 The role of social actors during recent developments in worker participation in ten countries of Western Europe

(Belgium, Denmark, France, Germany, Italy, Malta, the Netherlands, Norway, Sweden and the United Kingdom)

Henri Pinaud

Introduction

In the second section of this book the reader will find articles describing in detail recent developments in direct and indirect worker participation in ten countries of Western Europe. It is on the basis of that material that an attempt has been made in this chapter to outline answers to four major questions concerning the social actors in these different countries. But first it is essential to clarify what is meant by "direct and indirect participation".

The five main forms of participation

The three main forms of indirect participation

a)   "conventional collective bargaining" concerns the substance of work contracts and working conditions in the broadest sense of the term and involves employee organisations (trade unions), management and or employer organisations. In this form of participation the trade unions have a dual role. They stand up against employers, whose interests, as in all conflicts for power, are clearly different from their own and at the same time they assume the role of an independent opposition, monitoring the "rules of the democratic game".

b)   "joint consultation" and or "co-management" exists in regional, national and international organisations composed either only of trade union and management representatives or which also include government representatives (tripartite organisations). Such bodies can control considerable budgets such as unemployment compensation funds, social security funds or vocational training budgets. They may also have a consultative role, such as the Economic and Social Councils, the French Work Accident Prevention Committee or the International Labour Organisation.

c) "co-determination" differs from collective bargaining in the sense that it is a specific democratic institution in which the employees wield influence by means of specific procedures and in which the employees enjoy decision-making power through the intermediary of their representatives. They are thus able to make their voices heard on matters concerning work organisation on the shop-floor or at higher levels in the company hierarchy. By definition the decisions taken are no longer based on the interests of capital but also on the interests of the workers themselves. The best example of co-determination is the German "Mitbestimmung" system which grants staff and trade union representatives the right to sit on company supervisory committees and works councils. More watered-down forms of co-determination also exist elsewhere. French works councils, staff assembly meetings and various types of joint consultation are examples.

The two main forms of direct participation

d) organisational participation or "participative management" has workers either directly or indirectly involved in the operational management of a company mainly by means of various forms of shop-floor participation such as quality circles, semi-autonomous groups or systems in which workers are encouraged to assume greater responsibility for their work. Thus the workers become involved in the organisation of the production process rather than in the making of strategic choices or decisions.
Some forms of participation are half way between co-determination and participative management. Examples include health and safety councils. If they only implement decisions already taken as part of a general company policy they are nevertheless forms of participative management. But they are forms of co-determination to the extent that they contribute to drawing up health and safety policy. One can generally say that this is the case for works councils, project groups, etc.

e) "financial participation" is a procedure by which employees share in the profits and the capital of a company (profit-sharing and employee share-ownership systems).

The task at hand

We have attempted to provide some answers to four main questions. The first of these questions concerns the presence and importance of participation, particularly organisational (participative management) or financial forms and the extent to

12

which such participation is included in the strategies and action of management. The second question concerns how European trade union organisations view worker participation. The third examines the importance of the role of government and international institutions (such as the European Commission) in participation and the fourth concerns workers' representation, expectations, demands and feelings about participation.

Employers and direct participation

Organisational participation in companies

Since the 1970s, following social uprisings in many Western European countries and the crisis in demand for goods and services, employers, especially in non-protected sectors of industry, have found themselves faced with growing international competition and the rapid development and spread of technology.

Faced with targets which constantly had to be adjusted, private companies, and to a lesser extent, public sector companies have tried various forms of organisational adaptation to market fluctuations.

In companies with a traditional form of work organisation and virtually no technical modernisation, the first step was to try to introduce a dual form of flexibility - internal flexibility through stock management and external flexibility through dismissals (even if this meant rehiring when conditions improved) and more frequent use of short-term employment contracts and sub-contracting.

Other companies invested in the modernisation of their production processes (mechanisation, robotisation and computerisation) and implemented new production management methods, (lean production - zero stocks/zero delays/zero defects). The result was a reduction in the number of low-qualified jobs but the general principles of Taylorism were nevertheless preserved. The preservation of the Taylorist structures and practices also implied a need for external flexibility.

Some companies tried to make the Taylorist model more flexible by introducing participative management of human resources: a mixture of modernisation of the production processes, attempts at decentralising operational decision-making, decompartmentalisation and company coherence achieved more by persuasion and integration than by rules. In theory, the techniques of participative management allow for multiple forms of internal organisation adjustment - enriching and redefining jobs, flexibility, quality circles, project groups, semi-autonomous groups, autonomous profit centres, corporate culture, corporate projects, etc.

However these methods do not exclude the use of short-term employment and simply shift the external adjustments on to the sub-contracting company. Furthermore, the form and the essentially productivist goals of these methods are also closely controlled by management and as a result these methods have little effect on Taylorist organisation (Tchobanian, 1990).

Other companies attempted to introduce a more or less coherent mixture of part measures taken partially from one or another of the above approaches.

Recent research in France into different sectors of activity (part of the PAROLES 2 programme, cf chapter 17), has highlighted the difficulty in linking company modernisation with management-prompted forms of direct participation. Not only do the terms refer to totally different concepts, they are also sometimes diametrically opposed. This research was unable to establish a correlation between implementation of forms of participation and variations in the economic effectiveness of the systems of production of goods and services.

Participative methods of management which directly involve workers to a greater or lesser degree and in varying forms have developed throughout Western Europe with varying degrees of success. These countries include Italy, Germany, the Netherlands, Belgium, Scandinavia, Sandberg, the United Kingdom and France (see Part II). This development has had to contend with the strength of unions which have generally been hostile to the concept. Company hierarchy has also been a decisive factor, either as a catalyst or an obstacle in the implementation of this process.

This form of direct worker participation is therefore essentially a management initiative and is the main contribution of employers to the participation process in recent years. These moves on the part of employers are not new, but are part and parcel of their traditional attempts to ensure that the autonomous management of a company is not directly influenced by worker representatives. There has been a long history of employer resistance to workers' attempts to introduce "worker control" into company life (Tchobanian, 1991).

This employer offensive, of which one of the intentional or accidental side-effects was to short-circuit the union-elected or designated representatives in the company, has greatly hampered national union organisations, often leaving them on the defensive. This policy of seeking increased flexibility has also greatly contributed to making jobs and wages far less secure (increases in sub-contracting and job insecurity). It has also contributed to raising unemployment and, consequently, an anarchic destruction of the fabric of society. These employer tactics have been organised at European level since 1987 by the European Federation of Quality Circles Associations and since 1988 by the European Federation of Quality Management.

Financial participation

Financial participation in the form of profit-sharing has met with increasing success in private-sector companies in several countries of Western Europe. In some case government support has been provided (in the form of legislation as in France, Great Britain, Greece and Ireland) while in others there has been virtually no government intervention (Belgium, Italy and Scandinavia). However until today the phenomenon remains virtually unknown in former West Germany (cf Vaughan-Whitehead, Chapter 14).

But different forms of participation in capital (internal employee share-ownership plans encouraged by company buy-ups by employees, etc.) do not seem to have proved as successfull in Western Europe.

In France, for example, in 1990, only 600-800 companies were issuing stock options to some 40,000 employees. The possibility of company buy-ups by employees has often been regarded with suspicion by trade unions and has not taken off in France. Apart from one or two exeptional cases, the concept has not gained ground in Belgium either (van Leemput, 1993).

Only in Scandinavia and the United Kingdom, with its "popular capitalism" have attempts been made to develop worker participation in capital. With a weakened economy and rising unemployment, Denmark, followed by Norway and Sweden, have introduced share-ownership plans for workers in the hope of consolidating companies' financial health (Qvale, chapter 12). In Sweden convertible bonds (which after several years could be transformed into shares at advantageous rates) were offered during the economic boom of the late 1980s and today are issued amongst most workers of large companies despite trade union indifference or open hostility (Sandberg, chapter 11). In 1989 there were some 1,000 examples of financial participation in the United Kingdom, involving between 7-9% of the workforce (Gold, chapter 9). Since then, a mushrooming of laws encouraging share ownership systems has led to a rapid rise in the number of employee share-holders.

Trade union organisations and workers' participation

Indirect participation

Basic trade union strategy remains the consolidation and strengthening of indirect participation both within the company and beyond, by means of elected staff representatives and trade union representatives. Therefore European trade union organisations intend to continue to try to develop worker participation mainly by increasing the means and powers of bodies of worker representation and by developing collective bargaining.

In Italy, from 1974 onwards, the right to information became increasingly widespread in State owned and private companies. More recently, in the Zanussi group (1991), co-management was won in areas such as quality, productivity levels, safety, trade union training, personnel training and environmental issues. From 1976 onwards, collective bargaining in different professions produced a spread in the right to information in worker councils. During the 1980s large public sector companies set up joint consultative committees that operated at different levels. The most recent sectoral collective agreements, such as those in the chemical and metalworking industries, stipulate besides the right to information, the setting up of permanent bodies with equal worker-employer representation. These bodies process the vast amounts of information available and undertake joint initiatives to tackle issues such as the job market, training, job classification, health and safety, etc., (see Guarriello, Chapter 7).

In France the 1982 and 1983 Auroux laws (mainly inspired by the trade unions) and much of the legislation since then, have strengthened works councils and health and safety councils (which oversee operational budgets, have the right to call in experts, and to refuse work in dangerous situations and oversee a generally wider area of competence). These laws also stipulated an annual obligation for negotiations in companies on matters such as wages, hours, work organisation, the work environment and vocational equality. These laws paved the way for the election of worker representatives on the supervisory boards of nationalised companies. It is from this time on that one can discern an important shift in national intersectoral and sectoral bargaining. From the end of the Second World War until the early 1980s there were only a few hundred company bargaining negotiations each year. This rapidly rose to several thousand. National bargaining began to change, attempting to reach agreements on "content". This meant that these agreements would be applied comprehensively at company level. The 1988 and 1989 national intersectoral agreements concerning the introduction of new technology, changes in working hours, the work environment and professional equality were known as the "orientation" agreements or "framework" agreements. They only stipulated the general guidelines on which the signatories agreed, thus leaving it to different industrial sectors and companies to decide on and implement the details (see Pinaud, Chapter 5).

In the Netherlands, unions generally represent workers' interests through collective bargaining, mainly at sectoral, regional and company level. But it is through works councils and in particular by developing their bargaining powers and increasing the powers of worker delegates that the FNV believes it will win better participatory rights for workers. Obviously a main goal of union activity is to provide support for elected representatives and improve coordination between sectoral and company negotiation. This has become even more important in recent years as works councils have become potential rivals to the unions at company level. Despite trade union demands, neither the unions nor works councils have been granted the right to elect worker representatives to supervisory boards, except in some public companies and private companies in which the works councils have the right to put forward or propose candidates. Nevertheless the boards have retained their prerogative to appoint their own members (see Leisink, Chapter 8).

In Belgium, the participatory rights of the workers remain limited. The works council is mainly a body providing information and advice. While management directly appoints its own nominees to this body, workers' representatives are chosen every four years by all employees in the company in what are called social elections. In 1975, the obligation to set up works councils was extended to the private non-market sector. Until recently, only representative workers' organisations could nominate candidates. In 1987, the National Confederation of Middle Management also won the right to propose candidates. This presents a problem of balance between management and workers on the council, as middle management representatives often take a stand closer to management than to the other trade unions (Van Leemput, 1993).

In Scandinavia, reforms in the 1970s were instituted whereby workers and/or local unions in Sweden, Norway and Denmark were allocated one third of all seats on company boards of directors (see Qvale, Chapter 12). In Sweden, where there are no works councils, but local "union clubs" elected by the workplace members, there is a tendency to replace or supplement detailed negotiations with different forms of project groups or committees including union representatives and management (see Sandberg, Chapter 11).

The German system of co-determination in companies offers union members an important role in outlining and discussing claims and drawing up company agreements in coordination with sectoral or regional union organisations. Here, too, there is no doubt that the DGB regards co-determination as the principal form of worker participation (see Szell, Chapter 6).

One key characteristic of British industrial relations is the central role of collective bargaining in regulating the workplace. In the 1980s, collective bargaining and joint-consultation remained very much alive in certain industrial sectors and in larger companies, but overall there has been a serious drop in both. The 1990 Workplace Industrial Relations Survey (Millward et al., 1992) revealed that 71% of British employees had been covered by collective bargaining in 1984, but only 54% by 1990 (see Gold, Chapter 9).

It should not be forgotten that in several countries, a drop in union representation on worker representative bodies in companies has made union organisations fearful that these bodies are attempting to replace trade unions and their role in collective bargaining with employers. Between 1990 and 1991 more than 50% of representatives on works councils in France were elected on non-union lists. In the Netherlands, a third of those elected to works councils were not unionised. This percentage is much higher in some specific sectors of industry such as the commercial service sector where union membership is low (see Leisink, Chapter 8). The FNV recently lost a case it had brought against a works council for having signed an agreement with the employers which the union deemed as unacceptable.

In Belgium, according to Vilrokx & Van Leemput (1992), the trade unions - not the works councils - are entitled to conclude collective agreements with management. They are therefore well adapted to dealing with decentralised negotiations, though occasionally agreements are concluded at company level which are counter to general union policies.

Finally, the resolutions of the 7th ETUC statutory congress place great emphasis on developing European-wide social dialogue through collective bargaining and the action of worker representative bodies. These efforts are particularly relevant in the light of the directive for the European works councils.

17

Discussion of industrial democracy has mostly been prompted by European trade union organisations. But for the last fifteen years, direct worker participation as envisaged by trade unions in the 1970s (self-management or worker control) has not been a central concern for trade union organisations, except in Scandinavia, France and Malta and to a certain extent, Germany. Nor has it represented one of the main areas of confrontation between the social partners.

In Malta, various forms of direct participation have been introduced since 1971, in the public and nationalised sectors. There is even a Yugoslav-inspired form of self-management which has been operating since 1975 at a leading company called Malta Drydocks. This was set up by a Labour government (1971-1979) with trade union support. However, the company has encountered serious economic difficulties over the past decade due to the international recession in the ship-building industry. As a result the company has been able to operate with generous public subsidies.

Today, under a Nationalist government, it seems that direct participation will take the form of a cooperative system in the public sector, while the self-management system is unlikely to be expanded (see Zammit, Chapter 10).

In France, following demands for self-management in the late 1970s, three trade union organisations, the CFDT, and to a lesser extent the CGT and the CFTC, managed to have laws enacted in 1982, 1983 and 1986 by the Socialist government that gave workers some rights to direct expression in companies. The CGT-FO and minority groups in other trade unions opposed these laws, viewing them as a threat to the trade union movement and to staff-elected representatives in companies. The right to self-expression, which had been demanded since the 1970s, was nevertheless enacted in a very different context. The 1980s were marked by unemployment and de-unionisation and less importance was attached to the work environment.

The direct, legal workers' right to expression concerning conditions, quality, content and organisation of work was introduced with the aim of radically changing industrial relations by giving workers a legitimate right to intervene in certain decision-making processes alongside elected and trade union representatives. The right to self-expression has come up against many difficulties - the inertia of Taylorist structures and practices, inevitable hostility from within the company hierarchy whenever the participatory process is implemented, foot-dragging on the part of the employers, relative indifference or even opposition on the part of some active trade union members and staff-elected representatives and disillusionment on the part of workers in view of the relatively ineffective application of this law. The right to expression as legislated in 1982 and 1983 has lapsed into inactivity. A renewal of the topic of company democracy could give new life and a new form to the concept, taking into account the lessons of the last ten years. Whether or not this happens, French experience suggests that trade union involvement would be the same as it was in tackling the topics of the work environment and work organisation (see Pinaud, Chapter 5).

In the 1970s Germany's DGB was ideologically opposed to any form of direct worker participation. From 1980 onwards the trade unions, especially unions in the metalworking (automobile) and chemical industries, gradually softened their stance until eventually company agreements were signed which introduced employer-initiated forms of participative management (decentralisation of operational decision-making, quality circles, autonomous groups) in exchange for worker benefits such as training, classification, shorter working hours. Union projects on direct worker participation have been tested in German companies over recent years with the help of academic consultants. Recently, following the electoral success of the ecologists (the Greens), technical self-management pilot schemes have been set up in the public services of four regions, several departments and hundreds of communes (see Széll, Chapter 6).

In Italy participation has only been rarely regarded as a stable, institutional factor in industrial relations, despite the existence of article 46 of the Italian constitution which guarantees workers the legal right to participate in the management of companies (see Guarriello, Chapter 7).

In Scandinavia, the concept of direct participation entered the debate on industrial democracy in 1962, when the sociologists Emery and Thorsrud pointed to some of the weaknesses of traditional approaches to the democratisation of work and suggested an alternative by systematically redesigning jobs, technology and work organisation. After several years of field experiments and research, recent discussion in Scandinavia has shifted to the relevance of democratisation programmes designed to improve competitiveness and which suggest a possible powerful alliance between economic needs and human development in work life and society (see Qvale, Chapter 12). In Sweden, in particular, many unions have been active in developing new forms of work organisation - decentralisation of decisions on work planning, team work and the integration of traditional blue and white collar work. The metalworkers' union has been one of the leaders with its two programmes "Good Work" and "Work Solidarity Policy". But the unions have constantly emphasised their role in developing these new forms of work organisation. In the domains of work and production, unions have concentrated on developing work content and influencing individual union members or teams in their daily work. One challenging and important task for unions, and by no means contradictory, might be to develop a modified role, interacting with highly competent union members who are themselves capable of influencing their daily work, thus avoiding constant union intervention (see Sandberg, Chapter 11).

In the Netherlands, the ideal of worker self management has been supported by the trade union movement for years. In a policy document entitled "Work in 2000", the Social-Democratic FNV stated that "the FNV strives for democratic company decision-making. This implies that the FNV advocates a decision-making process in which workers have the final say and can as far as possible take decisions by themselves. Democratisation of companies should go hand in hand with social ownership. These goals can only be achieved gradually. However, action should be taken to reach these goals". (FNV, 1987, 6). In November 1990 the FNV organised a conference entitled "Economic Democracy and the Trade Union Movement". The policy document, which was accepted by the conference, was clear about democratic participation. "Worker participation is the main reason for the existence of and the main goal of the trade union movement" (FNV 1990:1). Nevertheless, the document does not explicitly refer to the concept of worker self-management at all (see Leisink, Chapter 8).

It should also be noted that the development of the social economy, especially cooperatives, does not seem to have been regarded as a priority by the trade union movement in Western European countries, even if the social economy continues to represent a major economic and social issue. One can at the very least speak of a certain ambivalence towards cooperative movements. Cooperatives have even come in for trade union criticism (as for example from the Dutch FNV) for their economic inefficiency and consequently for the poor wage and work conditions which they offer their workers (see Leisink, Chapter 8).

Furthermore, the position adopted by the ETUC in the resolutions of its 7th statutory congress (1991) should not be underestimated. In its "Preamble", point V ("For an Economic and Political Democracy") it states that "it is of fundamental importance that workers be assured the right to information, to consultation, to negotiation and to participation in European companies and in transnational companies operating in Europe, especially on issues concerning employment and technological and environmental changes. The ETUC asks that the statute of the European joint-stock company be adopted as quickly as possible and that it include clear provisions for ensuring worker participation at company or group level". Lastly, one should note the ETUC declaration dated March 1992 concerning the work environment: "Concertation, participation, information and consultation on the part of workers, their trade union representatives or their delegates in the company must be the fundamental principle at every level of health protection in the workplace...the right of every worker to be informed, to lodge a complaint and to participate in the workplace must be stipulated in writing." Be this as it may, it must be admitted that concrete efforts to achieve these demands in EC countries have concerned workers' representatives far more than the workers themselves.

Participation in capital and participation in profits

Trade union organisations have generally been opposed to this kind of participation and have remained ambivalent about cooperative and mutual fund forms of participation.

Trade unions initially felt that profit-sharing represented a dangerous precedent and the start of a move towards arbitrary forms of wages with employees and their representatives running the risk of being trapped by the demands of profitability. In more general terms it was felt that profit-sharing might challenge the principle of wage equality (equal pay for equal work) which trade unions had always defended. Furthermore it was argued that the spread of profit-sharing could replace conventional wage bargaining between the social partners in companies and also at sectorial level.

Nevertheless, it appears that trade unions have changed their stance in several countries of Europe (France, Belgium and Italy) and have become more pragmatic in the wake of concrete examples in different companies. As Vaughan-Whitehead stressed, (cf chapter 14) opposition to the concept is mostly to be found amongst national union leaders while the dévolution of wage bargaining has facilitated the implementation of collective forms of financial participation within companies.

On the other hand trade union organisations in Western Europe generally all continue to express if not opposition to, at least suspicion of participation in capital, particularly "worker share-holding schemes". But often their voices fall on deaf ears amongst employees themselves, as the privatisation of British Telecom illustrated.

Governments

Clearly governments have played an important role in economic democratisation. Government support has varied from country to country. After the Second World War, most countries of Western Europe sought to render their economies more democratic by nationalising important sectors of industry and by introducing legislation to ensure a form of industrial relations which was fairer to workers and the trade unions. These moves were greatly influenced by Marxist philosophy which held that democracy and economic and social justice could only be achieved through massive State appropriation of the means of production in key sectors of the economy. Thus, progress was enshrined in law.

Governments have also encouraged the development of various forms of direct and indirect worker participation either by working together with trade unions or as a result of union pressure. Government help has first been visible in constitutional acts, as in Italy, but also in legislation, as mentioned above, introduced by a Labour government in Malta, a Socialist government in France and Social-Democratic governments in Germany and Scandinavia.

In Sweden, the Social Democratic governments supported the unions by introducing the Co-determination Act (1976). In Norway, extreme "Taylorist" forms of job design (e.g. 100% machine pacing and very short job cycles) were outlawed, and 50% worker participation was introduced in new safety and work environment committees. Factory inspection was improved and comprehensive training schemes were introduced as well. But the conviction that there must be more general changes in legislation before increased direct participation is possible, has waned. Furthermore, the belief that legislation for generalised or new forms of community or employee ownership will automatically promote direct participation at work and increase productivity, has largely disappeared (see Qvale, Chapter 12).

21

These governments have also offered direct financial support to participative companies, such as the highly unprofitable Malta Drydocks and certain cooperatives in the United Kingdom. They also facilitated the implementation of pilot schemes in participation in the public sector and nationalised companies. Government funding of permanent study, research and training groups (in Malta) or academic research into worker participation has been an important boost to the spread and legitimacy of worker participation (the French PAROLES programmes, Sweden's Work Environment Fund, which supports research and development projects on work and the work environment, the Leadership Organisation and Co-Determination Research Programme and Norway's SBA - Norwegian Work Life Centre).

On the other hand, deregulation policies and attacks on trade unions by the Thatcher government in the United Kingdom have harmed democratic worker participation and encouraged the spread of participation in capital. In France, the 1970 and 1973 laws on applying for and buying shares have so far had little effect. The European directive on the creation of European works councils is being implemented throughout Europe after a long period during which obstacles were created to block any greater participation of employees or their representatives be it in the form of European works councils, European joint-stock companies or financial participation of workers in profits.

But the effect of all these government steps has been severely limited by the transient nature of politics and governments which remain in power for only a few years. The time required to develop and encourage the process of democratic participation is far longer.

The social basis

By the end of the 1960s most Western European countries had experienced numerous social uprisings in protest against poor working conditions and forms of work organisation that condemned workers to carrying out mindless tasks of no interest which offered them no dignity and no future (in France: Le Joint Français, Pennaroya, Renault, the banking sector, the post and telecommunications sector). These uprisings were mostly led by poorly qualified blue and white-collar workers, especially women and immigrants, and took the form of lengthy and hard-hitting "wild-cat" strikes. But these uprisings also expressed themselves in terms of high staff turnover, frequent absenteeism, a drop in production quality and sometimes wastage and sabotage. Some of these uprisings led to experiments in popular self-management such as LIP in France. In Belgium, some uprisings, although considered "wild-cat", were actively supported by trade-unions. During the late '60s and early '70s, even the General Christian Trade Union Federation (ACV/CSC) supported some factory occupations and calls for production under self-management as in Prestige (De Coninck & Vilrokx, 1977).

These social movements were a decisive factor in winning union demands for an improved work environment and direct worker participation. They also played an important role in changing employers' attitudes, encouraging and experimentation with new forms of work organisation (e.g. France, Scandinavia) and the introduction of new legislation. In Scandinavia, during the 1970s, a reaction among workers against the lack of participation both in managerial and union structures and rising concern about the work environment (including psycho-social factors) led to radical new laws (see Part II). In Sweden for example, around 1970, social unrest, symbolised by major strikes at the Kiruna iron-ore mines in the north of the country, undoubtedly contributed to the development of co-determination (see Qvale and Sandberg, Chapters 11-12).

These expressions of anger gradually diminished as unemployment rose, the trade union movement weakened and employers at least partially heeded the demands of the 1970s. But workers' concerns about the work environment and work organisation continued, as a look at the most recent social conflicts, especially in France and Belgium, proves. These conflicts have affected hospital staff, social workers, employees of the State owned railways and airline and long-distance road-haulage drivers.

It seems that the loss of influence that trade union organisations have experienced among workers (M. Regini et al., 1992) suggests disillusionment on the part of workers about traditional forms of indirect participation. And yet, with one or two exceptions, direct participation has so far not been one of the demands made by a social base weakened by the threat of unemployment and social exclusion. However, research into experiments in direct participation suggests that workers do have a deep-felt need for participation which must to be met as soon as conditions make this possible. This need is all the more apparent given the fact that workers' representatives express interest in matters concerning the quality of life in a company. One could argue that in France the development of direct participation in the workplace can be measured in terms of greater interest in these matters, either in the form of trade union demands or, less conflictually, in the form of health and safety councils (Le Tron, Pinaud 1992). This seems true for Sweden too, where there is a correlation between trade union interest in work organisation and direct participation on the one hand, and the implementation of these forms of organisation on the other (Sandberg, chapter 11).

Conclusions

The task we have set ourselves, as scientific researchers, is to pin-point the most important facts, the most favourable conditions, the major hurdles and an outline of the necessary means for developing democratic participation in Western Europe.

Faced with fundamental changes in Western European societies today, we must re-examine the role of trade unions and workers. With the danger of seeing unchecked liberalism and/or authoritarian regimes emerge, democratic participation (for workers, those elected to office and trade unions) must be seen as a strategic move and a goal. It is important to resist the idea that democracy, both in society and in companies, is a luxury at a time of rising unemployment and social division (between the employed and the unemployed, those with permanent and those with non-permanent work contracts, nationals and immigrants, "legal" and "illegal" workers and full-time and part-time workers). At a time such as this, democracy is indispensable if we are to succeed in finding any lasting solutions to these problems. Are we to argue, as did Laureano Lopez Rodo, vice-president of the Spanish Council under Franco, that democracy can only concern us when the per capita GNP reaches US$1000? It is true that we all live by bread but not by bread alone. The means and the ends are linked and democratic participation will make it possible for workers to earn their bread and win democracy.

By concentrating on indirect participation and particularly on conflicting forms of participation (such as collective bargaining), trade union organisations have allowed employers to occupy the fields of direct participation and participation in capital. As a result, trade unions have thus deprived themselves of an important means of improving or re-establishing links with workers. Surely now is the moment to seize the initiative and promote democracy in society, revitalise the trade union movement and respond to the aspirations of the workers (Maire, 1987). Otherwise, corporate culture will continue to dominate workplace ideology.

Since the 1980s, there has been a rising trend of de-unionisation in many countries of Western Europe. This has been accompanied by a regular drop in the number of unionised worker representatives sitting on company bodies, as in France and Belgium or on co-determination bodies, as in Germany. There, recent elections for the country's social security supervisory council showed a drop in votes for the DGB since 1980 and a rise in "free" lists. In France, Belgium and the Netherlands these drops in union influence are a consequence of what has often been a conflictual relationship between the unions and elected representatives in companies.

The various forms of participation, both direct and indirect, at company level and beyond, whether they are trade union or management sponsored, based on collective bargaining, co-determination or financial participation, etc., are not all contradictory or incompatible. Indeed they can be cumulative. When applied individually they lose both their meaning and their effect. Democratic participation is to be found within them as a dynamic whole. There is a need for a systematic approach to greater democratic participation.

These various forms of participation must be linked together, focused and fused. Trade unions are best placed to take up the challenge that democratic participation represents by integrating its diverse manifestations into a coherent strategy, by providing bearings and direction for such participation, by providing a forum for discussion and examination of national and international experience, by acting as a source of information and an arena in which decisions may be made concerning what should be handled on a conflictual basis and what should be handled on a participative basis. Such a strategy would provide trade unions with a chance to wrest back control of all levels of decision-making and all spheres of life (economic, organisational, technical, social, etc.) and get to grips with all forms of direct and indirect participation in an attempt to achieve true democracy in companies and in society as a whole (see Kester and Pinaud, Chapter 4).

We believe that social science institutions can be of help in advancing trade union debate on the subjects of democracy and social and economic development in companies and in society at large.

2 Participation and building social Europe

Janine Goetschy

Institutionalised employee participation in company decision-making will undoubtedly prove to have been one of the most controversial topics in the search over the last two decades to produce a European social policy. Participation has been at the centre of numerous ambitious, complex and extremely divisive draft directives of the European Commission. Even the most important of these have still not been completed. However, during 1993 and 1994 important progress was made in the drafting of these directives and by the end of September 1994 the directive concerning "the creation of a European works council or employee information-consultation procedures in companies of European dimensions" was adopted. In this chapter we will examine the broad outlines of this draft directive. Participation is not only breaking new ground in the attempts to draw up an 11-nation Social Agreement, it is also, in its different forms, playing an increasingly important role in transforming social relations of production and in trying to meet the social challenges posed by European construction.

The directive on the European works council in trans-national companies (22 September 1994): rapid and unexpected progress

This particular initiative was part of the plan of action of the December 1989 Social Charter and was the subject of a December 1990 draft directive. It was amended on several occasions and was finally adopted on 22 September 1994 by the Council of Ministers of Social Affairs under German presidency. Throughout 1993 Danish and Belgium presidencies had indeed helped harmonize the points of view of member states and get the matter moving. In 1991 and 1993 the draft directive was scuttled because a unanimous vote was required in the Council. Later it was tabled using new procedures stipulated in the 11-country Social Agreement annexed to the Maastricht Treaty which came into force in November 1993. This was the first European draft directive to be handled under the new

27

procedures. These procedures include novel provisions in three different areas. It provides for two consultation phases between the European social partners and the Commission, the first phase concerning the principle and the second the substance of the proposal. It also provides for the possibility of European-wide negotiations should the social partners wish so and, lastly, if the social partners do not intend to negotiate or if negotiations fail, the Commission takes up the baton once again by tabling its draft directive in Council. The novelty of the procedures lies in the fact that certain important social aspects, including employee information-consultation, can be adopted on the basis of a qualified majority vote of the 11.

It should be noted that the European social partners did not succeed in agreeing on the principle of launching European-wide negotiations on the subject of the creation of European works councils. The draft directive was thus to be adopted on the basis of an 11-country vote, the United Kingdom not participating in the decision-making process since it refused to sign the social chapter in the Maastricht Treaty. On 22 September 1994 the directive was adopted by a vote of ten member states, Portugal have abstained during the final vote. After more than 20 years of dithering, clashes and obstacles, it seemed that the qualified majority vote of the 11 had at last won the day and a directive on employee information and consultation was at last a reality.

Substance and impact of the new directive

What, briefly, is the substance of the new directive? It provides for the creation of a European works council or information-consultation procedures in companies and groups of companies which employ more than 1,000 workers in member states and more than 150 in at least two different member states after agreement between management and a special negotiating group made up of employee representatives. This agreement should define the scope, structure, terms, functioning and financing of the works council as well as the length of the mandate of those in it. Failing this such an agreement should specify the details of how employee information-consultation procedures might be implemented. The directive also includes a series of clauses aimed at solving the thorny problem of information confidentiality. This permits management not to divulge certain information under certain circumstances and requires confidentiality on the part of council members.

If after three years no agreement has been reached which allows the creation of a European works council or information-consultation procedures, or if management has refused to launch negotiations, minimum 'prescriptions' will be applied. These 'prescriptions', referred to in the directive as "subsidiary" provide for the creation of a works council which has the right to meet once a year with management and to be informed and consulted on developments and activities in the company regarding the company's future on the basis of a report drafted by management. Additional meetings can take place under exceptional circumstances which directly affect the workers' interest (such as company relocation, company

28

closure or mass redundancies). The future works councils will only be informed about and consulted on decisions which have a "European" impact. The running costs of the works council will be borne by the company.

Member states have two years from the date on which the directive was adopted (until October 1996) to incorporate the contents of the directive in their national legislation. If one then adds the three years allowed for negotiations on a future works council or any other form of consultation, it becomes clear that in practice these minimum 'prescriptions' can only become enforceable in 1999.

It should be noted that the text accepted by the Council does not include the amendments that the European Parliament tabled, which in essence sought to reduce the application threshold from 1,000 employees to 500 and from 150 to 100 for subsidiaries in at least two member states. These rejected amendments also sought to reduce maximum negotiating time in companies from three years to 18 months.

The directive will also affect companies whose headquarters are outside the European Union (in Japan or the United States for example) if they have subsidiaries in the EU which meet the criteria in the directive. Furthermore while companies whose headquarters are in the U.K. will not be affected by the directive, any subsidiaries in the other eleven member states will be.

The attitude of the social partners

What was the attitude of the social partners towards this draft directive on European councils before it was finally voted?

According to the European Commission, this was a "versatile and flexible" draft which respected the autonomy and the choices of the social partners in those companies concerned. It also respected "the much talked of principle of subsidiarity" in that it did not affect national systems of participation but instead, aimed to cover situations (in trans-national companies) which were not covered by national legislation.

As far as the positions adopted by the social partners with regard to this draft were concerned, the ETUC expressed support for it. However, the UNICE (Union of Industrial and Employers' Confederations of Europe) voiced repeated opposition to what it called "a rigid and coercive" draft. It proposed replacing the directive with a European framework agreement drawn up together with the ETUC and the ECPSE (European Confederation of Public Sector Enterprises) under the auspices of the European Social Dialogue. UNICE believed that any such developments should unfold as part of continued "Joint Opinions" issued by the Social Dialogue of March 1987 (a mutual position on information and consultation) adopted jointly by the social partners and considered to be a "pragmatic and balanced" text. Criticism of the Commission's draft directive included the fact that it damaged the existing systems of information and consultation and did not permit decentralised procedures. It was also held to be a measure imposed from above, contrary not only to the spirit of the Social

Dialogue, but also contrary to the new procedures outlined in the Maastricht Social Agreement and the principle of subsidiarity enshrined in the Treaty. It was seen as a measure that would reduce company competitiveness because of its cost and because it would slow down decision-making. It would reduce motivation among local management hierarchies, especially in small countries such as Belgium, Ireland, Denmark, Portugal and Greece where the large companies do not have their head offices. It was viewed as a potential dissuasion for investors from outside the EC. In addition to the UNICE, the employers' group of the Economic and Social Committee also made a minority statement against the draft directive, appended to the Committee's official position on the text (March 1991).

The content of the draft directive was based on the success of existing group councils or European works councils such as at BSN, TGP, Bull, Péchiney, Volkswagen, etc. which were run on a voluntary basis. But it was the lack of any positive action on the part of the UNICE over recent years in spreading these initiatives that pushed the Commission to opt for the directive. Faced with a directive which seemed poised to succeed, the UNICE made a last ditch attempt and proposed launching negotiations with the social partners on the subject. But it was too late.

The Hoover transfer has had the effect of speeding up matters. It enabled the ETUC and the EMF (European Metalworkers' Federation) to put pressure on Jacques Delors, the Flynn Commission and member states to approve the directive. Some consider that the Hoover affair would not have ended as it did if the directive had already been in force.

While stepping up pressure on Community institutions such as the European Parliament, the Commission and Council to get the directive through, some sectorial trade unions were at the same time actively fighting to get group councils set up on a voluntary basis. The EMF drew up a list of 30 companies to be targeted in its industrial sector. The FIET (which represents employees and technical workers) took similar steps mainly aimed at the banking sector and insurance companies. It is to be expected that European-wide sectorial trade unions will in the future be far more assertive as regards the structure of group councils, particularly regarding the way they are run, prerogatives and the role of unions in them. If fact, during an evaluation carried out at the beginning of 1993, these trade unions felt that although the number of such councils had grown constantly, the way in which they were organised left a lot to be desired, especially given management attempts to water down trade union power. In many cases agreements reached included no obligation to guarantee consultation, only the provision of information.

According to an ETUC evaluation conducted in 1994, 33 companies have now created European group councils on a voluntary basis; 18 are in the iron and steel industry, 3 in the banking and services sector, 2 in the food industry, 1 in the building industry and 9 in the chemical industry. Immediately after adoption of the directive, the ETUC asked employers not to wait for the directive to come into effect at national level but to start negotiations immediately.

How many transnational companies will be affected by this new directive? The president of the European Social Council, N. Blüm said in September 1994 that the directive would effect 4.5 million employees working in 1,200 companies. According to earlier, more detailed estimates (Sisson et al, 1992), some 900 transnational companies with over 1,000 employees had their headquarters within the European Union with subsidiaries in at least two member states. Overall, these companies employ 13,6 million workers. Of these companies the United Kingdom counts the most with 332 (6.1 million workers) of which only 28 are in the industrial sector. Germany counts 257 groups with 3.4 million employees. Here the industrial sector is well represented with 154 of the 257 groups. France counts 117 groups with 1.9 million employees of which 39 groups are in the industrial sector and the Netherlands has 83 groups with only 11 in the industrial sector, representing 1.1 million workers in all. Italy counts 32 groups split fairly evenly between industry and other sectors, representing 665,000 workers. As for transnationals whose headquarters are outside the E.U. (with more than 1,000 employees and subsidiaries in at least two E.U. countries), the same authors (Sisson et al) listed some 280, almost half of which were in the United Kingdom.

N. Blüm, president of the Social Affairs Council added that the cost of implementation of this directive was not particularly high for companies. The Commission estimates that it will cost some 20 DM per person for any given company.

What is the future for worker participation at Europe level?

Adoption of the directive on European works councils has prompted debate on concrete ways in which it will be implemented and the strategies of social partners in this new context.

Generally speaking what are the new possibilities that this social agreement offers and what are the chances now of seeing success in other matters regarding European-level participation? As the adoption of the directive on European works councils illustrates, the fact that the subject of worker consultation and information now demands a qualified majority vote among the 11 member states in the European Council will make adoption of directives concerning this matter much easier. Moreover, formalising consultation among European social partners in the European legislative process should help finalise the content of the measures proposed by the Commission, gives them added legitimacy and helps find an area of consensus between the social partners. Also, the fact that European social partners can independently negotiate European collective agreements which can cover several economic sectors, one particular sector, a region or a company should help encourage new initiatives in participation.

The diversity of these procedures and the methods used in drawing up Community-wide proposals and implementing them nationally should above all help remove obstacles created by UNICE which have prevented implementation of European measures on participation.

While the future of worker participation depends to a great extent on new compromises and the room for manoeuvre which institutional reforms from Maastricht will offer, the fate of participation is largely dependent on the economic and social problems which have to be addressed as a result of the acceleration of European integration and European Union, especially the possibility of economic and monetary union.

Expansion of the EU to include new members, with highly-developed industrial relations provides good grounds to hope for gains in the domain of employee participation. These countries (Scandinavian countries and Austria) very often have large experience in this domain.

Procedures for allowing worker consultation and information are designed to prevent continued social dumping as practised among subsidiaries of a company or two companies within a same group. At European level, worker participation is also regarded as one of the best paths for achieving "competitiveness, growth and employment". Indeed in the wake of the alarming 1992 and 1993 employment figures, there have been a number of calls made by politicians at European level for the need to link European integration more closely with job creation. It should not be forgotten that the "Joint Opinion" adopted in July 1992 by the ETUC, UNICE (representing European private sector employers) and the European Confederation of Public Sector Enterprises, entitled "A New Strategy of Cooperation for Growth and Employment" provided considerable momentum for this new awareness. Since then, two important initiatives have been drawn up. One was in May 1993 when the Council presidency asked the Commission to propose a "community framework for employment", known as the Green Paper (cf Flynn's Communication of May 27 on this matter). Although this was only a relatively general communication as far as the Commission was concerned and despite the fact that most measures designed to tackle unemployment depend on the member states themselves, concern about developing a centrally coordinated boost and Community-wide policies on employment clearly illustrate that it is no longer feasible to complete European economic integration without preventive or compensatory measures for employment. The second initiative was the fact that employment was at the top of the agenda at the Copenhagen summit in June when the Council called on the Commission to prepare a White Paper on the relationship between "growth, productivity and employment" in preparation for the December 1993 summit.

Now that European-level solutions are being sought to solve the problems of unemployment (according to the White Paper, a target of 5% unemployment is to be set for the year 2000), direct and indirect worker participation can be regarded as useful ways of introducing increased flexibility which will not jeopardise employment.

In fact many commentators believe that economic and monetary union will increase employer pressure on wage costs but also make it easier to compare the limits and effectiveness of wage negotiations. In the light of these developments, worker participation becomes all the more important as a way of ensuring improved productivity on the one hand and as a counter-balance to any potential austerity measures on wages on the other.

To conclude, at the time of writing, European economic integration is not a popular subject. There is increasing doubt about the wisdom of accepting further deterioration of national economies provoked by efforts to achieve economic integration. The Commission's Green Paper (17/11/1993) on social policy in general, designed to spark debate on the subject, suggests the implementation of a watch-dog organisation to oversee social policy during the period of transition to economic and monetary union. The aim of such a body would be to identify and hence soften the blow of measures introduced at national level to bring about economic union - a process in which the social partners will be called upon to play an important role.

Clearly, any examination of the relationship between worker participation in company decision-making and European integration should be carried out in the wider context of evaluating the influence of the various social partners in the various stages of the economic and social construction of Europe.

3 Guiding principles for a strategy for democratic participation

Gérard Kester

Introduction

The aim of this chapter is to stimulate debate on the guiding principles on which the development of democratic participation may be based. It makes explicit the assumptions that underlie the policy and strategy proposals made in the next chapter.

These guiding principles are drawn from an analysis of experiences in different parts of Europe and elsewhere in the world (see Part II). These principles also draw on the general body of scientific literature on participation and the diverse comments and suggestions on an earlier draft of this chapter made by trade unionists during the colloquium on "Democratic Participation and Trade Unions" held in Paris in February 1994.

These guiding principles are of a general nature and do not relate to any one specific country, nor to specific situations. They are presented as the basis for a policy and strategy debate.

Democratic participation is a fundamental human right

Democratic participation should be seen as a universal human right. The Universal Declaration of Human Rights and the European Charter of Fundamental Rights both implicity or explicitly regard participation as a basic right. The right to express oneself and the right to vote are considered to be fundamental components of the integrity and dignity of each human being.

Despite the fact that worker participation is declining in the Second and Third Worlds and stagnating in the First World, it has not lost any of its intrinsic values. Research continues to confirm that when workers are exposed to far-reaching participation schemes, they express appreciation and associate it with values such as equity, democracy, humanity, solidarity and efficiency. These values are cited by workers regardless of the era or culture concerned, suggesting that participation is a fundamental human need. Recent cross-cultural studies have confirmed this.

Acceptance of, indifference to or rejection of democratic participation is often a function of actual contact with it. When participation produces unwanted consequences for those involved, as for example in cases of badly-planned participation or as a result of manipulation, participation itself can be regarded as a trap. Insignificant forms of participation, what one might call "token participation" ("tea, toilet and towels democracy") generate indifference. Often, initially positive attitudes turn to apathy when workers discover that there is little or nothing to be gained, either morally or materially.

Appreciation of participation grows as workers gain a more meaningful and effective understanding and experience of it. The closer workers come to dealing with power-related matters, the greater their demand for participation. (Drago and Wooden, 1991). When conditions for true (non-politicised) self-management are achieved, workers equate it with equity, solidarity, participation and dignity (the 22,000-member self-managed Mondragon cooperative, see Greenwood and Gonzales, 1990). In a recent survey conducted in Guinea-Conakry, the principle values attached to worker participation by grass-roots worker representatives were very similar to those expressed in Spain - equity, democracy, humanity and efficiency (Diallo and others, 1992). Further research results could be cited, irrespective of culture or era, to suggest that participation is indeed a fundamental human need. The works of Blumberg (1968), Braverman, (1974) and Carole Pateman (1970) remain classics on the social, economic and political dimensions of this need. Recent cross-cultural studies of participation have confirmed this. (Bayat, 1991 and Prasnikar, 1991).

Democratic participation has its own intrinsic value *and* in addition is an instrument for achieving certain objectives. It has intrinsic value - "it does something *to* you" - and extrinsic value - "it does something *for* you" (Allan Fox, A Sociology of Industry, 1971).

Although democratic participation may be considered a universal human right, this does not mean that everyone will want to exercise this right. The same applies to the right to vote. Participation or non-participation remain a matter of free choice for every individual. Lack of interest in participation among certain groups or categories of workers does not affect this fundamental *right*, which must be defended for those who do wish to exercise it.

The right to participate is independent of trade union membership. In other words, trade unions do not have a monopoly on participation. Workers have the right to participate directly and without trade union intervention. This evokes another universal human right - the right to freedom of association. Anyone is free to join or not to join the trade union movement.

In view of gradual improvements in educational standards, an increased demand in participation is to be anticipated in the future. This has not escaped the attention of trade union circles. One French trade union leader has advocated participation at the cost of traditional trade union action, in response to the expectations of young employees in particular (Maire, 1987). And one French industrial relations analyst came to similar conclusions when he attempted to identify the conditions required to halt the decline in trade union membership (Rosanvallon, 1988).

Democratic participation is an issue for all political agendas it is not the exclusive preserve of any one political ideology

Participation used to be associated with or included into leftist and/or progressive political ideologies. Furthermore, mainstream intellectuals researching participation tended to enclose themselves in leftist territory. Whatever the initial intentions were, participation and self-management both suffered greatly under Socialist and Marxist regimes. Slogans, rhetoric, bureaucracy, corruption and manipulation made many people allergic to participation.

The challenge today is to launch participation once again as an ideology in its own right and to disassociate it from all major political systems, or better still, place it fairly and squarely in all political systems.

If the first guiding principle is accepted, it logically follows that democratic participation cannot be the exclusive property of any one political party or movement. It is a *universal* human right. Of course it is not surprising that the concept of participation used to be associated with or included into leftist and/or progressive political ideologies. Worker participation became a battle cry for socialism and worker self-management a show-piece for some Marxist or Marxist-oriented countries, although other Marxist ideologies and systems rejected both participation and self-management. Mainstream intellectuals researching participation enclosed themselves in leftist territory and many theories were formulated which claimed that socialism (Marxism was often included under this heading) was a necessary prerequisite for effective and meaningful participation (Horvat, 1982). Jaroslav Vanek stood alone for several decades in claiming that self-management was practicable on its own strengths (Vanek, 1970, 1971, 1975).

Associated as it has been with failing political ideologies and regimes, participation has become a dirty word. Privatisation calls for a "no-nonsense" approach rather than the introduction of participation. In Eastern Europe, many people have grown allergic to the idea of participation. The smear campaign against democratic participation conducted by deliberately associating it with failed, bygone ideologies must be countered by putting democratic participation squarely on the political agenda. If we accept that trade unions are going through a crisis today, then we are presented with an opportunity for change in which democratic participation can play an important role. The Chinese use the same ideogram for the concepts "crisis" and "opportunity". The immediate challenge facing us is the development of the European Union social policy and beyond that,

37

the internationalisation and globalisation of the economy.

How then, can the universal right to participation be consolidated, given this new perspective? Clearly, it is the trade union movement which has the historic role and duty to put participation back on the agenda and make proposals for appropriate forms and strategies for fostering participation. (see also guiding principle 6).

The origin of the right to democratic participation can be found in labour and not in capital ownership

The main achievement of mainstream worker participation over the past decades has been to demand democratic influence in the economic sector. Protagonists have argued that the contribution of labour to production is as much a basis for power as is ownership. Today there is a tendency to increasingly link participation to capital, not to labour. Management and employers encourage incentive and loyalty schemes and block further infringements on their decision-making prerogatives. Whilst recognising the importance of financial participation, it should be made clear that the principle of participation is not a function of proportional capital ownership but a right which finds its basis in one's labour.

With communism K.O. and socialism in intensive care, triumphant capitalism now seeks to rebuild labour relations according to its own logic. Any forms of participation which imply access to important areas of power are dismissed, with allusions made to the old and failed leftist systems. In their place, forms of participation are now on offer which can be traced back to the capitalist form of production. It is through ownership that workers may now obtain rights of appropriation (profit-sharing and/or workers' shareholding schemes) or control (access to shareholders' meetings or board of director meetings). Participation based on capital ownership is rapidly becoming the centre of debate surrounding privatisation in Eastern Europe and is also creeping into the vocabulary of popular participation in Africa (Rubanza, 1991). In Western Europe a revival of profit-sharing and shareholding schemes can be witnessed today (Russell and Russ, 1991). This may be largely a smoke-screen and simply an attempt to motivate the workforce but it could also be a double-edged sword which could lead to unexpected consequences such as greater employer control over privatised firms, since the employers will continue to be majority shareholders. Investments by social security and pension schemes could also be affected.

This trend must be identified, exposed and challenged. Only then can we hope to defend the tenet that the right to participation is based on labour. It is precisely this right that the trade union movement has taken up as its battle-cry for over 150 years.

The imminent dangers are clear. A way of thinking is being encouraged which makes a distinction between political democracy and economic (i.e. capitalist) democracy. The debate on democracy in many Eastern European and African countries will stimulate the idea of multi-party systems amongst the people there. Political democracy is a civic right, reflected in the right to vote. Political democracy cannot hope to achieve maturity unless it is sustained by forms of democracy at the grass-root level (Pateman, 1970). New, innovative ideas about citizenship reserve an important place for participation in the democratic landscape (Coenen and Leisink, 1993).

One particular challenge, then, is to redefine the role of capital in labour relations and in the development of worker participation. Vanek's propositions concerning the relationship between capital ownership, appropriation and control must be given the attention they deserve (Vanek, 1970, 1971, 1975). Vanek is not opposed to private ownership of capital as such, but he rejects the principle that such ownership should yield exclusive rights to surplus appropriation and to control. In a free market economy, people who produce make use of capital and pay the capital owner an economic return. Beyond this, the capital owner has no further claim on, let alone control over, how a company should be managed. Vanek develops his theory mainly for purely self-managed companies in which management is exercised by virtue of work and not by virtue of ownership (Vanek, 1971, p.20). He has developed a number of criteria regarding ownership as it relates to a self-managed company (see Vanek, 1975, Introduction). Under other forms of worker participation such criteria do not apply, but they could or should change the nature of the relationship between capital ownership, management and control of a company (Vanek, ibidem).

Capital should be at the service of mankind. It is not for mankind to be at the service of capital. Vanek's theory is, of course, open to amendments, elaboration and revision. Renewed efforts have been made to review the role of capital. For a long time, the dichotomy between capitalism and communism tended to polarise the two different modes of production. But just as the end of the Cold War gave rise to a debate on a new world order, so the disappearance of communism as a system could give rise to a new economic order. A start has already been made by Michel Albert in his book "Capitalism versus Capitalism" (Albert, 1991), in which he argues that the Anglo-American form of capitalism is far more inegalitarian and less productive than capitalism as it is practised in Scandinavia, Germany and the Benelux countries, all of which score higher marks both economically *and* socially.

Democratic participation is a dynamic process. Constant efforts must be made to render it increasingly meaningful, effective and democratic

Democratic Participation is a learning process for workers, worker representatives, trade union representatives, managers, directors, owners and governments. It is also a struggle. Once a certain level of power is attained, the desire for higher levels, other areas of power and more effective and meaningful forms of participation will grow. What is at stake in this struggle are the fundamental values inherent in the human right to participation - humanity, dignity, democracy, equity, social and economic efficiency and solidarity. Democratic participation is a dynamic process which has been constantly proposed, learned and defended - often through struggle and it must be constantly widened and adapted to new situations.

Democratic participation is a cumulative process of change in labour relations. In this process of change, an accumulation of institutionalised forms of worker participation allow workers to increase the independent, effective and meaningful influence over decision-making at different levels of management or policy-making in their workplace. Through their trade unions this influence may extend to all other levels of decision-making beyond the workplace. Characteristic of participation is its dynamic nature. It is a lengthy, on-going developmental process drawing on new ideas, new events, action, policies and strategies which either directly or indirectly increase worker influence.

A convincing presentation of the participation process can be found in Mothé's book entitled *"Autogestion goutte à goutte"* (Self-Management Bit by Bit). Mothé sees the participation process as a chain of little revolutions rather than a quantum leap in the form of one major revolution. Such a major revolution either never occurs, or simply leads to monopoly by the "Party".

The participation process is a process of consciousness-raising. Obviously this generates a conflict of interests and a power struggle between those seeking to increase their influence and those who do not want to cede or share power. The moment the participation process comes to a halt, the struggle comes to a halt. Consolidation or surrender? Stagnation leads to decline because the dynamic momentum is stifled. No new goals, demands or proposals are formulated. No new "thresholds" are passed (Bernstein, 1976). The internationalisation of worker councils (in multi-national companies) is an important step forward but other than this, it would seem that stagnation has set in. There are no new initiatives and there seem to be other priorities on the agenda for those engaged in the struggle. The employers' camp has seized the initiative by developing worker participation linked to capital ownership.

Participation should be developed and made more meaningful, more effective and more democratic. More meaningful by focusing participation on those levels, moments and places where decisions are taken and implemented and by concentrating on policy control rather than day-to-day management. More effective by assessing whether or not participation leads to greater humanity, equality, social and economic efficiency and solidarity. And more democratic by ensuring adequate worker influence over design, implementation and development of existing forms of participation. "Dynamics" should not be taken as meaning "more of the same". It should not be interpreted as simply an extension and/or transplantation of existing forms of participation in particular countries. "Dynamics" should take into account socio-economic changes taking place now or expected to occur. Mention has already been made of the internationalisation and globalisation of the economy, the dislocation of ownership, the far-reaching changes in labour relations (part-time work, lean production, increasing cuts in the workforce, etc), different styles of management, new systems of information management, etc. All these changes bring with them many new challenges in the struggle to develop democratic participation.

These general statements of principle need considerable practical elaboration and require skill and imagination. But they are also limited by practical constraints. There is no room for Utopia in a liberal market economy. Conversely, acceptance of practical restraints which limit the potential development of democratic participation amounts to surrender on the part of the labour movement. The dynamics of development towards meaningful and effective democratic participation can only be maintained by active implementation and endeavour.

The development of democratic participation requires an appropriate support structure

The participatory process is an on-going process of policy and strategy formulation, of design, shaping and re-shaping, based on a constant evaluation of experience. Constant monitoring is required. The academic community has often been eager to assume this monitoring role and this has led to the democratisation of universities. But problems such as stagnation and decline also rear their heads at this level. Today we are witnessing the "participation strip-tease".

The observation that participation is a dynamic process implies that this gradual approach to the matter requires coordination, organisation and support. The development of participation has to be conceived in a broad framework in which several inter-dependent processes evolve. These include policy and strategy formulation, the design or re-design of structures and procedures, the expression of opinions and expectations by workers, their leaders, management, employers, government and others. The search for conditions suitable for the development of participation should take into account these processes and inherent tensions. This is particularly true given that conditions for further development are often to be found in processes beyond the workplace. Vanek advocated a support agency with an economic, social and legal role, but he remained vague as to who should initiate and manage the body (Vanek, 1970).

In some European countries special legal measures have been introduced to encourage the development of democratic participation (e.g. France, Germany, Greece, the Netherlands and Spain). In most countries, support is lacking or non-existent. Support by "third parties", in particular, universities or similar institutions, is sharply decreasing.

This "participation strip-tease" can be witnessed in many countries. Stripped not only of party slogans and utopian ideals, but also of ideological context, participation finds itself in a political vacuum and has lost many of its supporters. Capitalism has much freer play in the Western industrialised countries (plagued by Thatcherism), in Eastern European countries ("this is not the time for new experiments") and in developing countries ("if you were on our side in the Gulf War we will reduce your debts").

Scientific support is decreasing. The writing is on the wall. The Documentation Centre for Participation and Self-Management at EHESS in Paris has had to close for lack of funds. The outstanding documentation work of the International Institute of Labour Studies (ILO) has been discontinued. The journal "*Autogestions*" is no longer published, the "*Arbetslivscentrum*" in Sweden has been forced to accept a drastically reduced budget, while specialised courses on participation and self-management at the Institute of Social Studies in the Hague have been discontinued. Even the father of the theory of self-management, Jaroslav Vanek, no longer has an assistant to help him with his pioneering work on the Programme of Participatory and Labour Management Economics at Cornell University.

In recent years there have been some attempts to provide support. The creation of the European Foundation for the Improvement of Living Conditions and the Work Environment is one example. Under its auspices, trade unions and employers' organisations of the member states reached an understanding that employees and their representatives should be kept well-informed and be consulted during the introduction of new technology and the development of an improved work environment (Dublin Foundation, 1990). Drago and Wooden make an important observation on the difference between information and consultation, on the one hand (the major concern of the Dublin Foundation), and power-sharing at higher levels, on the other. They base their observations on painstaking, empirical study. "...participation...changes employee desires, with participation at higher levels increasing employee demands for it and participation at lower levels reducing demands for higher-level participation." (Drago and Wooden, 1991, p.177). The Dublin Foundation is based on the principle of tripartism. Tripartism is very important but it has to be recognised that it can also encourage a status quo. It would seem that the Dublin Foundation requires closer scrutiny to ensure that it is run as an instrument for obtaining more meaningful, effective and democratic worker influence.

The trade union movement has to reinvest in the development of democratic participation

Failing political or other forms of support, only the trade unions can hope to become leaders in the development of participation. Trade union support is needed because the unions can act as brokers and as a bridge in the participation process. A force that can be trusted by the workers can bind together different levels, different moments in time and different issues at the heart of the participatory process. As a workers' organisation, trade unions are ideally placed to play this role and give democratic participation new direction and shape.

If trade unions should decide to opt out or adopt a low profile, the initiative will fall into or remain in other hands. This is the danger facing us today as participative management, quality circles, employee stock option programmes and other worker shareholding schemes become employer initiatives.

Democratic participation can be a catalyst for trade union renewal.

In the search for solutions to secure the meaningful and effective involvement of workers and to monitor participation, the importance of trade unions is obvious. Trade unions are in a strategic position to represent the demands of the workers with respect to participation.

The participatory process should be seen as an incremental process of influence. It requires a stimulus, in the form of the trade unions, to represent its new objectives and expectations at higher levels. Progress made in participation must be transformed into new policies and strategies, often at national level, especially when new legislation is needed to consolidate progress (Kester, 1980).

In fact, the trade unions have fulfilled this role since their earliest days. When we examine what happened in Europe and other parts of the world (see Part II) we see that the greatest momentum was achieved in the 1960s and the 1970s.

What is so perplexing is that the trade union movement has lost this momentum, and has become more defensive, abandoning its initiative in worker participation to conservative forces. Over the last ten years or so, participation has been regarded as something of a luxury and trade unions have had to concentrate on more urgent and immediate problems.

Trade unions which have only a luke-warm attitude towards participation obviously hesitate in taking up the challenge. It would appear that they are being lured into a rapid "decentralisation" of labour relations and are having to cope with the effects of privatisation and company reorganisation, spending all their energy on issues such as wages and the work environment, sudden lay-offs, deregulation, etc.

But there may be more to this than meets the eye. Apart from offering alternative forms of participation, managers and employers have found it a useful line of defence to decentralise collective bargaining and promote individualised labour relations, thereby dissipating trade union energy and concentration. This "progressive fragmentation" of labour relations has, in the United Kingdom, been brilliantly described by Flanders and Fox (1970).

New enthusiasm is needed to breath new life into efforts to develop worker participation. In Western Europe the participative rights that workers have won so far must be defended and expanded. In Eastern Europe as well as in many developing countries (in Africa) where the collapse of orthodox political parties has created a political vacuum, trade unions should ensure that they do not become simple "bread and butter" unions.

The French trade union leader Maire made an appeal to use worker participation as a spring-board for trade union renewal (Maire, 1987). The opposite is equally true. Trade unions are a prerequisite for a renewal of the development of participation.

The relationship between trade unions and their members is undergoing substantive changes. Personal objectives are becoming more important than professional and work-related objectives (individualism/privatisation). The challenge facing the trade unions is to formulate new general objectives in response to the changing needs of the workers. The trade unions also seem to be facing internal challenges. They must increase union democracy, re-orient their policies and reorganise themselves.

Collective bargaining or participation - an erroneous choice

There has been a tendency to view collective bargaining and participation as contradictory. It is true that two different orientations underlie both. Collective bargaining emphasises the worker as the wage labourer and focuses trade union action on the conditions of the employment contract, whilst participation emphasises the worker as a partner in production who can claim, on the basis of his or her work input, a respected place in the production process.

If the trade unions put all their energy into bargaining, employers will try to manoeuvre forms of participation so that they favour the employers. Trade unions have to take up the challenge because corporate culture is already invading the ideological arena of the workplace.

A two-track strategy would appear to be the obvious answer - developing both bargaining and participation.

Collective bargaining is for the most part an "ex-post" phenomenon, dealing with the social consequences of economic, financial and technical decisions regarding terms of employment and, possibly, the work environment. In spite of its diverse manifestations, it generally takes place at fixed intervals, once a year, possibly once every two years, sometimes once every three years.

Many decisions can, meanwhile, be influenced by forms of participation such as consultation, which in practice is virtually a form of informal bargaining. This is an active and on-going process.

King and Van de Vall distinguish between three possible roles for trade unions in participatory systems (King and Van de Vall, 1978, p.166), taking the examples of the United Kingdom, Germany and former Yugoslavia. The British trade unions view management antagonistically and abstain from involvement in the participatory system, thereby maintaining their role as an independent opposition body. The German unions are more inclined to view management as an industrial partner and to accept that inherent in sharing control is a duty to assume shared responsibility. In former Yugoslavia, the trade unions switched to a more macro-social and national orientation, but their ideological roles and party links made

44

them a virtual mouthpiece for the State and an instrument of its control.

The choice is not between the three union stances outlined above. The challenge is to try and adopt all three roles without falling into the trap of state control. Often, traditional and participatory roles are viewed as contradictory. The danger here is that unions may start to boycott or fight against worker participation, seeing it as a threat to their existence or power. But surely this is playing into the hands of the employers? Research in Sweden and France has shown that corporatism is invading the workplace (Sandberg, 1990, Le Tron and Pinaud, 1991).

The situation is essentially different when trade unions start to offer their full support for the development of participation, using it as a spring-board for trade union renewal and/or as a direct response to workers' expectations about labour relations and their ambitions for participation. Mention has already been made of the development of participation as a response to the conspicuous absence of young workers in trade union ranks (see also the alarming figures in Noblecourt, 1990, p.28-29) and the need to build up a sound economy for the future, with full worker participation in productivity and modernisation (Le Tron and Pinaud, 1991).

Trade unions can take up the challenge of participation, over and beyond their present role at the bargaining table. They can champion this new form of representation of worker interests by giving it direction, serving as a platform for debate, analysing international experiences, developing new perspectives, gathering relevant information and working out a strategy to decide what will be solved through bargaining and what will be handled through participation and coordinating these two spheres of influence.

All this will make the tasks of the trade unions far more complex. Flexibility and adaptability become key words. But given that worker participation is an inescapable demand of our times, trade union involvement in its development could help eradicate the paradox whereby, on the one hand, traditional union structures feel themselves threatened by participation while, on the other, workers demand union support for it.

It is important that different trade union roles be clearly assigned and specified so that the autonomy of each can be protected and unions can remain effectively accountable to their members for their actions in the different roles they play (Blumberg, 1968, p.139).

There can be no development without democracy and no Democracy without participation

Participation can be likened to the linchpin between general elections and grass-roots democracy. For most people, multi-party democracy means going to the polls once every four or five years. Elected parliamentarians cannot oversee the entire decision-making apparatus of a nation at its many different levels. Forms of direct and indirect participation can involve large groups of citizens in democratic decision-making on matters of short-term and long-term importance. This can take place in schools, offices, the workplace, etc. Participation is a necessary complement to political democracy as it encourages people to express themselves on a more continuous basis. In times of economic recovery (particularly today in Eastern Europe and Africa), social cohesion is not won through tough measures and certainly not through tough leaders! It is won by ensuring greater democracy during the period of transition.

The World Bank, the IMF, multi-nationals and many industrialised countries are justifying the drive for restructuring and privatisation in Eastern Europe and the Third World by claiming that it is part of the process of replacing one-party systems and military regimes with multi-party democracy. The main donor countries believe so deeply in this cocktail of capitalism and Western democracy that they now make it a pre-condition for provision of further funds for development and cooperation.

It is becoming increasingly and dramatically clear that economic restructuring is good for the economy but bad for society. A rapidly widening chasm is appearing between those who survive the privatisation game (the factory cleaners employed before prospective buyers arrived who were lucky enough to keep their jobs after privatisation) and those who lose the privatisation game (the factory cleaners employed before prospective buyers arrived who were fired after privatisation). Those who stay have reasonable prospects, especially if they can benefit from the "paying for productivity" schemes. "How the Other Half Dies" or "A Fate Worse than Debt" are two accounts by Susan George of the consequences of restructuring for the other half (Susan George, 1986 and 1990).

If collective bargaining is to be the preferred channel of worker influence and if the employers are able to succeed in their attempts to over-decentralise it, then progressive fragmentation (see above) will do its work and in the short run all trade union activity will inevitably be concentrated on the luckier half and not on the half that dies! Once trade union activity is focused on a limited group and on a limited scope of action, its opponents will find it easier to create disunity, by creating economically different categories of workers and widening the gap between those with jobs and the jobless.

The social tensions which this could provoke could be much worse than anyone now dares imagine. In an emotional speech, Walter Grab warned a 1991 conference in Chemnitz (Germany) of the dialectic relationship between democracy, prosperity and nationalism. "The phenomena of chauvinism, racism, anti-semitism and xenophobia are functions and results of economic crisis...The present transformation of State capitalism in Eastern Europe to free enterprise and the market economy is producing nationalistic rivalries and conflicts in Yugoslavia, Rumania, the Baltic States and elsewhere" (Grab, 1991, p.10). At the same conference other speakers (Chouraqui and Sandberg) warned of the growing levels of anomy or social vacuum and the disintegration of society. Developments over the past three years do not encourage us to believe that we are dealing with temporary phenomena. It is to be feared that these trends will develop and spread throughout the former USSR and Africa.

We believe that participation is not a luxury but an indispensable instrument for exerting influence on economic restructuring. People are both the ends to and the means of development and thus independent, representative, democratic organisations must be given a forceful role in this process (Wagenmans, 1990). In most Eastern European and African countries, trade unions are the best organised and most vocal interest groups. They are in a unique position to point out to governments or the international community the consequences for workers of the economic measures being taken. They can press for a fair distribution of the cost of these adjustments (Wagenmans, ibid). This is not a commonly-shared viewpoint. In a book on development and democracy in Mauritius, no mention at all is made of trade *unions*. The book is more concerned with "trade *winds*" (Bowman, 1991). But many influential works on development do reserve a central place for participative approaches (e.g. Le Boterf and Lessard, 1986; Pradervand, 1989; Clark, 1991).

If we believe that worker and trade union participation are a vital part of a true democracy, then the World Bank, the IMF and donor countries can set yet another pre-condition for development aid and cooperation. They can demand participation in and beyond the workplace. No participation, no money. The European Union, with its tradition of support for worker participation, could set an example.

Democratic participation should be a lever for solidarity

Solidarity is a central concept in trade union vocabulary. It takes many different forms and poses ever new challenges. The development of democratic participation raises the spectre of a growing and deliberate division between workers. A wedge may be driven between the employed and the unemployed, between tenured and non-tenured workers, between immigrants, migrants and nationals, between "legal" and "illegal" workers and between full-time and part-time workers. Group egoism and corporatism are easily generated when forms of financial participation in profits and in capital are introduced in companies. It can also happen when some forms of co-determination are introduced but only made available to full-time workers in a company. If the interests of one group of workers override general interests, then democratic participation runs the risk of becoming a game for the privileged. We need to search for forms of participation which take into account the interests of all workers. The democratisation of participation is not a luxury. Development of all forms of participation adapted to specific situations, at every level, from the workshop and department to the company, region, industrial sector and the country as a whole, is imperative in order that lasting solutions be found to the scourges of unemployment and social exclusion.

One important and classic sociological theory argues that a lack of solidarity has devastating consequences for democracy and can lead to social disintegration (Durkheim, 1893). Modern society, with its far-reaching division of labour and its social, economic, political and cultural plurality must come to understand the interdependence of different groups in society. Society must create institutions which can express this interdependence or solidarity. Trade unions and other organisations have an important role to play here. Participation can be institutionalised so that it promotes this kind of solidarity. This can be achieved by developing more forms of supra-company participation (local, regional, national and international participation) in which less privileged groups can express themselves, can exert influence, can share in the fruits of economic success and, above all, can co-determine their future. This form of "organic" solidarity is a major component of social justice and it is the major line of defence against further social disintegration and rising nationalism, racism and violence.

Solidarity also means adopting a global perspective. It would be a mistake to talk solely of European participation. A new wave of enthusiasm for developing democratic participation is not only needed in the countries of the European Union. Central and Eastern Europe and the Third World are also undergoing rapid and merciless transformations towards neo-liberalism. Trade union influence is weakening and erstwhile institutions of participation are vanishing. As we try and breath new life into democratic participation, for example, with the European social policy, we should be aware of the needs of other parts of the world. Democratic participation should be developed to defend global solidarity.

It is precisely this challenge - championing social and economic justice for all, which could encourage trade union participation in decision-making at different levels. The internationalisation of the economy and the global dimension of many of the issues of tomorrow require a forceful international labour response.

4 The decline, consolidation or growth of democratic participation?

Gérard Kester and Henri Pinaud

The previous chapters have presented an analysis of the development of democratic participation in its broadest possible context. This analysis has paved the way for a policy debate on the future of democratic participation for trade unions.

Having presented a complex argumentation in the previous chapters, we will now proceed to a more simplified format, intended to trigger debate. Three future scenarios for democratic participation will be presented.

The first is the "bread and butter" scenario, in which trade unions concentrate exclusively on collective bargaining.

The second is the "consolidation" scenario, constituting essentially a continuation of the trends of the 1980s and early 1990s. Collective bargaining and related forms of industrial action and protest remain the main trade union preoccupations while forms of worker participation initiated and/or supported by the trade unions since the 1960s and 1970s continue to be defended. This scenario could also be called the "status quo" scenario. It should be noted that in this scenario, recent forms of worker participation, such as managerial and financial participation, initiated by management and employers, imply only marginal trade union involvement.

The third scenario is the "growth" scenario which essentially breaks with the trends of the 1980s and early 1990s and offers active trade union support for and coordination of all forms of worker participation and seeks to strengthen democratic participation at meso, macro and international levels. This scenario is called "Scenario 21", in reference to the next century. In this scenario, existing forms of participation will be improved and expanded and new forms initiated.

These scenarios are presented for policy debate. They represent broad policy outlines, based on an analysis of pilot schemes and experiences in a select number of European countries (see Chapter 1) and on a number of general assumptions which have been made explicit (see Guiding Principles, Chapter 3). They may serve as points of reference in the debate on the development of policies and strategies on participation and in discussion of the institution of an appropriate framework to support democratic participation.

These scenarios are not "models" but projections of possible trends. They are presented in general and, by necessity, simplified terms. Concrete details must be worked out in each individual country. Many variables may come into play such as the size of the company, the sector (public or private), the industry, relevant technological, legal and commercial frameworks, trade union tradition and strength, etc. The scenarios have not taken into account all these variables.

In each of the three scenarios, propositions for the following five different forms of participation are examined: "classical collective bargaining", "concertation and/or co-management", "co-determination", "participation in management" and "financial participation" (see the introduction of chapter 1 for a brief explanation of these five forms).

The bread and butter scenario

The mainstay of this scenario is that unions more or less exclusively concentrate on negotiations on the terms of employment through collective bargaining. Collective bargaining is likely to become less effective in the long-term if unions do not actively seek to develop other forms of participation.

Some trade unions in Western Europe have expressed reservations about co-determination and other forms of worker participation. They have adopted traditional collective bargaining as their main form of action. As a result, trade union action is in no way opposed to, nor does it seek to influence employer and management-initiated schemes such as participation in management and financial participation. Collective bargaining is likely to become increasingly less effective because:

a) its scope will be increasingly limited as employers continue to develop and expand managerial and financial forms of participation. Those bodies in companies on which elected worker representatives sit, run the risk of being increasingly controlled by non-unionised "independent" employees who are all the more susceptible to employer pressure. Work environment issues will be increasingly discussed in forums generated by participation in management. These issues will thus become a subject of joint management and worker regulation. Financial participation will give employers the chance to deal much more directly with workers, using financial terms of reference. This may eventually mean that employers will offer workers a framework for discussing financial and remunerative matters which will render trade union bargaining increasingly redundant.

b) as employers increasingly negotiate directly with workers on issues such as the work environment and financial incentives, and respond to important worker concerns, trade unions will find it harder to win support for industrial action from workers and the general public. If trade unions refuse to acknowledge and embrace existing and new forms of participation but only concern themselves with collective bargaining and related forms of action and protest, they will become increasingly stigmatised as trouble-makers and are likely to find themselves rapidly losing support and membership. Employers can encourage this trend by stepping up their efforts to deal with workers within the framework of institutionalised forms of participation.

The consolidation scenario

The essence of the consolidation scenario is combining collective bargaining and co-determination at company level. Existing forms of co-determination will eventually lose their effectiveness if trade unions do not play a more active role in encouraging them and strengthening links between co-determination and managerial and financial participation.

The bread and butter scenario and to a lesser extent the consolidation scenario could provoke the following sequence of phenomena:

1) *a division in the representation of workers' interests. On the one hand representation in a trade union context, and the other, representation in a management context. This duality of representation would undoubtedly be exploited by employers.*

2) *a shift away from collective forms of representation to individually-based forms of representation.*

3) *individualisation of labour relations and the creation of different categories of workers, a consequence of increased financial participation.*

4) *a further split in the work force which in turn may lead to further decentralisation of collective bargaining.*

5) *progressive fragmentation (see chapter 3, guiding principle 6) which could lead to social disintegration and anomy.*

6) *a widening gap between two broad categories of workers. On the one hand there would be the productively employed, often enjoying material benefits as a result of corporatist schemes and hence requiring less and less trade union support. On the other hand, the marginalised workers with few material benefits or none at all, the part-time employed (a consequence of deregulation) and the unemployed.*

7) *a danger that unions will eventually find themselves mainly representing the dispossessed. In their struggle for social justice and solidarity, the union may gradually lose the support of those who have what they need.*

8) *management and employer encouragement of this trend. Governments may remain indifferent.*

9)   *increased isolation of trade unions, forced to deal more and more with only the negative aspects of the privatisation, materialisation and individualisation of labour relations.*

10) *the possibility of inevitable drops in union membership, power and influence*

In Chapter 1, it was concluded that over the past few decades mainstream Western European trade unionism has managed to consolidate its achievements in worker participation.

Co-determination is and will remain an area of contention between trade unions and management. Employers will continue to try and bring co-determination under their control. They may well succeed given that managerial and financial participation create a corporate culture in work organisation. Co-determination could well become a form of representation to which trade unions have no access. A number of studies have already illustrated this trend (Part II). The recent success of a workers council in a Dutch company in concluding a non-union collective agreement with their employer illustrates the extent of the potential de-unionisation of co-determination. Furthermore, the proportion of elected trade union officials on workers councils continues to decline (see Chapter 1). A reduced trade union role in co-determination is unlikely to be in the interests of industrial democracy. It was trade union pressure and power which originally led to a widening of the scope of co-determination. But as co-determination increasingly falls under management control it will undoubtedly become primarily a forum for information and consultation, thereby assigning trade unions to the same fate as outlined in the Bread and Butter Scenario.

If trade union involvement in work organisation, management and financial participation continues to be non-existent or paltry, the danger of such a fate for the unions increases. If employers and management continue to dominate this domain, they will make renewed and further attempts to reach agreements with workers on matters regarding the work environment and financial incentives while not ceding any of their prerogatives. The conclusions of studies of financial participation in the United Kingdom cited earlier suggest that in this form of participation employers continue to regard the distribution of shares to employees as a generous gift while refusing collective consultation and negotiation of economic decision-making (Baddon et al, 1989, p281).

Recent French research into participative systems suggest that a new kind of social actor - the employees themselves - is emerging, that a new form social relations is developing within companies and that the trade unions and the employees are drifting further and further apart. Until the end of the 1970s, trade unions did not believe that participation, the democratisation of work relations and direct worker expression were separate and independent of union representation. Industrial democracy and participation were more or less inseparably linked to the development of union power and collective bargaining. Obviously, relations with unions is still an important aspect of all relations in a company. Unions define rights and limit abuses, negotiate wages and defend the work environment. The unions are the memory of a company. But workers consider unions to be far removed from their work, its organisation and for life on the shop-floor or in the office. Unions are not directly involved in management changes and alterations in social relations. Being excluded or having excluded themselves from these types of participation, the unions are no longer at the centre of new socio-productive models in society. The best they can do is to stand on the sidelines. (P. Bernoux, 1993 and C. Thuderoz, 1993).

The danger of corporatism in the Consolidation Scenario cannot be over-emphasised. If the trade union movement does not take a lead in developing all five major forms of participation at different levels and uniting different categories of workers, then the gulf between the employed and the unemployed will widen. Within the category of the employed there will be further sub-divisions as employers succeed in their attempts at differentiating financial participation. The Consolidation Scenario represents a threat to worker solidarity as it puts increasing emphasis on collective bargaining. It is in the interests of employers and management to encourage financial and management participation and co-determination because they provide an opportunity for setting up institutionalised channels between management and the employees. As these channels and links develop, trade union power will correspondingly diminish. This may eventually lead to a weakening of employment contracts. If employers resort to these forms of participation in an attempt to eradicate trade unions, the unions will have no alternative but to respond by fighting for their preferred forms of participation and trying to win back the confidence of the workers.

The scenario for growth of democratic participation, or scenario 21 (scenario for the 21st century)

Trade unions are ideally placed to respond to challenges at the meso and macro-economic and social level. Only they are able to present a united front and offer a strong response, both in tripartite bodies and when negotiating other policy agreements. These meso and macro-forms of co-determination open up the possibility of elevating participation to even higher levels of decision-making.

The mainstay of scenario 21 is the development and spread of co-determination and increased active union involvement in all forms of participation including organisational and financial participation. If this scenario is played out, the following trends are to be expected:

1) collective bargaining, rather than becoming less effective, will flourish because, a) the domains it covers can be better defined and coordinated with other forms of participation b) trade union involvement in all forms of participation will represent a multi-track strategy and will prevent employers from using different forms of participation as tools in their fight against unions c) trade unions will win social support and will no longer be regarded as trouble-makers but as a constructive social partner.

2) *co-determination will have a greater chance defending the interests of the workers if it is actively supported by trade unions. There is considerable research evidence which suggests that active trade union support increases the scope and extent of co-determination (see chapter 1). Training, education, advice and other forms of support and encouragement are vital to ensure that this form of participation is fully exploited. It is here that trade unions can play a most effective role.*

3) *managerial and financial participation would better reflect the individual and collective interests of the workers if such schemes were actively supported and coordinated by trade unions. This is especially true if these forms of participation could be combined with co-determination and collective bargaining. This would provide a comprehensive framework in which workers' interests could be represented. It would ensure policy continuity and a better balance between individual and collective interests and between the interests of the privileged and the under-privileged. The democratisation of management and financial participation would elevate these productivity and financial incentive schemes to a higher and broader level. This is unlikely to happen without explicit trade union support.*

4) *trade union support for and involvement in all forms of participation would make it possible to balance individual, group and collective interests and thus promote social justice and social cohesion. This new form of solidarity would be even more effective if trade unions were willing to support, monitor, assist, coordinate, educate and train their members, worker representatives and workers in general.*

5) *different forms of participation (traditional collective bargaining, concertation, co-determination, participation in management and financial participation) are neither mutually contradictory nor incompatible. On the contrary, their effect can be cumulative. Implemented separately they lose their meaning and effectiveness. Implemented in harmony they assume a dynamic force - in other words they become democratic participation. Thus trade unions may enjoy a comprehensive hold over labour issues and all forms of labour participation.*

6) *ultimately, scenario 21 is a scenario of greater solidarity and democracy. It is a scenario for empowerment. It seeks to link the problems of the shop-floor and the enterprise to meso and macro-level problems and to local, regional, national, european and global challenges. It offers the possibility for trade unions to promote a democratic culture of solidarity in which workers fight for their own rights and the rights of others, not with the law of the jungle but by building and using solid democratic institutions in the world of work and the economy.*

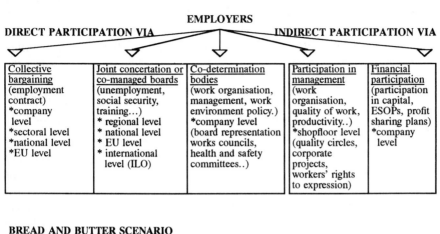

DIRECT PARTICIPATION VIA ———————— INDIRECT PARTICIPATION VIA

Collective bargaining (employment contract) *company level *sectoral level *national level *EU level	Joint concertation or co-managed boards (unemployment, social security, training...) * regional level * national level * EU level * international level (ILO)	Co-determination bodies (work organisation, management, work environment policy.) *company level (board representation works councils, health and safety committees..)	Participation in management (work organisation, quality of work, productivity..) *shopfloor level (quality circles, corporate projects, workers' rights to expression)	Financial participation (participation in capital, ESOPs, profit sharing plans) *company level

BREAD AND BUTTER SCENARIO

Collective bargaining is the main form of union action	Trade union action is mainly determined by the major issues of collective bargaining	Passive trade union attitude	No trade union involvement	No trade union involvement

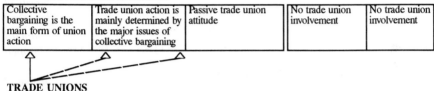

TRADE UNIONS

CONSOLIDATION SCENARIO

Emphasis on collective bargaining as in the bread and butter scenario, but in coordination with codetermination	A wider range of issues is considered	Active trade union role in the organisation, functioning and development of codetermination	Little or no trade union involvement	Little or no trade union involvement

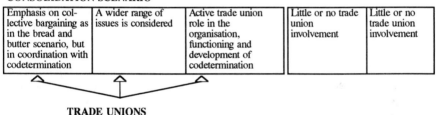

TRADE UNIONS

DEMOCRATIC PARTICIPATION GROWTH SCENARIO

Collective bargaining remains important together with all other forms of democratic participation	Trade unions seek to influence issues concerning the work contract, the economy and politics. Growth of influence at national and international level	As in the consolidation scenario, but incorporating financial and management participation so as to increase union influence on a wider range of issues and at international level (European works councils)	Rendering forms of participation in management and work organisation more democratic	More democratic control of financial participation; links to collective bargaining and collective forms of financial participation

TRADE UNIONS

Figure 1 Three democratic participation scenarios

Scenario 21 should not be regarded as a departure from the Bread and Butter and the Consolidation Scenarios. In the latter two, the power of collective bargaining represents the foundation of trade union action. This power must be preserved. In the Consolidation Scenario, the power of co-determination, especially at company level, gains momentum. Several countries in the European Union have valuable experience of collective bargaining (the United Kingdom being perhaps the leader). Others, such as Germany, have wide experience of co-determination.

Scenario 21 is not completely unknown. Unions in some countries already have considerable experience of financial participation, such as Denmark, experience of concertation at meso and macro levels (Italy, the Netherlands) and experience of direct democracy in the workplace (France). So important lessons can be learned in preparation for taking the next logical step at European level.

However, Scenario 21 is not simply a continuation of the first two scenarios. Rather, it is a response to a rapidly changing world, rapid and major changes in the labour market, a shift away from secure employment contracts to short-term contracts, away from full-time to part-time employment and to higher labour turnover. Ownership structures are changing too. They are being internationalised, even globalised. The problems of energy supplies, natural resources, the environment, migration, population, etc., all have major consequences for the world of labour and production. Technological changes, social changes (towards increased individualisation) and political changes (towards liberalisation) are creating new kinds of workers.

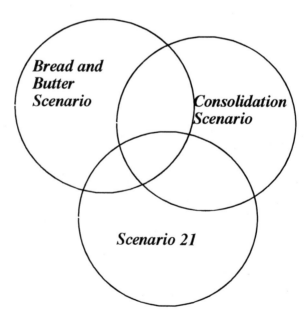

Figure 2 The partial overlap of the three scenarios

56

There is a wide spectrum of spheres in which new participation strategies could be explored. These include the environment, the labour market, quality of life in general, the creation of socially useful activities, adult education, non-discrimination, etc. The ETUC and, at the global level the ICFTU and the WCL, have all made their positions clear. In some cases specific demands have been made but it is vital that reliable, regular and effective institutions be created to guarantee trade union influence on European and global developments.

In the past trade unions have proved that they could achieve this. In the postwar years of reconstruction, diverse forms of national consultation flourished in many European countries. But over the last two decades decline and consolidation have set in everywhere except, perhaps, in Italy, where trade union participation in regional reconstruction constitutes an important innovation in democratic participation. Present, traditional institutions of labour relations cannot hope to cope with the meso and macro-level issues with which the world of labour is confronted today. In addition to the right to expression (often extended by trade unions to cover other issues - for example anti-racism demonstrations), co-determination is needed in regional and national concertation to ensure that broader issues are effectively dealt with. Solidarity contracts are a good example of the kind of innovative schemes required. Many issues can only be handled at international level. European works councils could play a leading role here but they run the risk of becoming bogged down in international corporatism. More, much more is needed. Above all, courage is needed, because when trade unions demand increased participation they must also accept increased responsibility.

It is not always desirable to achieve concertation by encouraging tripartite bodies (frameworks for policy agreement between the government, employers and trade unions). Tripartite institutions are extremely important but they carry with them the threat of creating a coalition of those who have what they need and marginalising the dispossessed and of concentrating on the present at the cost of the future. Consensus between strong social partners of production may well encourage vested interests to take precedence while traditional structures in which labour relations are handled gradually ossify. This will make it almost impossible to respond to the major labour problems of the future. Other frameworks for reaching democratic agreements, such as bipartite or multipartite structures might be envisaged, bringing into play consumer groups, environmentalists, anti-racism organisations and women's groups. Some steps involving these other social partners have already been taken. It is precisely in the domains that these groups represent that the major challenges of tomorrow will have to be faced. Social, political and trade union imagination and inventiveness in these domains is essential in the future.

Scenario 21 is a scenario of solidarity. Deregulation policies must be replaced by an economy of employment for all, social guarantees and equal rights for all. Other avenues should also be explored such as a shorter working week, a minimum wage, etc. The development of all five forms of democratic participation must reflect the interests of trade union members and non-members alike, the employed and the unemployed, the young and the socially excluded.

Trade unions may find themselves faced with a paradox, as far as membership is concerned. In the struggle to staunch falling membership, priority must be given to improving direct links with workers in the workplace and dealing with concrete bargaining issues. Further involvement in co-determination at national level and reaching policy agreements at international level will not in themselves produce any sharp increases in union membership. Nevertheless, the Scenario for Growth of Democratic Participation is an essential investment for the future.

Social support for a solid trade union policy on democratic participation seems likely. Industrial strife which aims to win social justice for all will be regarded as justified by society and in everyone's best interests. In the long-term, such a path is also in the best interests of both the economy and society as a whole and thus government and employer support might eventually also be won.

Conditions for the success of scenario 21

The sustained spread of democratic participation is only possible under appropriate conditions. The three most important conditions are a) a coherent national and international trade union participation policy b) a framework which would provide facilities for research, information, education, training, publications, consultancy and legal advice c) a permanent institutionalised framework of joint trade union-university research on democratic participation. We will examine these three conditions here in brief.

A coherent trade union policy and strategy for participation

It has been repeatedly argued throughout this document that trade unions are in a strategic position to take up the challenge of democratic participation by drawing up a comprehensive and coherent policy and devising suitable strategies.

On the basis of the analysis presented in this document, it is felt that several major issues deserve particular attention. First, the absence of any declared trade union policy on participation, at a time when employers are taking the initiative in participation, unhindered by any union counter-proposals. The trade unions need a firm stance on this issue. In addition to formulating short, medium and long-term objectives, trade unions must also outline the means and conditions required for achieving these objectives.

The absence of any trade union policy is particularly noticeable at international level. The internationalisation of the economy implies an internationalisation of labour relations. Tiziano Treu made a plea for action in this domain, "while economic integration is rapidly becoming a reality in Europe and might accelerate in other areas, the pace of social integration is much slower...international Fordism may benefit from the international dimension of economic action by the simple absence of any opposing social and political forces." (Treu, 1992, p18-24).

The information and consultation procedures enshrined in the European Union's present social policy (see Goetschy, Chapter 13) are totally inadequate as tools of labour influence. Several courses of action must be taken at European Union level:

a) recognition is required of a number of fundamental principles of democratic participation. These will form the basis of a social policy. These principles include not only the right to information and consultation but also the right to participate in decision-making on all matters which directly or indirectly affect workers, both the employed and the unemployed, both in the workplace and at regional, national and international level.

b) while winning recognition of the right to participation, this right must be sufficiently flexible to ensure that its application in particular countries is feasible, given the local social, political and economic conditions. There should be no "models". What are needed are "spearheads" of participation. Once an accepted set of principles for participation exists, those countries in which conditions are suitable would take the lead and then gradually encourage other countries to follow suit, with ETUC support. This would appear to be a far better solution than adopting a model acceptable to all countries and thereby reducing participation to the lowest common denominator.

c) given the internationalisation of the economy, a framework for democratic participation must be developed to allow workers, via trade unions, to influence economic and social policy in the European Union and beyond.

Given the different leanings of European trade union federations, it is by no means an easy task to mobilise and encourage them to develop new ways of reaching agreement on macro-economic issues. Nevertheless, a basic policy agreement at European Union level may prove to be the only way of achieving any further internationalisation of democratic participation. Many of the issues of tomorrow go well beyond national borders and beyond those of the European Union.

Trade unions in Central and Eastern Europe and many unions in Third World countries are struggling to get to grips with decisions affecting their workers and their societies. Many of these decisions are being made in other parts of the world. The European Union, the World Bank and the IMF, not to mention multi-national corporations, are developing highly undemocratic forms of economic aid and assistance which ignore the interests of workers. Forums for discussion of these issues do already exist (such as the annual European Union consultative rounds on the Lomé Treaty). But we need to evaluate the effectiveness of democratic participation at this level and search for ways of improving it.

At the international level it is also important to review the role of the ILO in the development of democratic participation. The vast majority of the ILO's conventions are concerned with collective bargaining and associated procedures.

But there is not a single convention on other forms of worker participation and only five more or less specific ILO recommendations (N° 94, 113, 127 129 and 135). These recommendations deal with communication and cooperation within companies, cooperatives and consultation (but not co-determination) at levels beyond the company. The latest of these recommendations was drawn up as far back as 1967!

How can a trade union movement which is already experiencing hard times, deal with policy issues for the workplace as well as national and international issues? This paradox has already been mentioned. Can unions afford to concentrate on developing industrial democracy at the international level while in many countries these same unions are losing rank-and-file support? The situation presents an alarming picture. Clearly the only solution is to ensure that the development of democratic participation at these differing levels is harmonised and that a complementarity and inter-dependency between these levels is achieved. Furthermore, the workers must be convinced of the utility of democratic participation. Only positive results will convince them.

A support structure for democratic participation

Simply drawing up a trade union policy for participation, at company level or beyond, is not enough. The implementation of such a policy needs to be constantly monitored and evaluated and those involved must be educated and trained. Democracy is a learning process and democracy can only be achieved if we learn lessons from this process so that the next steps forward can be taken. Participation is, as was argued in Chapter 3, a dynamic phenomenon which requires a permanent support structure. Perhaps the greatest weakness in the development of democratic participation over the past decades has not been the absence of policy but rather the absence of sustained support for implementation. It would seem to be of primary importance that the process of implementation be reinforced. This requires considerable investment. Investments are needed not only in the economy but also in democracy. Workplace participation is one of the most important manifestations of democracy. It has been argued that Scenario 21 will lead to greater social integration, social justice and social cohesion. If democratic participation functions effectively, the returns on adequate investments will be incalculable.

The following elements must be built into any such support structure:

(a)   research/evaluation/monitoring
(b)   information/publication/media
(c)   education and training
(d)   legal and other forms of advice and assistance
(e)   organisation and other forms of support

In the past, support in these areas has been weak, badly-coordinated and often arbitrary rather than systematic or lasting.

Research and evaluation are indispensable for the development of democratic participation. Frameworks need to be created in which workers can regularly express their experiences. These frameworks would permit workers to explain what they would like to implement in order to improve worker participation and widen its scope. Continuous feed-back would thus be created. This is a imperative if monitoring is to verify the extent to which stated objectives have been actually been achieved. Such feed-back would also permit re-adjustments to implementation.

Although this is not the place to go into detail about all the elements of such a support structure, some remarks should be made concerning education and training.

As stated above, a comprehensive education and training policy is needed to enable people to play their parts in democratic participation at every level. Worker education would concentrate on raising awareness of the phenomenon of participation in all its manifestations, as well as understanding of its dynamics, its potential, the links between participation at different levels, the importance of participation in terms of the development of democracy, etc. This kind of teaching should obviously not take the form of indoctrination or the promotion of a particular trade union ideology. It should provide platforms for well-informed discussion of policy, choices and methods of implementation.

Training will be needed to enable workers' representatives to acquire the skills and competence they need to play their roles in the organs of participation. Clearly both training and education will increase in importance and effectiveness as their form and content are continuously adapted to the results of research on real experiences in participation.

When so much weight is attached to both training and education, the importance of universities and research institutions becomes apparent. In Part III a review is presented of the current state of cooperation between trade unions and universities. It will be argued that university resources are increasingly being channelled into human resource management. Furthermore, academics and researchers are doing far too little to transmit their specialist knowledge to those social actors who could use it profitably. Research results are often presented in a language which is incomprehensible to workers and their representatives and relevant publications are sold at prices they can ill-afford. Typically, work on labour issues is chiefly published nationally or internationally for the academic community. When academic works are made available to the general public, it is employers who buy books about workers, landlords who buy books about peasants and "ladies" who buy books about women. It is striking to note that the sharp reduction in the amount of literature on democratic participation has by and large gone unnoticed in trade union and worker circles because they have never been target reader groups. If a renewal of democratic participation constitutes an investment in democracy, university and research institutions will have to assume their responsibilities. They are public institutions and should cater to the needs of society. Instead of exclusively serving as bulwarks of the economy they should resume their role as bulwarks of democracy.

It is at universities that future generations are moulded. Areas of academic interest are quickly reflected in the general education system. It is of great importance that subjects such as labour, trade unionism, democratic participation in its various manifestations and the democratisation of industrial relations in general are re-established as areas of interest to the educational system, along with other forms of democracy and development. Precautions must therefore be taken and special provisions made to ensure that the knowledge generated by research is put to use for policy-making and action.

Towards an institutionalised framework of trade union research cooperation in the area of democratic participation

One of the methods of ensuring a direct link between research on the one hand and policy, action, training and education on the other, is to design cooperation projects between universities and research institutions and trade unions. As will be argued later, such projects should include cooperation at all stages of research. Researchers should play a role in policy formulation, education, training and consultancy. Long-term cooperation is needed to produce an integrated programme of research, education, information, training, policy formulation and assistance. It should allow for a continuous evaluation of democratic participation in all its forms.

Can existing institutions fulfill this function? Research institutes within the trade union structures which exist (only in some countries) have never generally paid much attention to democratic participation over the years. And even when they have, they have lacked the necessary resources to respond to the needs of the broader spectrum of research outlined in this document. Moreover, most trade union federations in the European Union, let alone trade unions in other parts of the world, do not have research units of any great size.

The question to be asked here is whether a tripartite structure is the most appropriate form for a body which is designed to support the development of democratic participation in Scenario 21. If the trade union movement wishes to renew its role as the leader of democratic participation and thus seeks research and educational support, it can make a (public) appeal to universities to establish bilateral relations. Many employers already make frequent and intensive use of university facilities. A tripartite organisation means the creation of legal or formal agreements and the creation of platforms for the elaboration and discussion of these agreements. If research, evaluation, information and training are only implemented through tripartite agreements, consensus or compromise with employers will have to be reached at every stage. The employers will naturally want to defend the status quo. They have no interest in Scenario 21. But why should the trade union movement allow the agenda for democratic participation, research and education to be jointly determined by the employers?

The case argued here is that a specifically designed support base for democratic participation should be created, together with a permanent trade union-university cooperation project with a jointly drawn-up agenda of research, education and training and policy and action development. This argument will be picked up again in the postface of this book.

Part II
ANALYSIS OF EXPERIENCE

Introduction to Part II

Gérard Kester and Henri Pinaud

In the first part we have attempted to present a series of observations on the present state of direct and indirect participation in Western Europe. We have also formulated a series of principles and propositions which are intended to (1) rekindle union and academic debate on the subject of participation (2) present trade union strategy and policy options for reappropriating democracy both in companies and in society, in Europe and beyond (3) stipulate the conditions for successful implementation of the "Scenario 21" option, with specific reference to the need for cooperation between trade unions and universities and research institutes.

The second part contains the material which we drew on to make these observations and formulate our propositions. We asked European academics and researchers, some specialists in the field of participation and others with experience of cooperation with trade union organisations in their country, to analyse recent trends in the development of participation in each country

In drawing on contrasting or convergent situations in each country the chapters contained in this second part help elucidate and illustrate the conclusions that we put forward in Part I. These articles represent an exceptionally rich compilation of information about the subject gathered over a period of many years. Most of the articles have been subjected to scrutiny from the academic contributors, during 1992 and 1993 editorial workshops and from trade union representatives, during a European seminar held in February 1994. The articles were revised several times as a result of these meetings in an attempt to achieve scientific and social coherence.

Part II will examine aspects of worker participation, such as indirect participation (collective bargaining, national consultation committees and elected representative bodies) and forms of direct participation which have recently been introduced by employers such as organisational participation, financial participation, etc. Our intention is to study the conditions under which these various types of participation have emerged and developed and to examine the attitudes and strategies of those involved.

The most immediate question which springs to mind is how European trade union organisations regard worker participation. Do any trade union strategies exist in European countries? Are there any common denominators in these strategies and if so what are they? What roles do large international confederations such as the ETUC play? How is participation likely to evolve in the future?

Secondly, it is important to examine the realities and significance of participation, especially organisational participation, for employers. How does participative management work in different countries? Does it represent a break from or simply an adaptation of Taylorist-Fordian work organisation? What effect does it have on union influence inside and outside the company? What effect does it have on the influence, the level and the content of collective bargaining? What effect does it have on the role and the credibility of elected union representatives sitting on representation boards? Is there an organised strategy at a national, European or even global level, behind the development of these new employer-initiated forms of human resource management?

Thirdly, we need to examine the nature and importance of the role of governments and international bodies such as the EU, and their attitudes towards different forms of worker participation. It is especially important to examine the importance and influence of legislation on participation. It is also interesting to examine the value and limitations of State funding and State initiation of participation.

Fourthly, we need to question the workers themselves. What are their perceptions, what are their reactions to, their opinions of and their demands as regards various forms of participation? Under what conditions and in what areas should direct participation and expression develop?

We have concerned ourselves primarily with Western Europe and specifically with Germany, France, Belgium, Great Britain, Italy, Malta, the Netherlands and Scandinavia, specialist areas of the researchers and academics involved in the project. But we believe that it is of vital strategic importance to examine the subject of participation in global terms and for this reason this general outline includes countries of Central and Eastern Europe and the rest of the world.

5 Participation in France

Henri Pinaud

Participation in France has generally developed along the same lines as elsewhere in Western Europe, with some specific characteristics, of course.

1968 - 1981: A period marked by new ideas, experiments and demands

At the end of the 1960s and the beginning of the 1970s, Taylorist forms of work organisation were shaken to their foundations by major social uprisings against the inhumanity and mindlessness of routine and anonymous work, a poor work environment, economic competition prompted by the remorseless globalisation of the economy and the speed of technical progress. France came up with four different responses to the question of democracy in the private and public sector.

Academics and researchers, analysing the "scientific work organisation", attempted to suggest adaptations or substitutes on the basis of studies and experience in France and elsewhere. Thus the debate was influenced by G. Friedmann, A. Gorz, A. Wisner and the French school of ergonomics, Thorsrud and the Tavistock Institute's socio-technical school, Herzberg and even the American school of human relations. Conditions for and forms of industrial democracy and technical self-management were central to the work of all these academics, either outside or within the capitalist economic system (e.g. Gorz, 1975).

The second response came from the government. While commissioning several national studies on the work environment and company reforms (in particular Sudreau, 1975), the government concentrated on trying to encourage limited forms of direct worker participation in private companies. In 1973 the ANACT (National Agency for Improvements in the Work Environment) was set up. This was a tripartite body (the State, the unions and employers) which was to provide financial incentives to management to experiment with new forms of work organisation and improve the work environment.

During this same period many organisational experiments were carried out, largely based on Anglo-Saxon or Scandinavian examples. These were mainly aimed at improving the internal flexibility of companies given the very unstable economic and commercial context. These experiments included expanding and enriching work tasks, introducing job rotation, autonomous production groups, workers' research teams studying improvements in the work environment, management by objectives, etc. These schemes were often carried out with the help of outside consultants and were organised by management, who always refused any negotiations with trade union organisations, despite attempts by the CFDT in 1973 and 1978.

Major debates took place amongst union organisations in an attempt to respond to the qualitative demands of workers which were becoming increasingly important in comparison to the more traditional quantitative demands regarding wages, hours and employment. Furthermore, the form in which these problems were surfacing was relatively new. Conflicts were arising as a result of action taken at grass-root level by small groups of unskilled workers, often women and immigrants, who cared about their own situation.

The unions were ill-equipped to tackle these problems related to work organisation and the work environment. There were several reasons for this.

Firstly, as the CFDT wrote in 1976, "French trade unionism has devoted its energy to the struggle to compensate the effects of work organisation and the division of labour, but it has always found it difficult to alter the foundations on which these are based..." Furthermore, many of the issues which needed to be tackled were problems concerning individual or small groups of wage-earners. These problems were of an essentially qualitative nature and generally very vague. They tended to vary in terms of urgency and intensity. It proved difficult for unions to handle these problems using their traditional methods of all-encompassing claims, union action and bargaining for collective guarantees at national or sectoral level. A more suitable forum for settling these problems would have been the company or even the shop-floor, levels at which negotiations did not often take place before 1983. Handling problems at these level risked generating conflicts of interest amongst workers.

Consequently, rank-and-file aspirations tended to be tackled in an approach more adapted to centralised bargaining. This meant an absence of company agreements while claims regarding work organisation simply revolved around wage scales, and as far as the work environment was concerned, it was quite common to simply negotiate hardship bonuses. Thus there was a move away from qualitative solutions to quantitative solutions while a real debate on work organisation was replaced by attempts to wrestle with the consequences of scientific work organisation.

The difficulty that the unions experienced in handling qualitative problems and their distrust of the field that work organisation encompassed can perhaps be traced back to the influence of Marxist theory on French trade union ideology and strategies. This influence has channelled the French unions' concerns away from the companies into the sphere in which Capital and Science are to be found. The class struggle has stifled the fight for work organisation and the work environment. Another consequence of the French trade union perception of power is that since power is not to be found in the factory but elsewhere, this surely means that management, executives, technicians and foremen must be considered as simply go-betweens between the real power brokers at the top and the workers. What is the role of the middle classes who combine specialist knowledge and power? There seems to be no clear answer. This emphasis on the power of capital is very useful in analysing situations but creates serious imbalances between rank-and-file and general needs by eclipsing the very powerful mechanisms at play at grass-root level.

However, since the 1968 "uprising of unskilled, blue and white collar workers" and given recent employer experiments, trade unions are now going to have to incorporate working conditions and work organisation into their claim strategies. They will doubtless disagree about the methods and will perhaps not proceed in a coordinated manner, especially when it comes to the right of expression for workers.

The CFDT was the first, in 1973, to float the idea that workers are experts in organisation and the work environment. With this in mind, the CFDT demanded that workers be granted the right to direct expression on matters of work organisation, job content and work environment. Their aim was twofold, to respond to experiments imposed unilaterally by management and to achieve self-management. This form of direct expression was to be linked to union expression. The call came in the wake of the CFDT 1970 congress, where it had outlined the three pillars of its plan for society: self-management in companies, decentralised planning and social ownership (rather than State ownership) of the means of production and exchange. In a 1977 manifesto the CFDT called for further wide scale nationalisations and, to counter-balance this increased power of the State, the creation of workshop, office and company councils which would work towards self-management in nationalised companies.

In 1978, the French trade union organisation CGT also adopted the principles of self-management and the right to expression but the CGT-FO remained adamantly hostile to all forms of direct worker expression in companies.

From then on, especially from the mid-1970s, when union membership dropped drastically and regularly, this debate divided French trade union organisations and activists.

On the one hand there were those (mainly the CGT-FO) who believed that the trade union was a collective organisation which workers had fought to set up and that the union was the sole historically legitimate body able to defend the workers' interests and speak in their name. This was the principle of delegation. They also pointed out the danger that direct expression, which could be manipulated by employers, posed to elected institutions of representation (such as works councils and staff representatives) and to the unions themselves. They stressed that collective bargaining, at that time mainly conducted at sectoral level, was also

71

threatened. On the other hand there were those, like most members of the CFDT, who believed that workers had the competence and the legitimacy to make qualitative demands and that this was the first step towards self-management.

Nevertheless most trade union organisations closed ranks to oppose the worker shareholder schemes introduced under the 1970 and 1973 laws and to support, albeit it rather timidly, all forms of the social economy such as the cooperative and associative sectors and mutual insurance companies - non-profit organisations which were increasingly introducing forms of worker participation in their decision-making processes.

Throughout the years from 1968 to 1981 there was an explosion of new ideas, experiments, claims and discussions concerning worker participation in France.

From 1981 onwards: implementation and loss of momentum

The Socialist government came to power in 1981 and thanks also to the influence of the CFDT, introduced the Auroux Laws, named after the then Socialist Minister of Labour. These laws were designed to reinforce indirect worker participation: union activity in companies (obligatory company negotiations every year, increased support for works councils, the setting up of an (elected) health, safety and work environment committee in companies) and also to promote one form of direct worker participation in the area of work organisation, job content and the work environment, both in private and nationalised companies. Thus, with the support of the two largest union organisations (the CFDT and the CGT), these new laws attempted to legitimise new forms of social relations in which workers played a more active role.

Significantly, at the same time, management-initiated participation schemes found a theoretical base in participative management based on a blend of the experiments of previous years and ideas imported from Japan. In a matter of years both attempts were to lose momentum.

Collective bargaining and legislation on direct expression and participation

The laws on workers' rights to expression stipulated that the forms of implementation should be negotiated in companies by management and trade union organisations. These negotiations, the first in France on such a large scale at company level, were initially very successful (1983 - 1985) despite opposition from the CGT-FO. More than 5,000 companies signed agreements which affected millions of workers. Nevertheless, implementation of these signed agreements was to come up against several stumbling blocks.

Some of these stumbling blocks were in the agreements themselves. Having no precedent for their implementation, in most cases both management and unions negotiated very bureaucratic texts with extremely rigid clauses which were often ill-suited to concrete workshop or office situations. Procedural negotiations became more important than negotiations concerning the actual right to expression.

Other difficulties cropped up in regard to the type of work organisation in which the right to expression might be exercised. The greater the Taylorist nature of work organisation, as is the case in the vast majority of French companies, the less autonomy the workers have and the more their expression is stifled and ineffective. Furthermore, workers who had participated with interest and enthusiasm in the first direct expression meetings gradually turned away as their remarks, opinions and suggestions were neither followed-up nor applied. What is more, some employers often simply paid lip service to these agreements while others sought to introduce competing forms of participation.

In addition, the trade union apparatus, from the national level down to the countless union activists in companies, often provided no support to the expression groups or workshop and office committees. Macro-economic and macro-social conditions had changed. The situation was dominated by quantitative problems of employment, wages and hours as well as a trend towards deunionisation that was proving difficult to revert. Union membership dropped from 20% in the 1970s to less than 10% in 1990. Trade union interest in the work environment and work organisation, which had been at the origin of these direct participation projects, dropped off as the unions turned their attention to other demands. Furthermore, union activists and elected union representatives in representation bodies (such as works councils and personnel representatives) clearly were often unhappy about the prospect of losing power and influence.

From 1986 onwards the social partners displayed no interest in negotiations on direct participation even though it had proved to be efficient in certain situations, such as improving the work environment (Ministry of Labour 1990).

Even the CFDT, which had prompted these demands and the later laws on the right of expression, only succeeded with considerable difficulty and with a varying degree of success, in getting its organisations and company activists involved in the implementation of the right to expression. This was, undoubtedly, the result of a lack of clear objectives. As far as union activists were concerned, this right could not be incorporated into any union project for companies or for society in general (Pinaud, 1988, 1991).

From 1990-91 onwards there was renewed CFDT interest in direct worker expression. This was seen in the 1991 launch of a second joint research project (CNRS - CFDT) entitled PAROLES 2 which aimed to study democracy in private companies and the public sector. Plans for an international conference involving researchers and unions on the topic of worker information, consultation and participation in Europe provides further evidence of renewed interest. Official CFDT national and federal level statements (Kaspar 1991, Bertrand 1991, Notat 1991) now talk of a "democratic tripod or tryptic" in companies (unions, elected representatives and workers) which could transform work and make unions themselves more participative. This has produced few results in companies because of the lack of any new union demands. Furthermore, many union activists are preoccupied with the development of forms of participative management introduced by employers.

Employer-initiated direct participation

From 1981 onwards employer-initiated participative management developed theoretical models with a dual organisational aim in companies - decentralisation/autonomy and cohesion/coherence. These new forms of human resource management provided for various forms of direct participation, mostly aimed at qualitative improvements in the production of goods and services (Seyrieix, 1983). Some schemes involved groups of workers who were encouraged to organise themselves or solve production problems (quality circles, etc.) while others attempted (1) to decentralise operational decision-making towards middle management, supervisors and foremen and (2) to de-compartmentalise relations between the different departments of a company with, for example, the creation of "autonomous profit centres" and "project groups" and by introducing management by objectives. Other schemes attempted to mobilise workers by means of the so-called "company project" (the sum of a company's strategic aims) and corporate culture, often based on a company's history (the sum of the values, practices and behaviours shared by workers). Company projects and company culture are disseminated both inside and outside the company by modern means of communication such as newspapers, films, videos and company publications. The entire process was initiated by employers, often helped by outside consultants and always remained under their control without virtually ever having been negotiated.

The implementation of these models was quite widespread in the private sector - mainly in large companies undergoing rapid technological chance and faced with serious competition. Later they were introduced in the public sector under Chirac's right-wing government (1986-88). In 1987 the French Association of Quality Circles announced membership of 3000 companies and the existence of some 50,000 quality circles. But serious difficulties then arose, similar to those faced during the introduction of the right to expression.

The main problems were in the inertia of Taylorist structures and practices. Downward decentralisation of operational decision-making was hindered by management fears of losing permanent control (facilitated by computerisation) over company hierarchy. What is more, the hierarchy was often unenthusiastic or actively opposed to calls for direct worker participation in a context seen as authoritarian, distant and threatening to its traditional prerogatives.

As for the workers themselves they continued to show an interest in all forms of participation in decision-making and were keen to get involved in the process. But they quickly realised the limits to the autonomy that they were being offered as well as the limited power and cash incentives that they were being offered in return.

After a few years, these theoretical models of participation were questioned because of their rigidity, the high cost of their implementation and their fragility. Many companies tried to supplement them by introducing lean management. Nevertheless the principle of questioning scientific work organisation under certain conditions seemed to have been accepted and today the idea that direct worker participation means efficiency is gaining currency in both the private and public sector. New, more flexible forms are being implemented. They are better suited to the specific conditions of each company, to the socio-economic environment or to specific markets. They are a serious embarrassment to union organisations which have drawn up no new demands and lack any projects for democratic participation, especially since the crumbling of examples of self-management in Eastern Europe.

To complete the picture it should be stressed that management-initiated participation schemes have spread throughout the world, and especially in Western Europe. Today there are two main European federations which are tackling problems of quality and total quality using participative methods. One is the European Federation of Quality Circles and Quality Management. This federation was set up following an initial congress held in Brussels in 1987 and since then it has organised European meetings, e.g. in Strasbourg in 1989 and in London in 1991. In terms of methodology it remains strongly oriented towards quality circles and is particularly active in Germany and in Sweden. The other is the European Foundation for Quality Management which was launched in September 1988 with the support of Jacques Delors and at the initiative of large European companies such as Philips, Fiat, Peugeot, ICI, Siemens, PUK etc. This foundation seems more political and be stronger on strategy than the first. Under the influence of Europe's "big bosses" it will try to develop the concept of quality in Europe as well as new forms of human resource management, making particular use of teaching. Several programmes were started in 1989 including the development of quality teaching in European schools of commerce and the establishment of an award for quality for the best academic thesis on the subject. These two associations both claim to have several thousand company members.

Consequently the subject of direct worker participation in France during the 1990s will be tackled virtually only inside companies and by management, both in the private and the public sector. For this reason most discussion today is centred around management-implemented or proposed changes to work organisation and improvements in the work environment (is this a false image or reality, an adaptation to or break with the scientific organisation of work?).

The topic of participation is above all used by management in the private and nationalised sectors and in social economic companies. As the public sector modernises, it is beginning to spread there too. This kind of participation is thus generated, financed, limited, oriented, adapted and sometimes abandoned at the whim of management alone.

There is no doubt that in the private and nationalised sectors employers have made their choice and quashed the negotiated right to expression as a form of participation, arguing that it is inefficient and ill-adapted - faults which employers themselves have largely helped to create!

Their intention was thus to show that State or trade union intervention in company organisation and management was doomed either because of incompetence or ill-will. This desire on the part of employers to neutralise companies is not new in France and is part and parcel of traditional attempts on the part of employers to ensure that a company's autonomous management is not directly influenced by worker representatives. There has been a long history of employer resistance to various attempts by the workers' movement to introduce "worker control" in companies (Tchobanian, 1991).

Divisions in the labour movement

For their part, French trade union organisations (national federations down to activists) have so far not made this matter a priority. For them it is collective bargaining and to a lesser extent action taken by elected union representatives which remain the main forms of worker participation. What is more, trade union organisations remain very divided over the principles, the forms, the conditions and the concessions involved in direct expression and participation.

The unions are nevertheless united in condemning the unilateral nature of employer forms of participation and the "risk of economically dangerous and socially unacceptable management totalitarianism" (Maire, 1986).

The main bone of contention among unions concerns the possible loss of union influence which, some believe, direct participation may cause. Others (the CFDT) believe that direct participation can be a spring-board to union revitalisation (Maire, 1986 , Le Tron, Pinaud, 1991).

But trade union organisations also remain divided over their conception of industrial relations. At the national level, the CGT-FO and the CGT tend to share a conflictual view of things and generally negotiate on the consequences of management decisions while the CFDT would like to see a form of "proposal unionism" which would encourage counter-projects in companies.

These differences are also to be found in their vision and use of elected institutions of staff representation (in particular works councils) and union representatives in companies. Should elected union representatives in elected institutions of staff representation simply be seen as tools of the union and a mere extension of more or less conflictual union policy? Or could works councils and health-safety-work environment councils enjoy a certain autonomy and play a joint regulatory role based on the right to information, consultation and referral to accounting and technical experts? It should not be forgotten that more than half of those elected to works councils are not union members.

These are not simple disagreements between the national organisations - they reflect different forms of behaviour, practices, education and general culture amongst rank-and-file union activists.

Nevertheless it does seem possible that renewed interest in problems relating to the work environment and organisation, as mentioned above and expressed in particular by the CFDT, may spark renewed debate on forms of direct participation and ways of using it with traditional union action. Workers continue to express a desire for increased involvement in decision-making whenever they are offered the chance. Thus there is today an opportunity for re-introducing real worker expression and participation in companies, at the very least on a case by case basis when and where conditions make this possible, rather than introducing a national union strategy. Thus it is important to take into account the level of union strength in companies and, given the divisions in the French workers' movement, the distribution of this strength in the various different unions. But progress, as with any democratic process, will be slow, painstaking, conflictual and constantly questioned.

6 Trade unions and democratic participation in Germany

György Széll

Background

In order to understand the present situation and related problems, it is important to look at the history of trade unions and participation in Germany. German trade unions have diverse origins, as in most countries, and today's most powerful union forces are the result of a series of fusions. (Their predecessors played an important role in the unsuccessful 1848 revolution). The first of these fusions was in 1875 between the Lassalle faction which believed in State socialism and the Bebel faction which supported grass-roots democracy and councils. The first official union was created in 1863. By then there was already a formidable "carrot and stick" policy in play. The world's first ever national security laws were introduced in Germany between 1883 and 1888 by the reactionary Bismarck government in a bid to gain the support of the new working classes. But the Social Democratic Party and unions were forbidden. Money raised was used to finance Germany's navy. After 1945 another fusion took place between the Social Democratic trade union and the majority of the Christian and Liberal trade unions. The Communist unions will be discussed later within the context of the GDR and its annexation in 1990 by the FRG.

It should be remembered that when one talks of trade unions in Germany today, one is generally referring to the DGB, the confederation of 16 industrial and sectoral unions. This trade union brings together 11 million employees and civil servants. Ranked after the DGB in terms of size and power is the DAG (*Deutsche Angestelltengewerkschaft*), the white collar trade union with some 500,000 members, followed by the DBB (*Deutscher Beamtenbund*) with 800,000 members, the Christian CGB (*Christlicher Gewerkschaftsbund*), with 300,000 members and several other associations which do not have official union status, in other words, the right to strike.

There is little to say about democratic participation amongst those unions outside the DGB. They do not have a democratic tradition or democratic attitudes. One might even say that they are actually right-wing, with the exception of the DAG which is more Social-Democratic in its political orientation.

In the DGB one must distinguish between those union members on the left and those on the right. How do these union members define themselves given the present meaning of "left-wing or right-wing"? They define themselves in terms of democratic participation.

Co-determination

What the world has come to understand by "co-determination" is a historical compromise. Even before the First World War German trade unions were fighting for the right to participate in decision-making in an economy seen as a transition period to socialism. In 1916, during the war, some worker participation was granted in order to improve morale but many unions regarded these measures as mere "war socialism". Finally, after the war, in 1920, the *Betriebsrätegesetz* (the Works Council Act) was passed but even this was simply the least dangerous way for the employers to avoid the introduction of Soviet-style socialism.

Other measures for a democratic economy, stipulated in the Weimar Constitution (§135) remained unimplemented. In 1928 Fritz Naphtali drew up a coherent programme for a democratic economy for the ADGB congress (the precursor of the DGB), but the programme was never implemented because of the rise of the Nazis. (This programme has been partially implemented by the Histadrut in Israel).

Although it is hardly worth mentioning the National-Socialist period of fascism in our discussion of democratic participation, it should nevertheless be evoked. For fascism can justifiably be defined as passive participation of the masses and employees and not just the petty bourgeoisie. An illustration of this can be seen in the last elections for business councils in 1932 at which the Nazis won 25% of the seats.

This period should be mentioned for another reason too. The destruction of the best democratic aspects of German society weakened German political culture for many years. After the Second World War, all forms of participation and commitment where considered suspect, because both active democratic participation and passive participation under a fascist regime were considered as negative, with no distinction being made between them. For most German citizens, selfishness started to prevail over solidarity.

Before reunification

The post-war years were difficult period of reorganisation for trade unions. The Allied Forces occupying Germany did not make matters easier. In fact, the DGB was only legally recognised in 1949, a year after the split with East Germany. The

DGB's basic programme from 1949 onwards, as indeed was the case with Ahlen's first CDU programme, included demands for the nationalisation of key industries and banks and the introduction of economic democracy. The social market economy was the historic compromise arrived at in 1949 between the various social partners. Co-determination in the coal and steel industry was only achieved in 1951 after the threat of a general strike. Thus the belief that co-determination was introduced by the Allies to weaken reborn German capital is completely false. The same conflict was to be seen again in 1952 regarding the *Betriebsverfassungsgesetz* (the Works Constitution Act). The unions had to give in to the right-wing coalition government on a number of points. The most important of these was paragraph 1 of the Act - the duty to establish an atmosphere of trust and cooperation between the employer and the works council. This was designed to prevent the councils from organising strikes. Furthermore, the law-makers hoped to drive a wedge between the councils and the trade unions by forcing the councils to work for the good of all employees in a company.

The works council could be complemented by a *Gesamtbetriebsrat* (company works council) if there were several businesses or establishments within the same company and by a *Konzernbetriebsrat* (group works council) when several companies were owned by the same capital owner.

The "Personnel Representation Acts" (*Personalvertretungsgesetze*) were also passed for civil servants, at federal level and separately for each state (*Land*). Compared to the *Betriebsverfassungsgesetz*, these laws weakened the role of public sector employees and civil servants in democratic participation. Various other laws which differed in the different states then followed, depending on the political majority in power.

Against the will of the legislators, the unions, especially the DGB, were able to occupy the works councils and use them to their own ends. Today they dominate these councils. Councillors are elected for four years and a certain number (1 for every 300 employees) is allowed to stop work entirely to devote his or her time entirely to council duties (*freigestellte Betriebsräte*). Affluent companies even provide financing for assistants, often highly trained, to support the councils. To carry out its work the councils have the right to consult experts inside the company, or, if need be, outside the company. In the latter case the consultation fees must be paid by the company. Furthermore, councillors have the right to special training, usually organised by the trade unions but sometimes by the companies - a four-week course each year for those elected for the first time and a three-week course each year for re-elected representatives.

Co-determination is an extremely complex system which has developed gradually. The works councils Act was updated in 1972 under Willy Brandt's liberal Social Democratic government. As their rights to co-determination increased, trade unions at last found themselves gaining formal access to companies.

In 1976 the Co-determination Act (*Mitbestimmungsgesetz*) was passed in the

Bundestag. It affects all companies with over 2,000 employees or a specific turnover. Today there are 450 companies affected by the law. This law increases the number of worker representatives on the supervisory board to half the total rather than one third as specified in the works councils Act (*Betriebsverfassungsgesetz*). But in the case of a split vote, the chairman, always a representative of capital, has two votes. Thus the DGB's aim of achieving equality between work and capital has not been successful. What is more, the top-ranking managerial employees choose their own representatives to sit on the supervisory board and since 1988 they have also had special representation in the form of speakers' committees.

In addition to this form of co-determination in the true sense of the term, there is an exhaustive system of collective bargaining. Bargaining generally takes place at sectorial and regional level. There are framework agreements concerning hours, leave, retirement, wage rates, bonuses, overtime wages, training, etc which are normally fixed for a period of between three to five years. There are also annual agreements which are mostly concerned with fixing wage levels. These agreements can be amended by the company agreements (*Betriebsvereinbarung*), if there are opening clauses (*Öffnungsklausel*). These amendments are signed by the works council and the employer. These company agreements cannot undermine signed collective agreements, they can only improve conditions for the workers they affect.

There is a co-determination system at the macro-social level as well but not at the macro-economic level. All matters regarding social security (sickness, retirement and employment) are co-determined.

To sum up, then, the present situation in the Federal Republic is highly codified. When conflicts arise between the social partners, the industrial arbitration system is set in motion, calling on a large number of experts before rulings can be made.

This form of industrial relations, which used to be referred to as the "German model" has significantly improved the quality of life and the work environment in Germany over the last few decades. The country has the shortest working week and wages (in terms of purchasing power), social security and retirement benefits are the highest in the industrialised world. Work itself has been considerably humanised in ergonomic terms, there is good protection against accidents in the workplace and relatively widespread social peace.

But by the late 1970s, during the second global economic crisis, the pact signed by employers and trade unions was being questioned by employers. This continued with the pressure from increasing overseas competition, especially from Japan, and support from the 1982 right-wing federal government. Inflation rates and growth in productivity also played a role. At the beginning of the 1980s, wage increases were below the inflation rate. To try and solve the problem of growing unemployment, German trade unions, and in particular the leading union IG Metall, the largest trade union in the world, launched their fight for the 35-hour week. The worst clashes in post-war German social history were to be witnessed in the struggle to achieve this aim which eventually was achieved in 1994. This is a victory for the trade union movement and a sign of its strength in the face of the present crisis and the attacks of neo-liberals who have been trying, as in other countries, to weaken the worker movement in the name of a more liberal job market. In Germany, attempts to destabilise the trade unions have failed.

As far as democratic participation is concerned, a series of important steps has been made in Germany since the Second World War. Co-determination has been introduced in most companies. Two thirds of private sector employees and all public sector employees are guaranteed some form of direct co-determination. Social co-determination is available for all employees in the country. But it has to be admitted that this has been a long learning process for those involved, and it has taken almost an entire generation. Now there is no turning back. Co-determination has become a part of everyone's life.

However, there exists among most union leaders a certain distrust of direct democratic participation at grass-roots level and in the workplace. Representative democracy, as in politics, is still seen as the only way of guaranteeing stability and efficiency. Direct forms of participation are synonymous with the kind of anarchy or weakness that characterised the Weimar Republic. And of course the spectre of fascism and its passive participation still hovers, either as a pretext for increased power for union grass-roots or as an example of past errors. The generation of union leaders who lived through fascism is now gradually being replaced by the post-war generation. But this new generation of union leaders is sometimes a generation of technocrats more than anything else. They are known as "doers" (*Macher*). They do not have much faith in the grass-roots either, because they believe that the grass-roots lacks the ability to make increasingly complex decisions. Furthermore, the role of experts within the trade unions has constantly increased. Clearly this is the price to be paid for a highly codified system.

The situation today and the outlook for the future

The unification of the two Germanies in 1990 was the moment when Germany and all of Europe hoped that a new era of peace and democracy would be ushered in to replace the Cold War. Sadly, as a result of mismanagement of the unification process, more problems were created than solved.

Many unionists had dreamed of developing democratic participation with the help and support of the democratic forces of the ex-GDR. These were the forces which had destabilised the East German system and finally brought about its downfall. These were the forces which had chanted "We are the people" and not those who had chanted "We are one people" when the danger has passed. The latter, obviously the vast majority of them opportunists as there are everywhere, wanted a strong Deutschmark and mass consumerism as quickly as possible. They did not want more democracy but a strong leader to solve their problems. As we can see today, the rise of neo-fascism and xenophobia throughout Germany has meant that democracy has been the loser in unification. Problems such as unemployment and well-being dominate trade union debate. Today there is more preoccupation with preserving what has been won so far. Even "Social Europe" sparks little interest.

The democratic forces of the ex-GDR - the citizens' movements which today make up *Bündnis 90* and which merged with the Green Party in 1993 - are not really involved in the trade union movement. These representatives of direct democratic participation at grass-roots level are suspicious of large structures. And since the sole trade union confederation in the GDR, the *Freier Deutscher Gewerkschaftsbund* (FDGB) was tarnished by its close connections with the former system, the entire trade union movement was suspected of being sympathetic to Soviet-style socialism. Thus there is a vast gap between these democratic citizens' movements and the trade unions. There is a lack of involvement of the most talented people from the ex-GDR. This involvement is vital for the future of democracy.

The FDGB was literally destroyed after the dissolution of the GDR. The DGB and other trade unions created entirely new structures in Eastern Germany. Obviously this required considerable energy and resources. And since most union members in Eastern Germany are either unemployed or earn considerably less than in the West, the unions heavily subsidise these structures and their representatives.

Co-determination in companies and in the social system was the result of a long learning process so it is not surprising that the structures in place for participation in Eastern Germany do not yet work as they should. What is more, employers, most of whom have come from the West, are exploiting this weakness.

Union representation has not changed since the unification of the two Germanies. As was mentioned above, the DGB is now one of the largest confederations in the world with some 11 million members. It is still nearly as rich as it was, compared to most other confederations. And while union density is not on the level of Denmark or Sweden, 45% nevertheless remains a respectable figure. The problems are elsewhere, as in most other confederations. The union structure continues to be dominated by qualified blue collar workers. Although membership amongst women continues to rise, women still only represent 28% of all members but 45% of the total work force. There is also the problem of young workers who are increasingly less likely to get involved in union activities.

But today the greatest challenge for the trade union movement is that posed by the new managerial strategies, sometimes referred to as "lean management". As with the Japanese model, participation in the workplace and company agreements are favoured under lean management. The German trade unions fear, as the case of Japanese trans-national companies in Britain has illustrated, that this form of management will weaken the position of unions and company councils. Given the increasingly fierce competition between Europe, North America and Japan, Taylorist and Fordian measures now seem outmoded. One would be right in doubting the value of Ohnism, as the Japanese model is referred to, (so named after the technical director of Toyota who made the largest contribution to this strategy). But what is most important for the future of industrial relations and company and economic democracy is that man and hence his well-being has become increasingly recognised by management as the principal factor in production. Dreams of automated factories are now gone. What are important are the qualifications, the participation and the motivation of those working in a factory. If Europe can learn this lesson then it will have taken a major step forward. Democratic elements are also required and in this domain Europe has a vast experience and is well ahead of other countries.

Summary

If one regards co-determination as an important form of democratic participation, then Germany can still be said to be ahead of most other European countries. But the German unions must once again make use of their strength in Europe. Co-determination must be adapted to the structures, needs and traditions of other European societies. And it should be complemented by other forms of democratic participation at the macro-level (which the DGB has always striven for), meso-level and at shop-floor level.

But the spread of ideas and practises relating to co-determination through the various countries of Europe has not been successful, with the exception of Austria and the Netherlands which both have a similar system. The 5th directive of the European Community which intended to introduce co-determination at European level has still not been adopted. The Bullock Report in Britain which proposed the same system in the United Kingdom has not been followed up either. The only development to date is the appearance of European works councils.

Naturally the role of the ETUC is vital if further democratic participation in Europe is to be achieved. Today the DGB is its greatest supporter. Such support should be put to good use.

At the beginning of 1993 the DGB launched a debate on its new basic programme, which it renews every fifteen years or so. Its last basic programme was set out in 1981. This new debate presents an opportunity to ensure that greater democratic participation is enshrined in the programme and implemented. It is to be hoped that this opportunity will be seized.

7 Participation in Italian industrial relations

Fausta Guarriello

The 1970s

The debate surrounding participation in Italy has been influenced both by the conflictual nature of industrial relations since the Second World War and the ideological plurality of Italian trade unions. The CGIL, the largest of these unions in terms of membership, maintained very close ties with the most important Communist parties in the Western world until 1991.

Historical factors have thus influenced the debate on participation through the years. Only rarely in the past has participation been regarded as a stable, institutional factor in industrial relations, despite article 46 of the Italian Constitution which guarantees workers the legal right to participate in the running of companies. Since the 1970s the debate has tended to revolve around the stakes at the centre of the power struggle between the social partners. And it is no coincidence that the most important gains in worker participation in Italy have been achieved as a result of collective bargaining at sectoral, group or company level. Trade unions have invoked article 46 of the Constitution and have learned from the experiences gained in early management council schemes tested shortly after the war but quickly abandoned after the political changes of 1948, when left-wing elements withdrew from the government.

While true participation, that is, institutionalised participation in the form of joint decision-making or joint control of a company's activities, is unknown in Italy, several watered-down versions are to be found. The most widespread is undoubtedly trade union participation in numerous public sector companies and organisations. The trade unions play an important and sometimes dominant role in making decisions which affect the interests of workers, such as social security and the public services for the employment of the work force.

This style of participation practised since the 1950s at national, regional and municipal level has meant that trade union representatives are present in public sector groups of a collegiate structure. Union representatives also participate in decision-making in that their opinions are heard before decisions are actually made. One of the most important examples of this form of participation concerns decisions regarding temporary lay-offs of surplus workers in companies in financial difficulties or being reorganised, to whom unemployment benefits was paid by the social security department. Since the Regionalisation Act was introduced, other bodies in which trade unions participate have flourished. These bodies handle matters regarding regional affairs such as farming, fishing, tourism, craftsmanship, vocational training and social services. On a more informal level they also handle matters outside these domains, for example services offered to small and medium-sized enterprises. This is one of the main reasons for the success of the developmental networks of small and medium-sized enterprises in industrial areas, known as *distretti industriali*.

The question of which unions should participate in decision-making or should sit on the various public sector bodies and committees eventually gave rise to the concept of "the most representative trade union". Consequently this union became the main partner in the development of policies to encourage union activity in companies on a legal basis (Act 300, 1970 known as the Workers' Statute or "*Statuto dei lavoratori*"). As a result, these unions also earned themselves specific rights such as the right to establish union representation in companies, the right to meet in the workplace, the right to hold workplace referendums, the right to put up posters and notices, the right to official leave and the right to a union office on company premises. Since the 1970s and throughout the 1980s "the most representative trade unions" were allowed to negotiate derogating agreements which grant exemptions from certain conditions of service, in particular in areas such as night-work for women, reductions in hours and new types of fixed-term employment contracts.

In addition to participation in decision-making in public sector bodies, Italian trade unions, legally recognised in companies as a result of the Workers' Statute, have been able to counter-balance the powers of the employer. During the 1970s especially, the conflictual nature of industrial relations in Italy meant that union power was regarded as a check on the arbitrary powers of the employer. This counter-balance took the form of union action, in particular Worker General Assemblies which enabled not only union members but all workers (called upon to elect representative bodies) to participate in union decision-making. At that time union power was clearly expressed in collective bargaining at sectoral and company level and this produced important concessions such as the "single status job-grading" system, health and safety rights in the workplace, equal pay for men and women and the right to negotiate new forms of work organisation.

Thus participation was contractual in form and was first implemented in 1974, in the agreements drawn up by several large companies (Fiat, Alfa Romeo, Sit, Siemens, etc). These agreements enabled unions to implement a strategy aimed at winning the right to information. This was seen as a prerequisite to union control of the investments of large companies. This control was mainly concerned with investments in southern Italy, within the framework of a sectoral economic programme. The first results were the 1977 Act 675 on industrial policy. Legal experts, referring to the right to information regarding company strategies, saw it as a form of social control over the company achieved by conventional means and ranked it alongside those forms of company control legalised by the Workers' Statute and various forms of control in public sector groups. The right to information concerning any decisions in a company which could affect employment implied a certain form of regulation of the powers of the employer who, as a result of the debate stimulated by the information provided to the unions, had to take the workers' interests into account. The right to information was central to all the major sectoral collective agreements from 1976 onwards.

However, the grave economic situation following the 1973 and 1979 oil crises changed the future of this strategy. Given the new economic situation, information concerning employment, reorganisation, relocation and new technology, etc., was now designed to help unions avoid the social trauma of factory closures, mass lay-offs and forced early retirement by means of the wage guarantee fund or *Cassa integrazione*. The *Cassa integrazione* placed the social cost of such a reorganisation of the industrial sector in the hands of the national insurance organisation, in other words, the community.

During this period, participation through bargaining produced numerous management agreements, above all at company level, in which the unions agreed to measures designed to ride out periods of crisis (flexitime, early retirement, retraining, mobility, part-time work, solidarity contracts).

The 1980s

In the early 1980s efforts at unified action on the part of the three union confederations, already witnessed at the conclusion of the 1975 national, inter-sectoral agreements and the 1977 labour costs agreements (which both later became law), encouraged greater openness and cooperation between the government, the unions and employers. This came at a time when direct contact between the unions and employers was at a stalemate. The result of this brief period of neo-corporatism was the agreement concluded in January 1983, signed by the three parties (albeit with some arm-twisting by the government) and the 1984 agreement which failed when the CGIL refused to sign it, but which, nevertheless, became a government decree. This kind of union participation in major political and economic decisions prompted considerable debate which examined the institutionalisation of union power, as the CISL chose to put it. In actual fact real political trade-offs only partially took place given the weakness of the government and its inability to respect the terms of the agreement, particularly as far as proposals for parliamentary legislation were concerned.

Debate on participation was rekindled in February 1984 when the three confederations signed the IRI protocol. This protocol agreement was re-negotiated in July 1986. It was applied to a large, partly State-owned company and was the first in a series introduced in other big, public-sector companies such as ENI, EFIM and CISPEL. Consequently this period is referred to as the "protocol season". It was stipulated in these agreements that partners should "trade" the right to more detailed information before any decision-making affecting workers' interests, against a reduction in minor conflicts at shop-floor level.

What was new about these agreements was the institutionalisation of the right to information on employer-worker boards - the consultative committees established at group level (IRI), at finance holding level and at operational level. The problem at the heart of these agreements was the ambiguity of the role of the consultative committees, which, as far as IRI was concerned, should remain technical bodies without negotiating power, whereas the unions, in particular the CGIL and the works councils (*consigli di fabrica*), regarded them as vital prerequisites to negotiation. It was this ambiguity which led to the unsatisfactory practical implementation of the agreements, although hostility on the part of companies was also to blame. The latter refused to accept IRI's "philosophy" of keeping unions informed and holding discussions with them before making any operational decisions. Despite resistance to implementation of procedures to provide information prior to any important decision-making (for in fact anything regarding important decisions was rarely transmitted beforehand to the joint bodies set up by the protocols) the IRI group was nevertheless, thanks to this agreement, able to undergo a relatively smooth reorganisation during the 1980s.

In addition to these experiments carried out in the public sector, progress in the spread of participation was to be seen in the collective agreements at sectorial level drawn up throughout the 1980s and the creation of a series of collective boards such as the job market or new technology watch-dog committees. In some sectors of industry such as the construction industry, schemes of a more participative nature were organised. Sectors such as these already had first-hand experience of collective boards like the Construction Workers Providence Fund, professional training colleges and on-site joint safety committees.

Zanussi, a major private group, one of Europe's leading manufacturers of home electrical products and owned since 1985 by the Swedish group Electrolux, took a further step along the road to participation when it introduced a series of agreements which first enabled a restructuring of the group and then introduced joint decision-making on product quality targets and productivity via collective boards. After the signing of an October 1991 agreement, new collective bodies were set up with powers to take decisions and consult on subjects relating to the environment and safety in establishments with over 300 employees, in areas such as work organisation and the introduction of new technology in establishments with over 200 employees and in areas such as job grading and hierarchy in establishments with over 100 employees. But Zanussi remains the sole example of a generally participative strategy amongst the country's larger private groups, despite an important number of company agreements on workers' financial participation (the Fiat, Olivetti, Barilla, Parmalat agreements).

Another interesting experiment at Zanussi were the pilot schemes in joint manager-union delegate training following the agreements on participation. These were intended to facilitate implementation of the agreements. Joint training is not unknown in other industrial sectors (e.g. the chemical industry) and in specific participative areas such as health and safety.

Trends in the 1990s

Since the start of the 1990s trade unions have attempted to re-introduce participation in public-sector groups, taking advantage of the CGIL's new strategy for participation as outlined at its October 1991 conference in Rimini. The idea, which was discussed informally with the management of public sector companies - traditionally more open to the idea of participation - was to try and draw up a single protocol on industrial relations based on joint consultative committees at group and financial holding level as well as committees with decision-making powers at company level and a unanimous voting system. If a unanimous vote could not be reached, each party would be free to act as it wished. During such procedures each party would agree not to undertake any unilateral action or resort to conflict. The idea was forgotten however, swamped by the "discovery" of a major State financial crisis which gave priority to political debate on privatisation and the possible dismantling of public sector and partially State-owned companies.

There have been other developments in trade unionism in Italy today. First of all the agreement signed by Fiat and the three iron and steel federations Fiom, Fim and Uim regarding new businesses in the Avellino and Melfi regions of southern Italy, both particularly hard-hit by unemployment. The trade union agreement was made possible by a draft agreement between Fiat and the Ministry for Southern Italy. The ministry has since been abolished but at the time financed a large part of the operation with public funds. The aim of the agreement is to encourage high-level union participation in the planning and implementation stages of industrial ventures. This would take the form of negotiation at every stage such as hiring, training, fixing hours and wages (initially lower than comparative wages) and shift work. It would be an important step forward for all of southern Italy where major industrial projects often end up as "desert cathedrals". It would also be of benefit to the union federations which would gain considerable influence from the project.

Another form of union participation in work organisation in companies and in the public sector is enshrined in the recently introduced 1991 Act 125 on affirmative action for women. It permits privileged allocation of public funding for all affirmative action negotiated by "the most representative unions" with employers. Here again, one of the most important agreements is the one concluded recently at Zanussi where action to support women at work has been undertaken including rescheduling hours and allowing workers to regulate their hours according to their family, social or cultural needs. Act 125 has, in many companies, resulted in the creation of collective boards to oversee sexual equality. These boards are to study work organisation and other factors which may discriminate against women and to propose suitable measures for improving women's lot in the workplace.

In the wake of the serious economic and financial crisis that Italy faced when the Amato government came to power in June 1992, the three confederations and employer organisations signed a protocol with the government one month later committing all the social partners to starting talks on a reform of the collective bargaining system, beginning with a ban on the interleaving of different levels of negotiations concerning the same subject and the provision of new regulations regarding the powers, duration and form of bargaining. The protocol also provided for a wage freeze until the end of 1993 and formally eliminated the mechanism by which wages were indexed to the cost of living. In exchange, the government offered a greater commitment to tackling tax evasion and working towards a healthier national balance of payments.

The July 31 agreement marked the beginning of renewed interest in participation in the 1990s, all the more noticeable given the extremely difficult economic and political situation (for the April elections and the judicial enquiries had undermined popular support for traditional political parties). This agreement also marked the start of a definite trend towards an institutionalisation of procedures for participation in macro-economic decision-making. This was vociferously contested by a large part of the union movement including autonomous unions, spontaneous rank-and-file worker committees (*auto-convocati*), etc., and resulted in a series of strikes held throughout September, and now referred to as the "hot autumn". As a result of the commitments made in the July 1992 agreement, the new government, headed by the former governor of the Central Bank, Mr Ciampi, launched negotiations with the social partners in May 1993. These talks produced the outline of a new protocol on July 3, 1993. At the heart of this new summit agreement are reforms to the collective bargaining system. The duration of sectoral collective agreements are extended from three to four years and that of regular re-negotiations fixed at every two years. Negotiations at company level are also included and are to be held in the interval between two sectoral agreements. Wages cannot be renegotiated except within the limits of the company's margins of profitability and productivity.

The aim of the new agreement is to encourage a lasting effort on the part of the government and the social partners to achieve a satisfactory wage policy. Twice-yearly meetings are provided for, during which maximum wage rises are fixed, taking into account budgetary policy. In the absence of an indexing mechanism, these meetings also allow for possible wage readjustments, if, during the preceding period, the real rate of inflation proves to be higher than projections. Other measures include stimulating employment, such as the introduction of temporary employment (until now forbidden under the anti-fraud laws), special contracts for the young, new regulations to encourage solidarity contracts and wider application of the laws regarding the *cassa integrazione* and mobility. It should be noted that the employers' conviction that unemployment can be brought down through massive public subsidies to companies and a dismantling of the Workers' Statute, has once again been incorporated into the agreement, despite union protest.

The general pattern to emerge from these two agreements is a strong form of responsible union participation in decision-making on sometimes painful and unpopular economic policies but which are vital if the country is to survive this unprecedented economic, political and institutional crisis. Nevertheless it should be made clear that this trend has not been accepted without comment amongst trade unions. There remain some serious differences on participation. While the CISL and the IUL are convinced of the benefits of participation, CGIL has its doubts and there is open criticism from the autonomous unions, the spontaneous rank-and-file workers' committees (known as *cobas* and formed to express dissatisfaction with union positions) and quite a number of grass-roots (self-styled) representatives, especially in industrial areas badly hit by the economic crisis. One has to ask whether the confederate union's insistence that it look after the general interests of all, claiming that it is responsible and can mobilise opinion to support weak governments which are unable to impose the draconian measures adopted, is really a viable democratic form of participation for Italy.

The 1946 Constitution makes legal provisions for the right to collective protest on the basis of union freedom and worker participation in the running of enterprises. But in addition to the Constitution another set of informal rules and practises has grown since the 1970s. This has transformed participation into one of the cornerstones of union involvement in economic policy while at the same time giving the "most representative unions"' a quasi-public role in joint-decision-making together with the government and employers. This role often goes beyond the functions attributed to parliament, the seat of legislative power and a symbol of popular sovereignty, but shunted aside by these joint efforts carried out at the macro-level. But one is forced to ask what the point of this joint decision-making power is and whether it is to be found at all levels of the union organisation or whether it has remained a prerogative of the highest ranks.

The absence of any legal rules and regulations formalising joint decision-making powers within companies and the greater role played by the confederate apparatus, as witnessed during periods of cooperation (although not systematically - only at times of economic crisis), make it difficult to answer these questions. The schisms and contradictions that exist are not only to be found among the various ideologies but also within different practices. During this difficult period of political and institutional transition, the role of the trade union within the State will have to be redefined.

Symptomatic of this conflict is the proposition put forward by members of the spontaneous rank-and-file worker committees (*auto-convocati*) to hold a referendum to abrogate article 19 of the Workers' Statute which would eliminate the notion of the "most representative union" for worker representation in companies. This would have the effect of undermining the cornerstone of union power. It would also affect several legislative propositions, regarding union participation and the decision taken by the three confederations to remove their representatives from the management bodies of public sector structures so as to provide unions with real autonomous control. On the other hand, the proposition put forward by the CISL and the CGIL regarding an imminent fusion of the three confederations should be regarded as ambivalent as should their support for the law defining the right to strike in the public services and, more recently, their support for the privatisation of employee-employer relations in the public sector. This seems to encourage over-simplification of worker representation and is a move to replace the conflicting and pluralist model with a functionalist model. These relations, until now defined by a special statute different from the one in the private sector, are very similar in essence to the 1993 Act 29.

Today, it is not clear what initial participative outlines are to be found in the union strategy of working with the government and employers on important political agreements. While such agreement are vital in terms of political power they are nevertheless costly in terms of the erosion in union legitimacy that they generate at grass-roots level. The content of this kind of political agreement, as the 1993 protocol has illustrated, is often elusive when one examines the trade-offs. Wage-indexing, temporary freezes on collective bargaining, limitations on company negotiations and job insecurity are traded in return for questionable future improvements (economic growth, employment, financial cleanups and a check on inflation). Perhaps Europe's increasing influence on domestic Italian affairs, so often cited as an excuse to provide companies with more manoeuvring room, may end up having the effect of harmonising the regulations and laws defining democratic participation at all levels where economic decisions are made.

8 Trade unions and worker participation in the Netherlands

Peter Leisink

Worker participation in the Netherlands today is to a large extent synonymous with participation through works councils as far as participation in company decision-making is concerned. The majority of works council members are trade union members and many will bear in mind their union's views of topics under discussion while representing their company's fellow workers, which is their statutory task.

In addition to works councils, unions may also represent workers' interests at company level, especially in particular cases like company reorganisation. At regional, sectoral and (inter)national level, trade unions are the main if not the only channel of worker participation.

Worker cooperatives are not widespread. There has always been a number of them, notably in the construction industry, and the idea of self-management has also appeared popular with environmentalists starting their own farms or recycling businesses but their numbers are very limited.

Despite trade union demands for worker participation in supervisory boards, neither unions nor works councils have been granted the right to elect workers' representatives on the board. At present a works council only has the right, in some so-called structural public and private limited companies, to propose candidates or give advice on a candidate, but it is the supervisory board's prerogative to appoint its own members.

Management initiatives to introduce direct participation at shop-floor level, through quality circles for example, have until recently met with trade union criticism and rejection. It does not follow from this that management strategies for forms of worker participation and involvement have not resulted in informal consultation practices. However, little is known about their numbers, their workings and the extent to which employees involved actually value them.

This report will, therefore, focus on trade unions and works councils. But first I will start with a brief review of trade union policy on worker self-management.

Dutch trade union policy and worker self-management

The great majority of Dutch trade unions have always taken a somewhat ambivalent attitude towards worker cooperatives (Leisink, 1989a). On the one hand, it is recognised that industrial democracy should ultimately lead to self-management. On the other the few cooperatives that exist in the Netherlands have not been hailed as vanguards of the democratisation movement. Trade unions used to be critical of cooperatives because they felt that the coops often paid less and that the hours and the work environment did not meet standards fixed by trade unions through collective agreements.

In the mid-1980s the number of self-managed co-ops was estimated at about 150, involving some 4,000 workers (Henselmans, 1984). This estimate is too low since small-scale "labour collectives" flourished at the time but were not counted. A recent estimate by Voute suggests about 2,000 self-managed cooperatives, only very few of them being large cooperatives with over 100 "employees". Moreover, only a minority of the workers in cooperatives participate financially in their cooperative, so the majority are really only employees.

By the mid-1980s the economic crisis had made itself felt for a number of years and many workers had been made redundant. This led a number of trade unions to take an interest in coops as an alternative strategy to combat unemployment. On the 25th anniversary of the founding of the Association of Workers Cooperatives in December 1984 the Union of Metal Workers (*Industriebond FNV*) contributed one million Dutch florins to the Workers Participation Fund to finance worker cooperatives.

However, by the end of the 1980s, interest in worker self-management had dwindled. A support organisation, which had been set up with financial help from the Ministry of Social Affairs and Employment, was discontinued because the number of coops was too small to justify the organisation's continued existence. The employee stock ownership fund was no success, it continued its activities but the unions withdrew their commitment.

In spite of the actual number of worker cooperatives, the ideal of worker self-management has been upheld by the trade union movement for years. In a policy document entitled "Work in 2000" the Social Democratic Federation of Dutch Trade Unions (FNV) stated: "The FNV strives for democratic company decision-making. This implies that the FNV advocates a decision-making process in which workers have the final say and can take decisions by themselves to as great an extent as possible. Democratisation of companies should go hand in hand with a shift to social ownership. These goals can only be achieved gradually. However action should be taken to reach these goals". (FNV, 1987: 6).

In November 1990 the FNV organised a conference on "Economic Democracy and the Trade Union Movement". The policy document, which was accepted by the conference, was very clear about democratic participation: "worker participation is the main reason for the existence of and the main goal of the trade union movement" (FNV 1990: 1). Nevertheless, the document does not explicitly refer to the concept of worker self-management at all.

Worker participation in the 1970s - shop stewards and works councils

In order to understand trade union policy in the Netherlands adequately, it is useful to know that the Dutch trade unions are split along religious/ideological and sectoral lines. The largest federation is the Social Democratic Federation of Dutch Trade Unions (FNV), which resulted from the 1976 merger of the Dutch Catholic Trade Union Federation and the Social Democratic Dutch Federation of Trade Unions. Union density in the Netherlands is now about 24% and about two thirds of all union members now belong to the FNV. The Christian National Trade Union Federation (CNV) accounts for about 20% of trade union membership. Both FNV and CNV cover blue-collar and white-collar employees in the private and public sectors. The Federation of White-Collar Staff Organizations (MHP) as well as the General Federation of Trade Unions (ACV) mainly consists of white-collar employees.

Ideological and sectoral differences are clearly reflected in the policies which the unions have adopted on worker participation. Generally speaking, however, all unions have now accepted the works council as the central pillar of industrial democracy. This has been the dominant view since 1979. A short review of trade union policy will illustrate both the development of industrial democracy and the views of respective unions.

At the end of the 1960s many of the Social-Democratic and Catholic trade unions were critical of the legislation on industrial democracy, which dated back to 1950. The fact that management presided over the works council prevented the works council from effectively furthering the workers' interests. Moreover, the council's rights to information and consultation were too limited to affect management prerogatives based on private ownership. In short, these trade unions viewed the works council as a management instrument to integrate workers into the company rather than as a means of representing the workers' interests. Some unions were no longer interested in participation in the works councils. They set about creating trade union committees as independent power bases within the company. As early as 1964 the Union of Metal Workers (*Industriebond FNV*) launched an experiment in worker self-management through trade union committees. At the beginning of the 1970s it published two policy documents in which it explicitly opted for socialism and worker self-management. A few years later Social-Democratic and Catholic transport workers' unions and unions of workers in the food-industry followed suit (Beukema 1987; Leisink 1989b).

Other unions agreed with this critique of works councils but tried to influence company policy processes both by participating in the works council and at the same time building up trade union organisation at shop-floor level. Apart from the white-collar unions, which were not very important at the time, and the Christian Confederation of Trade Unions (CNV), which rejected the "polarisation" position

97

of the other unions, all the unions agreed on the necessity to fundamentally transform capitalism and to introduce some form of socialism and worker self-management. Some authors view these radical standpoints as mere rhetoric (Akkermans, 1985: 186-187). It is true that in the 1980s unions set themselves more pragmatic goals. However, writing off trade union policy as mere rhetoric ignores a number of facts.

When unions started to set up trade union committees in companies they were confronted by unexpected problems which they seriously misunderstood. The absence of a tradition of trade union action at shop-floor level manifested itself in various ways. Union members were hesitant to militate and feared reprisals by management. Moreover, union members were not used to bargaining over workplace issues by themselves. When major problems at work arose, they called for paid union officials. Members had grown accustomed to unions functioning as a kind of service institution. Neither members nor officials were prepared for a new style of unionism that required members to be actively involved and officials to assist the members with their activities in a professional capacity (Coenen, 1987 p.384-391). In addition, many industrial sectors in the Netherlands, such as the construction industry and the printing industry, for example, are mainly made up of small-scale companies, rarely employing more than 100 workers. These small firms are characterised by more personal if not paternalistic relations which do not mix well with trade union militancy. Union efforts to set up trade union committees were therefore directed at larger companies. This divergence, as far as trade union organisation at shop-floor level was concerned, made the structural accommodation of trade union committees into the framework of union organisation difficult. Consequently there was no statutory provision for the influence of trade union committees on union policy in general and on union policy concerning their own company.

These difficulties hampered trade union policy on worker self-management through trade union committees. Indeed, many trade union representatives found themselves helpless when it came to influencing company policy processes. At the same time, in 1979, the works councils saw their legal rights expanded with respect to company policy. As a result of continued trade union efforts and despite employers' opposition, a new Works Councils Act was passed by the Dutch parliament. Management was no longer to be represented on the works council and the works council's legal rights were strengthened. The list of company decisions in the field of personnel and social policy subject to works council approval was substantially extended. In addition, the works council was granted the right of appeal should management not pay due regard to the council's advice on economic and financial issues. Also, facilities available to works council members were expanded including, for instance, training, expert advice and the possibility of conducting works council activities during office hours.

In addition to the expansion of rights and facilities through the 1979 Works Councils Act, the 1980 Health and Safety Act further added to opportunities to influence company policy-making through the works councils, via the health and safety committees.

One result of the new Works Councils Act was that many trade union activists decided to participate in the works councils rather than attempt to influence company policy through union shop-floor committees. Most unions then changed their policy as well and accepted the works council as the central institution of worker participation. The attempts to organise trade union committees at shop-floor level as an independent means of democratic participation were discontinued. From then on, trade union committees and shop stewards were regarded as the rank-and-file to back up trade union members in works councils.

At present 90% of all companies employing 100 or more workers have a works council and 56% of companies employing 35 to 100 workers have one (Van der Burgh & Kriek, 1992). In small companies with 10 to 35 employees, worker participation should legally require a consultative meeting between the employer and all employees twice a year, but only about half actually do so (Verstagen et al. 1987).

Worker participation in the 1980s - the focus on works councils

The change in trade union policy in terms of equating worker participation with works councils is remarkable for a number of reasons.

Firstly, the works council is not a trade union prerogative in the Netherlands. All workers, whether they are union members or not, have the right to elect works council members and it is the statutory task of the works council to represent all workers employed by the company. It appears that many workers who are not themselves unionised, elect union candidates. As a result, the percentage of unionised workers in works councils is about three times that of total union density - 67% to 24%. (Looise & Heijink, 1986: 109; Visser, 1987: 21). However, these findings also suggest that one third of all works council members is generally speaking non-unionised and this figure is much higher in particular sectors of industry such as the commercial service sector where union membership is low. In these sectors worker participation is therefore a non-union affair. In addition, it should be noted that even in those works councils where the majority of members are unionised, the diversity of opinion is potentially as great as the number of trade union federations in the Netherlands. This pluralist situation means that no single union can use the works council as an instrument of union policy. Moreover, no one union can recruit new members by pointing to their success in works councils at company level. On the contrary, the works council has established itself as a potential competitor with the unions at company level.

The change of union policy is also remarkable given the works councils' lack of contact with their rank-and-file since their very inception, as has been illustrated (Hövels & Nas, 1976). In this respect, the unions' decision to get trade union committees and shop stewards to back up union members in the works council is to be judged positively. However, it appears that more direct and practical union assistance is needed to bring about cooperation between works councils and trade union representatives. According to research, only in half of the companies where some form of union organisation exists at shop floor level, (which is no more than 40% in the case of private sector companies), do works council members get in touch with their union rank-and-file to consult on works council topics (Looise & de Lange, 1987, p.192). Trade union policy to encourage and to assist in cooperation between works council members and shop stewards appears to be the significant factor which decides the extent of this form of cooperation (Leisink, 1989b, p. 354-371).

The trade unions' policy to opt for the works council as the central institution of worker participation has not been substantially modified since 1979. The works council has indeed been given additional tasks, such as implementing a shorter working week, as a result of collective agreements drawn up between employer organisations and unions in several sectors of industry. Also, the confederations and some major unions have increased their expenditure on centres which provide professional advice to works councils on legal, financial, organisational and technological issues. The expenditure on the training of works councils has remained relatively high, the costs being paid by employers. Despite this commitment to works councils as the main institution of worker participation in company decision-making, there are tensions between unions and works councils related to the unions' own role as a channel of worker participation.

Unions as channels of worker participation

The main way in which unions represent workers' interests is through collective bargaining. Collective agreements in the Netherlands are mainly multi-employer, industry-wide agreements. Single employer agreements are to be found in big companies like Philips, Akzo and Shell, although there seems to be a slight overall increase in smaller companies (Visser 1992: 351). Today about three quarters of all employees are covered by collective agreements. At sectoral level unions also represent workers' interests on vocational training boards, pension funds and so on.

Apart from the sectoral level, unions operate at regional level, where their main aim is to influence regional labour market policies through the tripartite Regional Manpower Service Boards. At national level, the trade union confederations are represented in the tripartite Socio-Economic Council, which is the government's main advisory board on socio-economic policy, in the Foundation of Labour, which is the national platform for consultation between the trade union confederations and employer associations and in a number of other bodies concerned with social security, employment policy and so on.

I will elaborate on union activities at sectoral and company level since these are most directly related to worker participation through works councils.

Traditionally, a division of labour has always existed, with unions concentrating on collective bargaining over pay and conditions and works councils concentrating on influencing company policy on issues such as health and safety, personnel and so on. It was, and still is the formal prerogative of unions to bargain over pay and conditions and works councils are not allowed to enter into company agreements on these issues if these have been dealt with by unions. However, this division of labour is now under increasing pressure and the way in which this is handled may have serious consequences for the future of worker participation.

On the one hand unions have broadened their scope of activities. Collective bargaining is no longer restricted to pay and the work environment in the narrow sense of these terms. Increasingly, collective agreements cover issues such as the introduction of new technology, training, the quality of work and affirmative action in recruitment of immigrants, women, the long-term unemployed and the disabled. By broadening the scope of their bargaining, unions have penetrated areas which works councils used to deal with.

On the other hand, works councils have tended to become involved in pay and work environment issues, often with the help of employers who welcome decentralisation. A 1988 survey of works councils in private sector companies indicated that about one third was in some way involved in defining the terms of employment (Huiskamp & Risseeuw 1988: 14). The percentage of works councils which actually negotiated on issues of pay, hours and the like was limited to about 12% - one case being the engineering consultancy firm Grabowski, where the unions lost a legal dispute about an agreement between the company management and the works council. However, the works councils' involvement may also take other forms such as consultation or the right to express disapproval of certain decisions, as in the case of Océ, a manufacturer of photo-copying machines. It also seems that the works councils' involvement has grown in company agreements which supplement sectoral agreements and which may include issues such as hours, travel expenses, bonuses and so on. The problem here is that the unions' authority on pay and conditions tends to be eroded because of increasing works councils' involvement at a time when unions feel that only through collective bargaining may they hope to win back the membership they lost during the 1980s.

The suggestion that the very existence of works councils and their growing authority as representatives of workers may have contributed to the decline of union membership in the Netherlands has led some unions to re-evaluate the role of their union representatives at shop-floor level. As one official of the Union of Metal Workers (*Industriebond FNV*) put it, the union must be visibly present at shop-floor level providing individual assistance and handling collective bargaining in order for workers to join the unions (Vos 1986). Although the driving force behind this new approach to trade union organisation at shop-floor level does not seem geared primarily to strengthening worker participation, it may nevertheless contribute to it. Be this as it may, a number of unions, including the Social-Democratic unions in the construction, engineering, printing and services industries have, since the end of the 1980s, adopted a policy of strengthening worker participation through works councils and encouraging union organisation at shop-floor level to support works councils and collective bargaining.

In their efforts to build up a union presence at shop-floor level some unions have consolidated the role of shop-stewards by stipulating in collective agreements that shop-stewards be entitled to move freely around the shop-floor, assisting union members with grievances and so on. Union efforts to win a legal basis for workplace union activities were not successful, however. Employer opposition and a growing conservative concern about the State's interference in the economy led the 1980s' centre-right government to repeal a bill on workplace union activities. Instead, in 1990, the national employer organisations and union confederations agreed on a recommendation by the Foundation of Labour, listing a number of union representatives' facilities about which employers and unions might conclude agreements. The recommendation also states explicitly, however, that shop-stewards are not to interfere in worker participation through works councils (Stichting van de Arbeid, 1990, p. 5). By accepting this restriction, unions will be hampered in implementing their policy of supporting works councils through union representatives and balancing power relations between worker representatives and management. As far as employer organisations are concerned, all proposals to strengthen works councils have met with strong resistance (De Bruijn, 1992: 4). This is even more so at a European level.

The future scenario: towards cooperation between unions and works councils

Generally speaking, workers' attitudes to works councils are positive. They see them as representative of workers. For instance, 60% of non-union workers always participate in works council elections while 80% to 85% of union workers do so (Klandermans et al 1992).

Despite relatively low union density, overall attitudes to trade unions are positive. They are also seen as representative of workers. Less than 10% of non-union workers feel that there is no need for unions in a welfare state (Klandermans et al 1992). Over the past few years between half and two thirds of the workforce have felt that unions are doing their job well (Van den Putte et al 1992).

Given the role which each of them may play as workers' representatives, it will be clear that the relationship between unions and works councils is crucial. This is borne out by the fact that this issue features prominently in union conferences and in public debates on a reform of the Works Councils Act. The unions' policy programmes are explicitly in favour of close cooperation between unions and works councils based on a division of labour which would reflect the unions' prerogative in the areas of pay and the work environment. Everyday reality provides the observer with many examples of successful strategic alliances of unions and works councils but there are also examples of an absence of contact and even of open conflict. It is clear that lack of cooperation, not to mention conflict, damages workers' interests and worker participation considerably. But apart from that, there are other arguments in favour of cooperation between unions and works councils.

Firstly, unions in the Netherlands are increasingly faced with the problem of representation. Union density is down to 24% and some categories of workers such as migrants or those with atypical work contracts, including many women, are seriously under-represented. Although works councils cope with the problem of communication with their rank-and-file, unionised works council members could play a significant role in keeping their unions informed about shop-floor reality and workers' perceptions of problems and interests. Open dialogue and intense interaction between union officials and unionised works council members is needed to achieve this.

Secondly, unions could help works councils tackle the problem of a "sectarian" definition of workers' interests. Overtime regulations, for which works councils have the right of approval, illustrates this problem. Many companies have enough overtime work available to enable many unemployed to get a job. Obviously, the company's need for flexibility is a major management argument against hiring new workers, should works councils suggest it. However, as far as the fellow-workers of those on the works councils are concerned, it is in their interests to earn overtime pay and works council members might find themselves faced with a conflict of interests if they wanted to replace overtime by extra jobs. Unions that take a broader, non-sectarian notion of workers' interests might help their members on works councils to develop a more solidarity-oriented approach to worker participation at shop-floor and company level.

To conclude, cooperation between unions and works councils is an issue of great importance in the context of the Dutch system of industrial relations, not only in the context of democratic participation as an end in itself but also because of the significance of such cooperation in achieving those other, equally important objectives - equity and humanity.

9 Trade unions and democratic participation in the United Kingdom

Michael Gold

Broadly speaking, we can identify five strands contained in the concept of "industrial democracy" as the term has developed in the United Kingdom since 1945:

- collective bargaining
- joint consultation
- sectoral, regional and national representation of labour's interests on a variety of government committees and quasi non-governmental organisations (QUANGOs) through individual unions and the Trades Union Congress (TUC)
- worker directors on the boards of companies or trustees of occupational pension funds
- participation at shop-floor or workplace level, for example through quality circles, particularly in the redesign of jobs and the introduction of technological change

All these, except the last, involve indirect forms of democratic participation. In such forms, representatives elected by the employees are responsible for participation in decision-making, with the trades unions virtually always constituting the sole channel for representation. Indeed, the centrality of the trades unions in British industrial relations - in the absence of any statutory basis for works councils as in most other EU member states - is the first key feature to be grasped in any discussion of industrial participation in the UK. Direct forms of participation, by contrast, involve each employee as an individual without intermediaries. In the last ten years, as we shall see, such forms of direct employee involvement (which include financial participation) have burgeoned. It should be noted, regarding terminology, that "participation" in the UK tends to signify these direct forms of involvement.

The second key feature of British practice is the centrality of collective bargaining as the principal mode of workplace regulation. Negotiation has traditionally determined not only substantive outcomes, such as pay, working time and holidays, but also the procedures through which such outcomes are to be settled. This approach, which, apart from the Irish Republic, is without parallel amongst other EU member states, is known as voluntarism. Voluntarism involves the freedom of employers and unions to negotiate their relationships without legal regulation, a principle which has been jealously preserved over the years despite increasing government intervention since the 1970s. Indeed, the voluntarist approach to industrial relations issues is so firmly entrenched that the classic analysis of collective bargaining in Britain is even entitled "Industrial Democracy" (Webb and Webb, 1897). In other words, industrial democracy is actually identified with collective bargaining, the cornerstone of voluntarism.

To gain an overview of trends in the UK in recent years it will be argued here that "industrial democracy" in general - and "participation" in particular - express a power relationship between employers and employees (either collectively or individually) which can be analysed in a three-fold framework.

Framework

First of all, industrial democracy schemes can be analysed by level. Any participatory scheme takes place at one or more levels in the sector concerned - for example, at department, plant, division, company or sector level. Participation and joint consultation occur typically at departmental and plant level, though the latter also occurs at higher levels. Collective bargaining takes place at all levels, whilst worker directors operate at board level - in the case (now abolished) of British Steel, for example, at divisional, company and sectoral levels. It is important to distinguish such levels because strong shop steward presence in the plant, for instance, may be counteracted by unilateral management decision-making at board level.

Second, within each level, there is a range of topics which may or may not be covered by participatory arrangements. Plant-level joint consultation committees are usually restricted to discussing topics like working conditions, improvements in work organisation, canteen and social facilities and so on, but at the same level shop stewards may be able to bargain over staffing and bonuses. At each level, a spectrum of topics may be influenced by employees or their representatives. Clarke and others identify four areas for management decision-making: wages and redundancy, work methods, work discipline and finance (Clarke et al., 1972, p.85). At each level, each topic area cuts more deeply into management prerogative.

Finally, within each topic area, there is a degree of influence obtainable by labour. This extends from a minimum degree of influence to a maximum: for example, listed in order of increasing influence, we can specify:

- provision of general information to workers by management

106

- joint consultation; passive participation in management
- active participation in management
- self-management (Globerson, 1970, p.256)

This formulation reveals too that degrees of influence depend on the methods adopted by labour to achieve its aims. That is, at each level and for each topic area, greater degrees of influence are obtained through some methods rather than others. In the UK, unions prefer collective bargaining to joint consultation, though self-management would provide a still greater degree of control, other things being equal. Degrees of control are related to "organisational variables" - such as density of unionisation, company size, technology, ownership and management style - and to "environmental influences" - such as the class structure, educational system and attitudes towards authority (Guest and Fatchett, 1974, chapter 2).

It should, in principle, be possible to slot any participatory scheme into this three-dimensional framework. The significance of this approach, however, is that industrial democracy forms an ever-changing "frontier of control" (Goodrich, 1975) as defined by the interface of level, topic and degree between management and workforce. In the British context, industrial democracy can be understood to refer to any scheme or process whereby management and workforce mediate control at a given level of industrial activity, within a given topic area and with the intention there of securing a greater degree of control.

In this way we can locate any scheme within this framework and so trace developments more easily. As the rest of this article will demonstrate, industrial democracy in the UK has remained a live issue throughout the entire period under review (1945 to the present). What does change is the precise location of the term in the three-dimensional framework. In other words, emphasis changes. This ranges from joint consultation in the 1940s and early 1950s to workplace collective bargaining from the mid-1950s and from a brief period of interest in worker directors in the 1970s to the current espousal (principally, but not exclusively, by management) of various forms of direct participation.

The reasons for these changes in emphasis are extremely complex. Full employment in the 1950s and 1960s allowed shop stewards to encroach their influence at workplace level and turn consultation into negotiation. During this period, growing industrial concentration led to the growth of multi-plant bargaining, and with it the recognition by some unions that there was an "influence gap" at company level. This, along with British entry into the EEC in 1973 - and subsequent discussion of the draft Fifth Directive on company law reform - provided the context within which the labour movement could tackle the question through worker directors. The return of the Conservative government in 1979 abruptly ended moves in this direction and a series of anti-trade union laws - along with a policy of deindustrialization and changes in the employment structure - shifted the balance of power in favour of employers. In an evermore competitive environment, their interest centred on employee adaptability and commitment, and hence on human resource management techniques centring not least on forms of direct employee involvement. However, these points become clearer as we develop post-War trends in greater detail.

1945-51

The Second World War had demanded an immense industrial effort during the course of which "the trade unions accepted a massive responsibility for the planning of production at every level of industry - national, regional, local, and in the works". (Industrial Democracy, 1948, p.7) By 1944, for example, there were around 4500 joint production committees in engineering alone. This emphasis on production continued after the War too, as it was seen, following the election of the Labour government in 1945, as the means to achieve full employment, to pay for social services and to keep prices down. The tripartite National Joint Advisory Council (NJAC), formed during the War, agreed in 1947 to promote joint consultative machinery throughout the private sector at all levels, whilst the Labour's nationalisation programme established similar procedures in the public sector.

These measures set the framework for developments in industrial democracy for the next generation. Whilst after the First World War the Labour government had questioned management at its very roots, attention after the Second focused on its performance. The gradual incorporation of labour through co-operative decision-making led to a change in the basis on which management was legitimated. Consent, rather than prerogative, aided by the development of more "democratic" styles, has been the hallmark of management authority right up to the 1980s and still today through human resource management techniques. Indeed, in 1946, the Conservative Party produced a report on the future of British industry which spoke of the "urgent need to continue the valuable work of many joint consultative bodies set up during the war years". (Eaton and Fletcher: 1976, p.87)

However, this consensus was not to last long. As economic conditions improved - and in the context of the Cold War - shop-floor collective bargaining became more important, especially in those industries characterised by piece rates. The devaluation of the pound in 1949 and the Korean War led to inflationary processes and subsequently, in the 1950s, to "wage drift" as shop stewards moved out of the control of national union leaders.

1951-64

The mood of the 1950s and 1960s is captured by Coates and Topham:
"It was full employment, underpinned by a technological revolution, based on the War effort, of the fifties and early sixties, which not only disoriented a movement that had come increasingly to concentrate its fire against "inefficiency" and to ignore the traditional protests against "wage slavery": but also created, in

factory workshop organisations of unparalleled strength and security, the mood to begin another push for the old objectives." (Coates and Topham, 1975, p.55)

Employers during this period became increasingly concerned at workers' "slackening pace", wage drift, restrictive practices and the rising level of unofficial strikes (Understanding Labour Relations, 1958, p.10). A swing in the balance of power towards shop stewards at the workplace and growing tensions between the stewards on the one hand and the "official" union movement on the other are the key features of this period. For these reasons, the decline in interest in joint consultation dates from this time. It is not surprising that shop stewards preferred the greater degree of influence they could achieve through collective bargaining. Indeed, employers' attempts to reassert some sort of control through productivity bargaining merely reinforced the trend - namely, that collective bargaining at workplace level had become the paradigm, at this time, for industrial democracy. Management tried to buy out restrictive practices and piece rate systems, but at the expense of extending collective bargaining to formerly non-negotiable items.

1964-70

Many of the trends apparent in the previous period continued under the two Labour governments (1964-70). The stop-go cycle of economic policy continued and the pound remained weak, culminating in the 1967 devaluation. At national level, the government tried to cope with the crisis of productivity in a variety of ways, including voluntary prices and incomes policies and the preparation of a National Plan and tripartite joint statement of intent. These measures required the participation of the TUC and national unions, but did little to stem shop-floor militancy which grew against the background of the increasing pace of economic rationalisation and concentration.

The Donovan Report, published in 1968 to analyse solutions to the UK's industrial relations problems, noted that 95% of strikes were unofficial (Donovan Report, 1968, p.98). It blamed inadequacies in wages structures and disputes procedures, as well as insecurity of employment and technological developments which affected grading systems. Amongst other measures, it proposed strengthening collective bargaining, a process it considered as quite separate from industrial democracy. Chapter XV of the Report, "Workers' Participation in Management", focused almost exclusively on the TUC's proposals for trade union representation on company boards. These were rejected on the grounds of possible conflicts of interests which could arise for worker directors.

The result was a Labour Party White Paper on industrial relations reform, "In Place of Strife" (1969), which acknowledged the centrality of collective bargaining by advocating, amongst much else, conciliation pauses in unofficial strikes, strike ballots and the imposition of penalties for certain breaches. The ensuing furore within the labour movement gave an easy advantage to the Conservatives who won the 1970 general election with industrial relations reform as part of their manifesto.

However, a review of the events of the 1964-70 Labour governments reveals that the vestiges of joint consultation and productivity bargaining as well as the attempted regulation of collective bargaining through legal sanctions were unable to deal with the effects of structural change in the economy. At this stage, only the TUC had mentioned worker directors as a means to achieve greater influence over the formulation of corporate strategy. The Conservatives were still to attempt to establish an entirely new legal basis for industrial relations before the notion of worker directors was to emerge as the last novel solution to the "British problem". From then on, under the Thatcher government, it was to become a matter of relying on mass unemployment and legal reform to gradually reduce union immunities and promote individualist values at work.

1970-79

The Conservative government elected in 1970, then, passed in the following year its Industrial Relations Act, which introduced new individual rights at work, established an Industrial Relations Court and required the registration of unions and employers' associations - along with much else, all backed by punitive sanctions. It was vigorously opposed by the labour movement and subsequently repealed by the Labour government elected in 1974.

Job satisfaction

However, the Code of Industrial Relations Practice established by the Industrial Relations Act contained specific reference to job satisfaction and participation, concepts which were to lay the foundation for the Thatcher government's espousal, at the end of the decade, for employee involvement (Macmillan, 1973, p.iii). In June 1973, the government set up the Tripartite Steering Group on Job Satisfaction and, on its recommendation, the Work Research Unit in November 1974 which continued analyses of the links between job satisfaction, job redesign and productivity.

From the unions' side, there was considerable scepticism over these projects which were often seen as a means to divert attention away from other features of the working environment such as low pay, excessive overtime, shift working and job insecurity. For these reasons, once a Labour government had been re-elected in 1974, the union movement returned to its principal interest - the extension of collective bargaining.

Extension of collective bargaining

The Trade Union and Labour Relations Act (1974) swept away the discredited

110

Industrial Relations Act whilst the Employment Protection Act (1975) conferred a series of new rights on employees, such as rights to information, maternity leave, time off for union duties and so on, all of which established new areas for negotiation at the appropriate levels of industry. Health and safety were dealt with in the same way.

Unions and economic policy

In addition to strengthening collective bargaining, the Labour government had another strand to its policies on participation: it aimed to increase the influence of the unions over the national formulation of economic and industrial strategy. The formation of the National Enterprise Board (NEB), a state-holding company designed to take an interest in the "meso-economic" sector of the economy (the top 100 leading companies), alongside tripartite Sector Working Parties and, of course, the Bullock proposals for worker directors, constituted the backbone of the "Social Contract" with the TUC. Voluntary pay restraint was to be secured in return for greater union involvement in planning investment and industrial strategy. The reality was rather different. It was not long before the government, despite the TUC's submission to pay policy, was acting independently. Faced by recession, it deflated the economy, cut public expenditure and sharply restricted the powers of the NEB to invest in large businesses. The NEB ended up as a home for ailing companies and the Sector Working Parties as little more than discussion forums.

Worker co-operatives

Another controversial, but ultimately unsuccessful, strand to the Labour government's economic strategy coincided with Tony Benn's tenure as Secretary of State for Industry (1974-75). During this period, a number of "new co-operatives" were supported with public finance as a defensive strategy to save jobs (Coates, 1976). The three most well-known were Meriden (motorcycle manufacture), Scottish Daily News (printing) and KME (engineering), though there were others too. All of them were set up following work-ins but all eventually collapsed, for a variety of reasons. These included a harder government line following Benn's replacement, the weak market position of the co-operatives themselves (which had led to their original closure as private enterprises in the first place) and internal divisions within the workforces involved and the wider labour movement. Indeed, it is now perfectly clear that the most successful and long-lasting worker co-operatives in the UK have been those supported by agencies like the Industrial Common Ownership Movement (ICOM) as co-operatives rather than as gallant attempts primarily to assert the right to work in unpropitious circumstances.

The Labour government, then, had proved unable to tilt the mediation of control in favour of organised labour through economic and industrial policy. Things did not progress much better in relation to board-level representation.

As we saw above, the Donovan Report did not favour worker directors as it feared the problem of split loyalties on the board. However, a number of factors changed the climate during the 1970s, notably the UK's entry into the EEC in 1973, a few months after publication of the draft Fifth Directive with its proposals for representation of labour at board level, and the growing feeling that such representation would help to secure employees' commitment to corporate decisions. In 1973, the TUC adopted proposals for 50:50 mandatory worker/management representation on supervisory boards through union channels, in the belief that worker directors would help to achieve influence otherwise outside the scope of collective bargaining (in relation to areas like merger, acquisition and investment policy).

In 1975, a Committee of Inquiry was appointed to advise the government on board-level representation in the private sector under the chairmanship of Sir Alan (later Lord) Bullock. Its Majority Report, published in January 1977, recommended: single board representation in all companies with over 2000 employees; a 2X + Y formula, where the 2X referred to equal employer/employee representation and the Y to a minority of "independent" directors agreed by the 2X; union channels to elect worker directors; a union Joint Representation Committee (JRC) to organise elections; and an Industrial Democracy Commission to advise on the operation of the legislation (Bullock Report: 1977).

Employers' organisations were implacably opposed to the proposals, but the union movement was split as well - in three ways. The first response, adopted by the TUC and the Transport and General Workers' Union (TGWU), was unreservedly in favour. The second response was also in favour, but with reservations. For example, the white-collar union APEX (now merged with GMB) felt that proposals for a Joint Representation Committee in each company did not sufficiently come to grips with the problem of the monitoring of policy implementation at lower levels, to achieve which it called for departmental councils too. The third response, however, was to reject the very principle of worker directors. Major unions adopting this position were the engineers, AUEW, and the electricians, EET/PU (now merged to form the AEEU). The influential AUEW rejected "the view that there is a point beyond which collective bargaining cannot develop" (Investigation, 1976, p.2) and called for company-level collective bargaining and the promotion of co-operatives. The EET/PU was concerned "that worker directors represent the absorbtion of trade unions into a scenario of corporate élitism..." (Evidence, 1976, p.6). Split union loyalties, constraints on the disclosure of confidential information and possible disunity of unions during elections were further reasons advanced by a number of unions for their opposition to Bullock.

In view of this fragmentation, the Labour government moved cautiously, and eventually published a White Paper in May 1978 which proposed that companies should be allowed to work out details of board-level schemes for themselves, but that there should also be statutory fall-back rights: legislation would permit a two-tier board system covering companies with over 500 employees. JRCs would have the right to discuss corporate strategy with the board and the right to require companies to ballot the workforce on whether they wanted representation at that level (Industrial Democracy, 1978).

In the event, the general election of May 1979, won by the Conservative Party under Margaret Thatcher, cut off all further movement in this area. In consequence, British evidence on possible results of worker director schemes is very patchy. The most well-known scheme in the 1970s - now long defunct - was undoubtedly that at British Steel (Bank and Jones, 1977). However, worker directors had to relinquish union office and withdraw from branch meetings, in addition to which some experienced problems over time-off. There were only one or two worker directors on each divisional board and no attempt was made, or perhaps could be made, to help them overcome their split role - to British Steel and to the workforce - when faced with widescale redundancies in the industry. Only one other worker director scheme has ever been tried in the public sector: the Post Office. Introduced as a two-year experiment in 1978, the worker directors were not re-appointed in 1980.

Apart from this, the only other significant experience in the UK with board-level worker representation is restricted to those companies which have union-nominated trustees on the boards of their pension funds. By the mid-1980s, there were some 100,000 occupational pension schemes in the UK, mostly managed by insurance companies. However, larger ones are administered by boards of trustees, around half of which have at least some employee representatives (a small minority elected through union channels). Their control over extremely large amounts of financial capital has nevertheless been limited by a number of factors, notably tight legal definitions of the role of trustee, limited access to alternative sources of advice and, generally, minimal training (Gold, 1981; Schuller, 1985).

1979 to the present

In contrast to earlier periods, the 1980s witnessed a surge of interest in various forms of direct participation. The reasons for this development are complex, and a series of background factors must be taken into account. First, at the political level, the Conservative government enacted a series of laws to curb what it deemed to be excessive union power. The closed shop, picketing, strike ballots and internal union democracy were just some of the areas governed by statute. In relation to industrial democracy, Section 1 of the Employment Act 1982 requires companies with over 250 employees to disclose details of employee involvement schemes in their Annual Reports, but that is all (a process known as "Section 1 reporting").

Secondly, the structure of employment has continued to change, with the decline of manufacturing offset against the rise in services (in 1979, 38.7% of the UK civilian population worked in industry but only 29.4% by 1989; in services, the figures for the same years rose from 58.6% to 68.4%). Over the same ten year period, the female labour force rose from 39.1% to 42.8% of the total, whilst numbers employed in the public sector (general government and public corporations) fell from 7.4 million to 6.1 million, not least as the result of government privatisation campaigns. These have entailed two kinds of policy to benefit the private sector: the sale of public assets, notably in energy, transport and telecommunications, and the contracting out of services formerly supplied by local authorities, such as street cleaning, council house maintenance and the provision of school meals. Unemployment, of course, rocketed from 5.0% to 6.9% of the total labour force (all figures derived from OECD, 1991).

Thirdly, product markets have become increasingly competitive which has led to moves towards decentralisation and, in many companies, human resource management techniques, such as flexible work organisation systems, employee development and training, stress on communications, performance appraisal and so on. Further, even less welcome moves by employers - such as de-recognition of unions in sectors like printing and the conclusion of single-union deals in particularly Japanese-owned companies - have also increasingly affected unions in recent years. Union resistance has not been assisted by their fragmentation - despite mergers and amalgamations there are still (in 1993) 69 unions, with widely varying internal structures and policies, affiliated to the TUC.

These developments, set against a background of continual technological change, have reduced trade union membership density from 58% in 1984 to some 48% in 1990 (Millward et al., 1992), and with it, union influence at all levels. This is a serious matter in a country where participation has been voluntary and organised almost exclusively through union channels. Overall, this shift from collective to individual rights at work and approaches to employment issues has led to major implications for the conduct of industrial relations - or employee relations as the area is often now termed. These include the extent to which collective and individualist systems can co-exist and the extent to which individualist practices are diluted in their operation (Guest, 1989, pp. 54-5).

Collective bargaining and joint consultation remain buoyant in certain sectors and in larger companies, but overall there have been serious declines in the coverage of both during the 1980s. The 1990 Workplace Industrial Relations Survey (Millward et al.,1992), for example, reveals that 71% of UK employees had been covered by collective bargaining in 1984 but only 54% by 1990. Similarly, 30% of private manufacturing companies had joint consultative committees in 1984, but only 23% six years later. However, management-sponsored forms of direct participation or employee involvement schemes are increasingly common, including:

- downwards communications systems, such as employee reports, company newspapers and magazines, briefing sessions and so on
- upwards problem-solving forms of employee involvement, such as suggestion schemes, quality circles and total quality management
- financial participation, such as profit-sharing schemes, employee share ownership and so on. By 1989 there were over one thousand such schemes in operation covering between 7% and 9% of the workforce (P + European Participation Monitor, 1991, p.14).

A recent study of these forms of employee involvement in 25 different organisations revealed that:

"In relation to industrial sectors most of the companies in manufacturing had long experience of representative participation and this had been maintained whilst more recent forms of employee involvement, most notably downward communications in the early 1980s and problem solving techniques in the late 1980s, had been added. In the service sector, there is a much shorter history of involvement, with representative participation being virtually non-existent. Employee involvement appears to have been given more emphasis in recent years and a variety of schemes had been introduced over a short period." (Marchington et al., 1992, p.x)

This study revealed that, of the 25 organisations, 9 distributed employee reports; 19 had their own newspapers; 19 operated briefing systems; 15 had suggestion schemes; 5 had quality circles; 19 had customer care/total quality management; and 13 operated a profit share scheme (Marchington et al., 1992, p.14). However, this research was qualitative and did not aim to ascertain the extent of different forms of employee involvement across the entire economy.

For this purpose, a survey carried out by the Department of Employment is probably more indicative. This study focused on a statistically random sample of companies required under the Employment Act 1982 to declare in their annual reports the action they had taken to promote employee involvement (they therefore all had over 250 employees). It showed that 81.7% of companies used some form of direct information/communications system; 66.6% consulted employees or their representatives on a regular basis; 76.9% had introduced financial participation of one kind or another; and 70.8% promoted a common awareness amongst their employees of the financial and economic factors affecting company performance. "Interactive practices" formed the most prevalent type of employee involvement, reported by 80.1% of companies - these included meetings/management line communications, briefing groups, access to senior management, union and staff association channels and quality circles (Hibbert, 1991, pp.659-664).

The actual effects of all this involvement is more difficult to assess. If we focus on financial participation alone, one team of researchers suggests that employers are often unclear about their motives for introducing one scheme rather than another and that they therefore do not always understand how desired outcomes may accordingly be generated (these include improving employee commitment, relating pay more closely to performance and encouraging wider share ownership as a principle). Systems for evaluating the results of the schemes are, as a result, usually lacking. "Financial participation schemes, then, have some resemblance to an "act of faith" on the part of management." (Baddon et al., 1989, p.280) Whether this observation also applies more generally to other forms of employee involvement remains open for the time being.

Recent union responses

In view of the employers' almost exclusive concentration on employee involvement, it is not surprising that the trade union movement has meanwhile become increasingly aware of the way in which international links, notably through the European Union (EU), can support their own demands for improved forms of representational industrial democracy. The TUC was, for example, in the forefront in supporting the draft "Vredeling" Directive on information and consultation in companies with complex structures and has more recently, of course, promoted the draft European Works Council Directive (Cressey, 1993).

It is true that some rank-and-file trade unionists have expressed concerns about the actual operation of European works councils as envisaged in this draft Directive. For example, there are concerns about how a works council system would graft on to the UK approach to industrial relations, based as it traditionally has been on trade union structures, and about how effectively EU group-level company information could feed back into the appropriate levels of union activity. Nevertheless, the measure has been generally supported because it is a major step forward and opens up new areas for union negotiation - and also, of course, because a hostile government and hardened employer attitudes domestically have acted as a clamp on other union initiatives. Indeed, the TUC believes that priority should now be given to the implementation of this Directive along with the draft Fifth Directive and the European Company Statute since it is here that progress can best be made towards greater industrial democracy - and genuine democratic participation - paving the way for further advances at national level.

Conclusions

"Industrial democracy" as a term has been closely associated in the UK from the very beginning with the development of collective bargaining. Furthermore, in line with the voluntarist traditions of industrial relations in the UK, it is inextricably linked with trade union channels of representation. "Participation", by contrast, tends to refer to the various direct forms of employee involvement which often bypass union channels.

Interest in industrial democracy has remained fairly steady over the last four or five decades, though its form has varied by level, kind of topic covered and degree of influence sought by the parties. Over the last ten years, however, direct forms of participation have become popular amongst managements, though it is important to stress that they often operate alongside existing consultation and negotiation structures. In the growing service sector, on the other hand, a sector not noted for its union density or collectivist traditions, direct forms of participation may be introduced by managements without challenge.

Other forms of industrial democracy have been attempted. Perhaps the most significant was the attempt to introduce worker directors on to the boards of large companies in the 1970s. However, employers objected that it would jeopardise their right to manage whilst the labour movement split in its views. Both sides tended to couch the argument in collective bargaining terms: the employers feared that the proposals would introduce collective bargaining into the boardroom, whilst a number of influential unions feared that they would dilute their bargaining strength. This illustrates once again the dominance of the collective bargaining culture in British industrial relations.

With respect to the future, on the one hand, declining membership and the rise of human resource management techniques at the workplace present challenges. On the other hand, participation in European debates and initiatives - particularly the European Works Councils Directive - presents opportunities. The British labour movement has faced serious challenges before, and its response now is to consolidate through mergers, improved service to members and recruitment in new areas of employment. In addition, it needs to counter the blandishments of those advocating individualist approaches to workplace relations by demonstrating the benefits of collectivism - not least through the construction of a genuine social Europe based on a range of appropriate forms of democratic participation.

10 From self-management to cooperatives in the contours of worker participation in Malta over two decades

Edward Zammit

Introduction

In order to understand the experience of worker participation in Malta one must take into account the historical circumstances that have shaped Malta's economy and society.

As a result of many centuries of colonialism, Malta has traditionally developed a fortress economy and a society accustomed to receiving instructions "from above" rather than to self-government. Vital decisions affecting people's lives in a most fundamental way used to be taken in remote centres of power. Until relatively recently Maltese elected representatives were allowed only a small measure of autonomy in purely "local" affairs. After independence was won from Britain in 1964, the economy remained for many years heavily dependent upon direct advances by the British Treasury and upon the presence of a large British military base on the Island. This provided direct employment to many thousands of Maltese workers and made an important contribution to the balance of payments. Even today, there are still visible traces left of the long colonial experience (Zammit, 1984).

Growth (1971-79)

In 1971, the newly elected Labour government (MLP) sought to put an end to the country's traditional "servile status" and give "Malta to the Maltese". Its aim was the eventual complete removal of all the British services stationed in Malta and a simultaneous move towards economic self-reliance. This goal was given the highest priority by the Maltese government and was reflected in its economic policies. Success was closely linked to an ambitious programme of social reforms and harmonious industrial relations. Worker participation featured prominently in this programme.

119

An early challenge faced by the government in 1971 was that presented by Malta Drydocks. This leading company had a long history of industrial strife. Ever since its transformation from a British Admiralty Yard into a commercial firm during the early 1960s it had been running up financial losses which were a cause for national concern.

The workers in this company pride themselves on being the vanguard of the Maltese labour movement. Their claim that a prolonged strike prior to the election of 1971 played an important part in the Labour party victory seems to be well founded for the strike helped expose the weakness of the former government.

In its election manifesto, the MLP had promised to introduce workers participation, or rather a form of co-determination, with equal numbers of council members appointed by the government and by the General Workers' Union (GWU). The key to the solution sought by the government was to pass on to the workers the responsibility for the running of the Yard. Despite a host of initial problems, this move gave a new lease of life to the company and provided a psychological boost to workers and their trade union to pursue this new course.

These innovative policies triggered a heated public debate in which unions, government, the opposition party, employer organisations and the general public took part. Early in 1974, an opinion survey among workers in participative firms showed that their attitudes towards participation were overwhelmingly positive (Kester, 1974). In a tug of war over the objectives, forms, scope, etc. of participation and its development in Malta, the various parties each continually tried to seize the initiative in order to safeguard their own position and interests. Eventually, the government started to bring this new policy increasingly under its control. The concept of participation well suited the new, more prominent role played by the State in economic activity. Participation was expected to contribute towards a more cooperative and productive labour force, and provide an opportunity to introduce much needed reforms in the social relations of production.

Between 1975-1979 worker participation spread. At first, specific institutionalised forms of worker participation were devised for individual firms, but later these stabilised into three major designs:

(1) A self-management structure for the Drydocks was established by legislation in 1975, the highest decision-making organ of the firm being solely composed of directly-elected representatives to whom the management of the firm was accountable.

(2) Para-statal and state enterprises were grouped in a special Ministry of Para-statal and People's Industries. There, a uniform pattern of participation was established in 1977 at the level of the board of directors. The ultimate aim was that these firms should eventually become self-managed like the Drydocks. This new sector and the Drydocks existed in parallel to a private sector.

(3) In the course of 1978 workers' committees were elected in most government departments. Their role was mainly to advise management on production matters. In practice, however, they usually served as an additional form of worker representation to the trade unions.

Thus by mid-1979 almost one-third of the wage earners in Malta enjoyed some formally institutionalised form of participation. (Zammit et al, 1982)

The overall approach has been pragmatic rather than ideological or legalistic. It has been a flexible approach, giving scope for persons and institutions to apprentice themselves in the new relations, and giving them time to respond to the government's initiative. There was hardly any ideological underpinning. It was direct experience with worker participation that brought to the surface new ambitions, perspectives, objectives and concepts regarding the nature of work and organisation, company hierarchy, company social relations, decision-making prerogatives, the structure of company ownership etc. Thus the development of government-initiated participation opened new and diverse perspectives, expectations and short and long-term goals. The major participants (workers, managers, trade unions, bureaucrats, employers and political leaders) all tried to guide participation in their own direction. Thus while for employers, participation meant that workers had to assume greater responsibility at work, for trade unionists it was an opportunity to achieve their claims without a fight.

The government's approach to establishing participation structures and procedures was flexible. Instead of following a predetermined strategy and imposing a uniform participation framework, it took every chance it could to develop whatever form of participation was feasible at a given time under specific circumstances. Legislation regarding worker self-management at the Drydocks helped consolidate the process.

During this period, the General Workers' Union organised numerous educational activities including seminars, workshops and short courses on the experiments in worker participation which were going on in various companies. These activities were usually intended for those involved in company participation programmes. However there was rarely any follow-up on the suggestions which emerged from these sessions. These were usually shelved until they re-emerged at some subsequent seminar. Thus there was little improvement in the participative experiments and this proved to be a major flaw in the system.

The supportive role played by the union in this process cannot be over-emphasised. It exposed itself to fierce criticism for allegedly abandoning its traditional defensive role. Nevertheless, it spared no effort in encouraging workers to pursue the objectives of participation.

Stagnation (1980-1987)

After the initial euphoria, further development in worker participation failed to materialise. Perhaps the lack of any sustained participative policy and long-term strategy was to blame. What is certain is that there were no adequate support structures. Many para-statal firms found themselves forced to revert to traditional forms of management when, following a period of economic difficulty, their assets were transferred in part or in full to private capital. Moreover, inter-union rivalry in the public service between the two biggest trade union movements - the General Workers Union (GWU) and the Confederation of Malta Trade Unions (CMTU) - meant that the workers' committees acted more as extensions of the dominant union in that particular industrial sector. They simply served as a channel for workers' grievances and requests for an improved work environment. The encroachment of these workers' representatives on managerial/ministerial prerogatives became regarded as an abuse rather than a new challenge.

This brought about the de facto demise of management committees. What did survive was a small number of elected worker directors - a symbolic more than a real form of participation which in the 1980s was extended to a number of large public/para-statal bodies.

The increase in the number of worker directors certainly aroused a general awareness not only of their existence but also of their potential influence on corporate policy, union power and worker access to information. At the same time, the lack of clear guidelines on various issues concerning worker directors was indicative of the unobtrusive and subdued nature of the board-room penetration which had characterised the overall development of worker participation for almost two decades (Zammit & Baldacchino, 1988).

In fact the only workplace where the participative system remained in its consolidated and unadulterated form was at the Drydocks. However, the financial losses which this firm starting registering in 1982 proved to be a severe setback to any further development of participation. The Drydocks' negative economic performance continued throughout the 1980s and its continued existence was only made possible by bank overdraft facilities. The government intervened to provide the necessary cash-flow as it controlled the major commercial banking institutions in Malta (Baldacchino, 1988). Thus the heavy economic burden that the self-managed Drydocks represented had to be shouldered by the whole country. This made the public question the value of self-management as it operated at the Drydocks. However, in spite of these setbacks, there seemed to be no evidence that the workers' keenness to participate had diminished (Zammit & Baldacchino, 1988).

In fact the survival of self-management in this important firm was mainly due to the workers' positive attitudes towards participation. This generated a determination on their part not to let anyone tamper with the system. As a result, all the major social, economic and political forces in Malta felt obliged to express their formal approval of some form of worker participation - although wide divergence both in the aims and forms of participation persisted.

The popular appeal of worker participation was reflected in the platform of the Nationalist Party, the other main political party in Malta, in power since 1987 and which has affirmed its support for participation. Likewise, private employers have made some cautious comments expressing interest in the concept. The General Workers' Union, with almost 60% of the unionised labour force, was and still is directly involved in shaping and directing participation. The union shared national policy-making under the Labour government - thanks to its close links with the government. It was represented on the boards and committees of participative enterprises. It was thus in a position to convey shop-floor experiences and expectations to higher levels and, conversely, from the higher levels to those below.

The search for a new direction (1987-1992)

The unions' central role came to an abrupt end following the defeat of the Malta Labour party in the May 1987 general elections. With the Nationalist party (NP) in power, a confrontational stance soon developed between the newly-elected government and the GWU. The first controversial issue concerned the appointment of worker directors in para-statal corporations. The government had failed to appoint a worker director on the newly-formed boards of these bodies. After protracted negotiations, the government and the GWU reached an agreement. The government pledged to enact immediate legislation on direct worker elections of one worker director on each board of two of the biggest parastatal corporations. The electoral procedures were to be agreed upon by the GWU and the government.

The Nationalist party was perhaps anxious to demonstrate its pre-election promises to support worker participation in management and to further liberalise existing forms of board representation. Thus the post of worker-director became contested in an open election and was not determined merely by trade union nomination. The GWU, still smarting from the electoral defeat of its social partner, the MLP, was keen to boost morale by a strong show of support for its sponsored candidates in the election of worker directors. Even the other trade union organisation, the CMTU, came out strongly in favour of elected worker directors. The election became a test of inter-union strength and rivalry.

At about the same time, in February 1988, a Federation of Worker Directors (FWD) was set up. Its main aim was "to promote industrial democracy in the workplace and to combat those forces which threaten it". In order to honour its electoral promise the government formed an inter-ministerial committee to study the implementation of a system of worker participation. (Zammit & Baldacchino, 1988).

Another confrontation that ensued during this period was that between the government and the Malta Drydocks Council regarding a disputed pay increase for the employees following an agreement between the Council and the union. The Council, supported by the union, insisted that the government issue the necessary extra cash to meet this increase in the wage bill - something which the government was reluctant to do due to the economic losses incurred by the company. This impasse was settled only after long negotiations which culminated in the signing of an overall agreement between the Drydocks' Council and the government regarding the future of the company. This included an 80 million Maltese liri (US$200 million) aid package to be provided by the government over a ten year period. This was aimed at restoring the company's economic viability. The agreement also allowed the Council and the GWU to make provisions for any wage increases. The government's financial commitment thus became clearer while the Council had to shoulder the responsibility of administering these funds in the best interests of the company and the nation.

The survival of worker participation, particularly in the Drydocks, would not have been possible without the crucial support of the union which constantly had to adapt itself as the situation changed. It often had to assimilate new ideas and stick its neck out in defence of new policies. At the same time, the union was also searching for a new identity - which it has not, as yet, found.

Throughout the 1970s and 1980s, the GWU's links with the MLP, particularly in the form of a statutory fusion, were severely criticised both by the trade unions grouped under the Confederation of Malta Trade Unions (CMTU) and the Nationalist party. Following the MLP's second successive electoral defeat in 1992, the union and the party formally agreed to end this fusion and their respective general conferences made the necessary amendments to their statutes. The current aim is to promote national solidarity among trade unions.

The GWU feels that by ending its fusion with the MLP it has removed one of the major obstacles to setting up a Trade Union Council which might incorporate all Maltese trade unions. This policy seems to echo the MLP's 1992 electoral manifesto which stated that a TUC would be more conducive to the participation of trade unions in policy-making especially in areas where their interests are concerned.

The Nationalist party, re-elected in 1992, has pledged to implement the proposals of a government-appointed committee on the development of worker participation in the workplace.

Among other things this Committee has recommended the setting up of "a support unit" to promote worker participation in those sectors of government departments and para-statal enterprises which are mostly congenial to the operation of a worker participation scheme. The ultimate aim is that these sectors will adopt a cooperative structure which would enable the workers to participate in the profits accruing from increased productivity.

For this purpose, both the Department of Labour and the Board of Cooperatives have been placed under the responsibility of the Ministry of Education and Human Resources and a Parliamentary Secretary has been entrusted with this specific task.

It is thus envisaged that any future initiatives in worker participation in Malta emanating from government sources would take the form of worker cooperatives.

To date, Maltese cooperatives have tended to be concentrated in the agricultural sector. In order to facilitate this development, it will be necessary to establish new autonomous structures aimed at promoting the establishment of new worker cooperative ventures particularly in the services sector.

It is further proposed to establish a technical support unit which will offer the necessary marketing, accounting, legal and other managerial skills which both the new and the existing cooperatives badly lack.

Nevertheless, some serious doubts may be raised about the extent to which the promoters of worker participation - in one or another of its forms - will succeed.

The reasons for these doubts include the following:

(a) Popular demand for worker participation is no longer as great as it was a decade ago. Nowadays, the values of individualism and materialism predominate and politicians are as usual keen to satisfy popular demands.

(b) The experience of worker participation at the Drydocks with its militant workforce and heavy financial losses has tarnished the public image of worker participation as a whole.

(c) Present union leaders, being confronted by an unfriendly government, are keen to develop a sound, working relationship with it by adopting moderate and conservative policies rather than policies inspired by past ideologies. This way union leaders seek to avoid the fate suffered by other unions elsewhere. They also feel that present social conditions are not ripe for promoting worker participation.

The above reasons explain why the present Nationalist government, despite its pre-election promises, has been dragging its feet on matters relating to worker participation. Consequently, the prospects of any dramatic breakthrough in this area at present seem rather bleak.

Nevertheless, if a clear message were to be received from Brussels endorsing worker participation as part of EU policy a new situation would emerge. As the present government is actively seeking entry into the EU it would eagerly harmonise its policy in that direction.

11 Participation and co-determination in Sweden

Åke Sandberg[1]

General background

Labour relations in Sweden have varied over the past 25 years. There has been a growing emphasis on productivity rather than democratisation and on cooperation and participation on the one hand and formal negotiations on the other. These shifts in emphasis over the years reflect policy changes among unions and employer organisations at national level. At local level such changes are sometimes less evident. The reasons for these changes are to be found in more general shifts in Sweden's economic and political situation.

In order to understand the situation in Sweden it is essential to possess a basic grasp of some of the major characteristics of labour relations in Sweden and a familiarity with the country's economy. Important factors include the historical dominance of social democratic governments which have worked closely with the trade union movement and the strength of the union movement itself, both nationally and at the workplace.

The Swedish trade unions owe much of their strength to the country's welfare system and pro-active employment policy. The latter guarantees support for new companies starting up business in "weak" areas of the country and encourages vocational retraining with the ultimate goal of full employment. Unlike most other European countries Sweden managed to keep unemployment figures very low throughout the 1980s.

In the early 1990s unemployment stood at just over 1%. The sense of security that the country's social, employment and industrial policies had given workers and trade unions was a major factor which contributed to workers' and unions' positive attitudes towards technological change and co-determination. Another important factor not to be neglected was the country's relatively small size and its dependence on exports.

The Swedish trade unions' solidarity wage policy calls for equal pay for identical jobs, irrespective of the industrial sector or region. The policy also calls for limited wage differences between different jobs. Given that such a policy means that inherently weak companies will vanish, it is a mechanism which fosters industrial renewal, provided that it is complemented by other policies offering support and help to new companies and new industries. The policy also helps generate extra profits for the most successful companies because additional pay rises are not permitted although local "wage drift" above the nationally agreed levels does occur and thus modifies the overall situation. Extra profits help successful companies to expand and grow. But they also encourage a concentration of power and capital. The "wage-earner funds" was an attempt to counter-balance this tendency (Meidner 1992).

Today the "Swedish model" of industrial relations has been radically watered down. Increasingly, employers opt for locally-based wage negotiations while nationwide industrial relations, previously the stronghold of Swedish trade unions and the core of the country's welfare state, have diminished in importance.

Historical background

During the 1960s a generally optimistic view of technological development prevailed in Sweden. Robert Blauner's concept of vocational retraining for workers with the advent of automation was widely accepted and it influenced trade union views on the subject. However, by the end of the decade some of the negative repercussions of radical technological and structural change in production were beginning to be felt. Employers found themselves faced with personnel problems such as increased staff turnover and absenteeism as well as production-related problems. The latter became apparent with the realization that Taylorist principles of organisation were not effective in complex production processes. Problems related to planning and quality emerged. Shop-floor action such as unofficial strikes spread in protest against the increasingly degrading nature of work. In almost half of these stoppages the root cause was issues related to the work environment and workplace control (Korpi, 1978). Gradually, union demands were formulated and calls were made for a change in work organisation and greater democratisation of the workplace. This marked a shift in trade union policy. Until then union policy had always been to reject shop-floor participation for fear of eroding union independence. These new developments must be seen against a backdrop of vigorous economic growth and full employment in Sweden at that time. Levels of education were high, young workers were numerous and it would be fair to say that the general climate was radical.

During the mid 1960s the above-mentioned production and staff-related problems were examined in detail by the technical department of the Swedish Employers' Confederation (SAF). This gave employers an advantage over the central union confederations LO and TCO when, at the end of the decade, various projects were launched in an attempt to humanise the work environment (gauged in terms of job satisfaction) and increase productivity. The Development Council for Cooperative Issues, set up by SAF, LO and TCO in 1966, formed a special research group known as URAF which in turn launched ten developmental projects in different companies throughout the country. The aim of these experiments in industrial democracy was to adapt work organisation along "socio-technical" lines. One common feature of these projects was the introduction of more or less "autonomous groups".

In state-owned companies in particular, this socio-technical approach was complemented by a variety of democratic bodies - departmental committees comprising three workers and a supervisor or regular departmental meetings for all employees. One project run in the civil service involved the participation of employee representatives in various more or less autonomous work-groups.

Initially some of these experiments proved to be very promising. But conflicts arose when attempts were made to actually implement the changes that had been debated. This is understandable when one appreciates the diversity of the strategic aims involved. On the one hand it was hoped that these new systems would raise productivity and solve a variety of social problems while on the other the projects were regarded as phases in an on-going process of democratisation. Furthermore, in the private sector there was a significant drop in willingness to cooperate whereas in the public sector researchers and trade unionists openly opposed management.

In the private sector the employers' confederation had been persistently pursuing its own course and interests, working in close collaboration with different companies. This trend intensified when joint projects collapsed. Gradually the "new factories" programme began to take shape, launched by the employers' confederation and using new models of production technology and new forms of work organisation. The programme's slogan was "coordinated independence". The idea was that semi-independent sub-systems in production would permit direct, albeit limited, employee influence over day-to-day work issues but with strengthened, overall management coordination.

Like the employers, the unions, when they set about investigating co-determination, drew on the lessons learned in these experiments in industrial democracy. It was LO in particular which, in 1971, voiced radical demands for representation and democratic influence in the workplace together with more general calls for more democratic work organisation and direct worker participation. LO also proposed wage earner funds to give local and central unions a voice in company affairs and give wage earners a share in capital growth. This move was also intended to increase the availability of risk capital on the stock market and lend support to the solidarity or equal wage policy by transferring "excess profits" to funds under the control of national and local trade unions. Companies were to issue shares to these funds.

In 1976, 1979 and 1991 the Social Democratic Party lost legislative elections. Conservatives and the employers' association had claimed that wage earner funds would lead to a monolithic society similar to those in eastern Europe, stripped of political democracy and freedom. The Social Democrats subsequently altered their policies and drew up a modified scheme for wage earner funds with limited capital. These plans were introduced when the Social Democrats were returned to power in the 1982 elections. The capital in collective funds was less than the value of the so-called convertible bonds (that could be converted into shares) which were offered to individual employees at favourable prices as part of a new management strategy. Today the funds are being dismantled by Sweden's present centre-right government.

The calls for increased worker influence at all levels of a company met with management resistance. Employers did not want to see employee participation go beyond direct participation in the office or on the shop-floor. This led to a further shift in trade union policy. By mobilizing political support the unions demanded legislative action. Their efforts led to the 1976 Co-determination Act which, together with further legislation enacted at the same time, is generally referred to as the "labour legislation offensive" in Sweden. The unions followed up with an educational offensive, disseminating information about the new legislation, computerisation and work organisation. The unions organised specialist courses and broad-based study circles in the workplace.

Thus after the mutual union-management efforts of the 1960s to improve job satisfaction and productivity, by the mid-1970s the Swedish unions were demanding democratisation of work through legislation and agreements. Their slogan was "from consultation to co-determination". This was also used as the title of a training manual published by LO. Meanwhile employers continued their socio-technical approach, concentrating on production and technology. The latter half of the 1970s thus saw both sides gain considerable understanding of the issues, improve their strategies and consolidate their positions. The unions were dissatisfied with the employers' reactions to their grievances. Union members were mobilized and ideas for industrial and economic democracy were discussed in great depth. Similar discussions took place within the Social Democratic Party. Braverman's ideas (1974) on the degradation of work were a dominant theme of research and union debate at the time. Workers and unions had suffered with the introduction of new technology and computerisation. Workers' skills had evaporated and the 70s generation of computers often proved to be ineffective work tools.

Co-determination

It was intended that the Co-determination Act be quickly followed by national and then local co-determination agreements. In national negotiations LO and PTK (the latter representing white-collar unions in the private sector) demanded a union right to veto and self-determination in matters regarding computers and work organisation. However, employers were attempting to "integrate" co-determination into the normal decision-making processes of companies. They preferred the term "co-influence" to "co-determination". There was an enormous gulf between management and the unions and in the private sector particularly, it was a long time before any agreements were reached. One of the stumbling blocks was that no amendments to the labour laws had been made to pave the way for the kind of co-determination agreements that the unions expected. The only issues of co-determination which could be negotiated within companies and which provided for the right to strike or organise lock-outs, were those which had been raised in centralised collective bargaining on wages. In the absence of any national agreements LO and PTK decided to strictly apply the provisions of the Co-determination Act regarding the provision of information and the right to regular negotiations in instances where no agreements existed.

National co-determination agreements covering issues such as technological change and streamlining were later concluded on a gradual basis in various sectors of industry. The last of these agreements, concluded in the private sector in the spring of 1982, was the "Development Agreement". It emphasised new technology, productivity and cooperation. These national agreements were supplemented by sectorial and local agreements. Issues such as power and influence were played down. The change in union attitudes between 1976 and 1982 can be summed up in a phrase much used at that time "from co-determination to development".

The early 1980s saw tremendous efforts in Sweden to increase productivity by developing and modernising production technology. Both labour and management agreed. Success would depend on developing and exploiting workers' talents and making full use of expert know-how. These efforts were being made against the gloomy backdrop of the economic recession which had hit Sweden. Those years were marked by high costs, inefficient production and relatively high unemployment and that economic context was the driving force behind the labour movement's decision to support the national drive to build "a future for Sweden". The winds of conservatism were blowing by then and from 1976 to 1982 a non-socialist government held sway in Sweden. During the same period employers emerged as a powerful rallying force and a major political lobby, capable of influencing public opinion.

By now the trade unions were feeling the effects of strategies implemented in the 1970s. Those strategies had emphasised legal and formal aspects of issues under discussion, minimizing content and production-related issues. As a result, formal negotiations had dominated over any genuine search for creative new solutions to problems. But such strategies proved ineffective for the 1980s. Concrete action to promote change in the workplace was required if the unions were to do anything more than simply expressing general objectives and voicing grievances. But any action presupposed excellent local union organisation within the workplace, a thorough understanding of workplace changes and company strategies and minutely-planned strategies able to combine cooperation and bargaining when dealing with employers. Meanwhile employers had begun to realise that if they wanted concepts such as the "new factories" to gain currency in the workplace they would need some form of legitimacy. This they hoped to

131

win by involving the trade union movement in development efforts.

The outlook for the future

Efforts to increase Sweden's industrial competitiveness have recently provoked renewed emphasis on the organisation of management-union projects to introduce and exploit new forms of technology. Attempts have also been made to ensure that as work organisation develops, employee resources are utilised to the full. The integration of work tasks for individuals and for groups is one way in which companies can try to meet the fluctuating and increasingly tough demands of the market. Employee competence and ability as a prerequisite for productivity is part of a new concept which is helping to encourage cooperation between management and the trade unions. However this should not be regarded as a return to the 1960s. The trade unions and their members have gained vast experience and understanding of co-determination and production issues since then, thus preventing a return to the past.

The combined effect of joint development projects run throughout the 1980s, together with the country's economic recovery, the resulting very low levels of unemployment and the re-election of the Social Democratic government generated a new atmosphere in Sweden towards the end of the 1980s. Once again the independent role of trade unions was being stressed as a basis for participation. One concern voiced regarding recent changes in work organisation was that apart from creating new and more rewarding jobs, it would also make work far more stressful. Employers began emphasizing the business aspects of work and the great potential for group and individual performance. A much-cited phrase at the time was "we are all businessmen".

Conclusions

By the end of the 1980s industrial relations in Sweden were riven with ambiguity and contradiction. The vision of the 1980s, which first emerged in the 1960s, of an economy devoid of problems and bound by common interests, gained ground. But these "common interests" had expanded beyond the boundaries of those enumerated in the 1960s when the drive for productivity was backed up by calls for a better working environment and, a decade later in the 1970s, demands for job satisfaction. In the 1980s competent and satisfied employees were seen as a precondition for productivity and competitiveness.

Many commentators have suggested that the ideas floated in the 1970s such as work democratisation and increased collective influence for workers and trade unions were now dead and buried. But there are signs that suggest that these ideas were still very much alive during the boom in the country's economy at the end of the 1980s. The Swedish Metal Workers' Union undertook a critical analysis of new forms of work organisation and management and conducted a survey to find out how they were perceived by their members. The foundations of a new, independent strategy were laid by the union in 1985 and developed in 1989. LO published a new report on democracy and influence at its 1991 annual congress. As part of its attempts to find new strategies for renewal the Social Democratic government commissioned a survey of the country's "worst jobs". Trade unions had become more explicit in their demands, making their goals more specific and calling for "good work". There was a union shift "away from development towards a good work policy" while employers were shifting "away from development towards business".

But the early 1990s did not create very favourable conditions for union implementation of their "good work" policy. Although union membership has been growing since the beginning of the 1990s following a steady fall in the late 1980s, other developments have proved less beneficial for the trade unions. The Social Democratic government lost the 1991 elections to a centre-right government. State subsidies for union training programmes have been stopped and a generalised state unemployment benefit system is being introduced to replace the purely union administered system. Economic recession has hit Sweden with unemployment figures rising rapidly to levels similar to those elsewhere in Europe while cuts have been made in the welfare system. New management strategies have been devised by management which stress the individual worker and trade unions now run the risk of being by-passed if they cannot do their utmost to find new strategies which combine direct worker participation and the participation of union representatives.

One major blow to the "good work" policy was the 1992 decision by the management of Volvo to close two innovative car assembly plants in Kalmar and Uddevalla, designed on the principle of team work rather than the conventional assembly line system. Working together with progressive managers and researchers the unions had played a decisive role in the development of the Uddevalla plant. Yet when the closure was announced there were no protests from either the Volvo unions or the national trade unions. Only the local Uddevalla union and one of the Kalmar unions contested the closure. Production over-capacity and losses in Volvo were the reasons cited by management to justify the closure but it is more than likely that high unemployment, the sapped strength of the unions and their inability to defend the "good work" policy contributed to the decision taken by the company. (See Sandberg ed. 1995).

Perhaps the most crucial of all changes has been the new strategy introduced by employers in Sweden regarding wage negotiations. Employers now seek to avoid national-level negotiations, preferring negotiations at company-level instead. The employers' confederation is nevertheless trying to maintain centralised control over local agreements that member companies may draw up. Local-level negotiations are nothing new in Sweden but this recent change has led to a dramatic drop in the importance of nationally-negotiated agreements and renders the possibility of a solidarity and equal pay policy more difficult. Ironically, multinationals are at

133

the same time centralising their decision-making at European or transnational level. In a country such as Sweden this may debilitate trade unions dramatically because an important part of their strength has always been concentrated at national level. More recently however there have been signs which suggest that the trade unions are reacting to this shift to local-level negotiations and transnational level decision-making. As with collective bargaining, the unions are today attempting to create integrated systems for tackling development issues, wages, work organisation and employee competence.

Notes

1.   This chapter is based on a section in Åke Sandberg et al., *Technological Change and Co-determination in Sweden*, Temple University Press, Philadelphia, 1992. Further references are to be found in that publication.

12 Direct participation in Scandinavia from workers' rights to economic necessity

Thoralf Ulrik Qvale

Introduction

The concept of direct participation entered the vocabulary of Scandinavian industrial relations in 1962 when Einar Thorsrud and Fred Emery pointed out some of the weaknesses of traditional approaches to democratisation of work and suggested an alternative (Emery & Thorsrud, 1969). At this time the labour movement was calling for further collective bargaining rights and greater worker or union representation in company decision-making bodies. Although the movement's approach, which relied on regulations to limit managerial prerogatives and on representative, indirect worker participation, had its merits, the two researchers criticised its failure to allow the individual worker increased control over his or her own work environment. A more general criticism was that it did not sufficiently mobilise or involve rank-and-file workers and that adherence to "scientific management" techniques (Taylor, 1911) no longer made it possible to respond to increasing shop-floor problems of a psychological or social nature (see also Trist, 1973).

An alternative was put forward in which the individual worker was granted greater freedom in his or her daily work by a systematic reorganisation of work, tasks and technology. These proposals were based on the experience and theories of the socio-technical system (Tavistock Institute, London, see Emery, 1959; Emery & Trist, 1969). Practical application of these new theories would draw on research on and changes in the British coal-mining industry during the 1950s and '60s (Trist et al, 1963). Emery and Thorsrud also suggested that increased participation in daily work situations would encourage workers to develop new ideas which could be channelled into the bargaining and indirect participative processes. As a result the representative aspect of industrial democracy could potentially become a very dynamic factor. Adapting the Tavistock ideas to the realities of Norwegian industrial relations meant that for the first time ever, industrial democracy was seen as closely linked to social, psychological and economic factors. The British coal-mining studies had clearly shown that an alternative form of work organisation (autonomous work groups) was superior both from a human and a productivity point of view.

However it was still not clear whether the concepts of organisational and technological "choice", which had been tried out at some pits, could be applied to other sectors of industry and permit greater individual and group decision-making. At this stage it was generally assumed by both industrialists and trade unions that an increasingly impoverished work environment (job fragmentation, monotony, few opportunities for learning, decreasing influence over decisions affecting one's own work situation) was the price to be paid for increased productivity and, hence, higher standards of living for workers.

The first phase of direct participation

The first phase of developing direct participation involved practical field experiments in Norwegian industries between 1964-68 (Emery & Thorsrud, 1976). The Federation of Trade Unions and the Employers' Confederation jointly sponsored the research. Later, similar experiments followed in Sweden (Sandberg, 1982; Gregory, 1978) and to some extent in Denmark (Agersnap & Junge Jensen, 1973; Junge et al, 1974). The feasibility of increased direct participation was thus tested and demonstrated under a variety of different conditions. Autonomous work groups, job rotation, job expansion, multi-skilling, cross-training and participative planning were some of the schemes involved in these experiments. Reactions on the shop-floor level were generally positive but spreading these new models through industry proved to be a slow process. However the involvement of Norsk Hyrdo, Norway's largest industrial company, and the Swedish car manufacturer Volvo, caught the public eye and gave these changes a high profile, prompting considerable public interest in this new approach to solving work-related problems.

The attention of the labour movement was clearly focused on how much decision-making power and autonomy could be transferred to individual workers and work groups. Essentially interest was in participation and industrial democracy as values per se but other parties involved, such as Norsk Hydro and Hunsfos linked these concepts to strategic issues such as human resource development, business strategy, competitiveness through improved utilisation of new technology and secure employment (Emery & Thorsrud, 1976). Volvo was largely motivated by the need to do something to reduce high labour turnover and absenteeism, to attract Swedish workers to its assembly plants and to fend off new legislation introduced to try and solve some of these same problems.

Gulowsen's (1972) study confirmed that worker and work group autonomy (their right and ability to make decisions) could be developed fairly extensively in existing industries through fairly minor technological modifications, the introduction of training and redesigning work organisation. He also suggested a more general theory that work groups could not influence higher-level decisions (e.g. where to work and what to produce) unless they had control over more directly work-related decisions (choice of work methods, job distribution within work groups, production standards, recruitment, questions of group leadership, etc.). Another study (Qvale, 1976) showed that in a plant reorganised into five autonomous work groups (more than 100 people altogether), the workers gradually increased the scope of their production and work planning. Initially one group planned production over a period of one week. Three years later, three groups were jointly planning and scheduling production for three month periods.

At this stage research and practical interest shifted somewhat from participative work organisations (e.g. autonomous work groups) to "participative redesign" (Susman, 1979; Elden, 1979). The preceding phase had illustrated that joint efforts to copy concrete solutions (e.g. autonomous work groups) from other companies, failed in most cases. The main reason for this was that autonomous work groups were being introduced without consideration for the conditions required to permit this style of work. Furthermore, because most companies in those days regarded the question of direct participation and autonomous work groups as something confined to the shop-floor and limited to manual workers, there was little top management commitment to setting up the necessary conditions when these had been identified by workers involved in the projects. This created considerable frustration and "autonomous work groups" as a concept fell into disrepute. "We tried it but it didn't work" and "the workers didn't like it" were comments that were often heard.

Clearly the researchers had not succeeded in conveying an appreciation of the "systems perspective" required in the development of participation and redesign. In successful cases there turned out to have been considerable researcher involvement (Elder, 1979). However, these valuable lessons were not passed on.

The second phase - frustration

In the second phase of change, those affected by these changes concentrated on forms of direct participation as an alternative to representative, bureaucratic forms of work democracy. However, attention was still mainly on a socio-technical analysis of worker participation and the redesign of job and work organisation. In a number of projects which had survived from the first phase, frustration arose in "experimenting" departments over the lack of more general support from experts, top management and central unions, which would have ensured the spread of participation throughout a company.

The third phase - new political priorities and legal reform

The third phase began in the 1970s following labour disturbances in the early years of the decade. A reaction among workers to the lack of participation both in managerial and union structures and increasing concern about the work environment (including psycho-social factors) led to radical new legislation throughout Scandinavia (Gustavsen & Hunnius, 1981). The new Swedish Co-Determination Act expanded local union bargaining rights to include all managerial decisions deemed relevant to union bargaining. Wage earner funds were set up in Sweden with the aim of gradually shifting ownership to communities and employees(IDE, 1981b; Hammarstrøm, 1987).

Extreme Taylorist forms of job design (e.g. 100% machine pacing and very short work cycles) were outlawed in Norway. 50% worker representation on new, improved safety and work environment committees, better factory inspectorate and extensive training were introduced.

This legislation, which addressed psychological and sociological factors and attempted to increase direct participation, was inspired by theories which saw a relationship between mental health and control (Gardell, 1977, Karasek, 1979). This led to a shift at national policy-making level. Direct participation was now seen as an occupational health issue and the unions' political right to bargaining and participation in decision-making bodies was stressed. Whether this innovative new legislation and practical application of collective agreements would actually produced the desired effect, remained to be seen (Qvale, 1976).

The fourth phase - new initiatives and programmes

A fourth phase in the development of direct participation in Scandinavia began in 1980 following a rethinking of the issues at stake. Throughout the 1970s the importance of direct forms of participation and the shortcomings of bureaucratic, indirect forms of participation had been increasingly demonstrated. Automation of mass production techniques and the need for more flexible work systems had started to take the industrialists' attention away from "scientific management" techniques and bureaucratic forms of organisation. There was a growing consensus between management and workers that bureaucracy and Taylorism were the crux of the problem. Marxist dogma was losing its foothold. But the expected breakthrough - the positive effects of new agreements and legislation on participation in the work environment which took into account psycho-social issues, did not really materialise.

Far more profound and systematic changes in companies, unions and the environments in which they existed were clearly necessary before there could be any hope of sustained development of direct participation. The need for a "new paradigm of work" (Emery, 1978) a new form of organisation (Thorsrud, 1981; van Beinum, 1990) and new research (Gustavsen, 1989) reflected this new orientation. New research strategies were being identified which would develop and implement a new paradigm. The possibility of reorganising the shop-floor was one of the results of the search for more general forms of participation and planning at company level (Emery, 1977). By now debate had moved beyond decentralising decision-making to workers, and now placed a premium on organisational learning and learning in the workplace as a basis for taking a constructive part in the development of a company. Designing a suitable infrastructure for this kind of general collaboration became a key concern.

As will be shown in the latter part of this chapter, the new challenge was now to find a balance between an "open participative development process" and ensuring sufficient creativity and competence in workers to find concrete, useful solutions. It was feared that a purely participative orientation might lead to increased management dominance, as demonstrated by Mulder (1971). On the other hand it was clear that there were weaknesses in a pure design orientation (e.g. the implementation by experts of new socio-technical solutions in the shop-floor, as in Volvo). Paternalistic management does not normally generate the kind of longterm commitment and improvements needed.

The LOM Programme (leadership, organisation and co-determination (1986-91)

In Sweden a five-year joint research programme, entitled LOM, began in 1985. The programme hoped to link academic and research institutes to the labour force by organising cooperation projects. (Gustavsen, 1988). Building on communicative theories (Habermas, 1984, 1987; Wittgenstein, 1953), the programme (Gustavsen, 1992) also represented a systematic attempt to strengthen the basis for action research and to supplement what had become known as "the Tavistock tradition" with a new outlook and perspective. Key components of the programme were the organisation of "dialogue conferences" involving all company employees, the creation of an internal development organisation and the establishment of networks between researchers and companies.

Another Swedish initiative - financial incentives for improvements in the work environment

At the same time (1985) a special company tax was introduced in Sweden in an attempt to cool the overheated economy. The imposition of this tax led to the creation of a fund which gradually grew to over US$2 billion. When the recession hit several years later, companies were able to reclaim their contribution to the fund, provided they spend the money on improving the work environment. By mid1993 the Work Life Fund has provided financing for 12,000 company projects (Hofmaier, 1993).

Norway - a new collective agreement (HABUT/HF-B, 1982)

In Norway a new national collective agreement on participation in company development was signed by the Employers' Confederation and the Trade Union Federation in 1982. The aims of the agreement were to promote internal policy and strategy development in individual companies in an effort to encourage shop-floor changes. "Search conferences" were used. These involved what is referred to as "broad participation". In other words all or most employees and managers attended two-day conferences during which the company's overall situation was closely examined. Important areas for improvement and development were identified and a plan of action drawn up. These schemes also financed internal "agents of change" (one representing the unions, the other representing management). They were expected to devote their time to promoting the new project, organising search conferences and establishing networks between various companies involved in the project. If local unions and management jointly applied for financing from the scheme they were automatically eligible. In addition they received professional advice on organising search conferences.

A 1990 review of the Norwegian collective agreement on company development led to greater focus on productivity. It also expanded the above scheme to include other sectors of industry and different regions and proposed financing for research support. Until then the scheme's impact on company productivity had been minimal (PSO, 1992) and there was a feeling that it should be more focused. Consequently HF-B adopted a similar strategy to SBA (see below). Whether or not progress will be made remains to be seen.

SBA - The Norwegian Work Life Centre: participation for productivity/change (1988-93)

In 1988 all the major Norwegian labour organisations joined the government in launching a new programme to encourage participative forms of management and organisation throughout all sectors of industry. This new programme led to the creation of SBA, the Norwegian Work Life Centre. This was a major attempt to capitalise on experience gained in previous experiments in work democratisation. The programme was proposed by a joint commission appointed by the government. It had submitted its report in 1985 (NOU, 1985:1). The basis of the report was the labour movement's demand for increased board level worker representation in the private sector beyond the legal requirement of 33%. Nevertheless the commission, which included the chairman of the Trade Union Federation, agreed to confine its recommendations to measures which would promote direct participation, i.e. measures that would promote productivity and hence also job security. The report was thus a symbol of the eventual penetration of the concept of "human resource utilisation" into the highest level of work. This concept had first been introduced in 1960 by Emery and Thorsrud. The report also marked the first time ever in Scandinavia that a programme of this kind spanned the private and public sectors. The reasons for this were threefold. Firstly, there had always been less systematic efforts to promote participation in the public sector, secondly, the efficiency and quality of the services provided by the public sector were important to the overall competitiveness of industry and thirdly, the private sector depended on close cooperation with public institutions for direct

140

access to the resources it needed.

Faced with the threat of increased unemployment resulting from intense international competition, the two sides agreed to exploit their relatively high level of mutual trust and their ability to work together to promote productivity and change (Harlem Brundtland, 1989; Qvale, 1989).

LOM evaluation

The LOM programme evaluation report (Naschold et al 1992) was drawn up on the basis of an international comparison. Major technology/work life programmes in Japan (organised by MITI) and Germany (most notably *"Arbeit und Technik"*) were used as yardsticks to measure the results of the US$12 million, short-term (five years) Swedish scheme. Although as a result the comparison is in some senses unfair, it still illustrates the important connection between industrial policies, technological development and the development of company organisation, networks and participation. The strategic effect that a programme like LOM could have on Swedish industrial relations is clear. The research programme was successful in many different ways. Its innovative process-oriented methods were seen as a potentially useful strategy for meeting challenges from Japan and elsewhere. LOM's impact on the performance of 148 companies participating in the programme cannot easily be assessed because of the short duration of the programme. The results are not (yet) very significant in terms of network-building, national penetration and, hence, in terms of overall economic effect. The evaluation team questioned the exclusive process orientation of the programme which precluded any attempts at design orientation. On the other hand, LOM's radical process orientation was seen as the key to its strength and one of the programme's essential characteristics.

The contrast between LOM and the extreme expert design orientation of, for example, Volvo (in the Kalmar and Uddevalla plants which have only recently been closed), is obvious. Volvo did not succeed in integrating the innovative, new sociotechnical design of the plants into a more general transformation of the company's overall organisation, which would have produced the Japanese *"kaizen"* effect or "continuous improvements". This was pointed out by Womack et al (1990). The LOM programme therefore became an important contribution to the debate on form and content in participation and productivity development. But LOM failed to achieve sustained development in companies and this seems at least partly due to a lack of professional input in terms of content (Cole, 1993).

The work life fund approach

The evaluation of the work life fund has only just begun (Hofmaeier, 1993). The considerable resources made available have provided the programme with a broad impact, involving as it did 12,000 companies compared to less than 200 in the LOM programme. Despite the fact that the LOM programme is a research programme and the work life fund is a straight-forward financial initiative, the resources spent on each project in the work life fund approach are far greater than in LOM. However, preliminary results of the evaluation suggest that in cases where the work life fund has helped companies look at improving the work environment and linking this to strategies to improve productivity, both productivity and the work environment have benefitted.

The Norwegian SBA programme

The above debate continued during and after the Norwegian SBA programme was implemented. This programme aimed at working with both "process" and "content". It had a clear objective - to improve competitiveness in individual companies (Qvale, 1991). SBA differed from LOM in many respects. For example, it was not a research programme in itself but rather an attempt to apply on a wider scale the strategies and experiences gained from the Norwegian shipping and oil research programmes (Roggema & Thorsrud, 1974; Walton & Gaffney, 1991; Qvale, 1984, 1993). Nevertheless it was found to be practical and strategically important to involve academics and their institutions in encouraging change in work.

The main strategy of the programme was to encourage participative methods of change in companies and to link the companies into networks and to relevant, external institutions It was thought that setting up a direct relationship of cooperation between companies and outside institutions would stimulate change.

SBA was therefore a programme aimed at developing and changing the "ecology" or external environment of both public and private-sector companies. It was thought that the lessons of the programme would gradually be diffused through these (changed) institutions rather than by the "lighthouse effect" that successful cases produced. It was assumed that working with relatively sophisticated companies would increase the chances of actually bringing about needed changes in the institutional infrastructure of companies. SBA's project partners could act as "demanding customers" in dealing with public institutions, regional administrative and political bodies and labour organisations.

The national labour organisations and the government had the greatest stakes in SBA. They were both funding its activities (US$12 million) and staffing it. The idea was that the two sides should exploit their considerable mutual trust and their consensus on basic values, the concept of power sharing and the need for change to try and bring about institutional change and, by learning from the SBA's projects, change their own policies and behaviour.

SBA evaluation

Evaluation of SBA (Davies et al, 1993) was carried out by an international team which included the key LOM evaluator. Its conclusions were that the programme had been successful at company level and had succeeded in creating regional networks. These networks would need further development after the end of the SBA programme, in cooperation with public companies (such as educational and research centres, local development agencies, etc.). The combined use of broad participative methods and concrete design input was described as innovative and successful. The programme involved more than 500 companies in 90 projects and managed to mobilise considerably more resources than its own, including contributions and investments from companies, science foundations, unemployment funds, educational resources, etc).

However, like LOM, the programme was considered to have been under-resourced and too brief given its ambitious aim of trying to improve national competitiveness. Its main shortcomings lay in its inability to actively involve the top leadership and hierarchies of labour organisations and obtain their active support. In actual fact it was they who kept industrial relations, agreements and bargaining issues outside the SMA's legitimate scope of work. According to the evaluation committee, these limitations in the scope of the SBA projects constituted a major hindrance to implementing changes in work and made the use of a potentially very powerful tool for change impossible. In Australia, the driving force behind current rapid development is "award restructuring" (a series of new, innovative collective agreements at company level) promoted by the Australian Trade Union Federation (Emery, 1993).

Payment systems based on traditional Taylorist/bureaucratic paradigms, which still dominate in Scandinavia, undoubtedly hinder change towards more participative forms of work in which learning and the utilisation of human resources are key elements. The SBA programme clearly revealed the inertia in large labour organisations which, in spite of initial agreement about the need for change and a willingness to be flexible, proved unable or unwilling to change their own behaviour in practise. The conclusions of both the LOM and the SBA evaluations concord on this point. Unless labour organisations change, the Scandinavian (corporative) model of cooperation in work and politics is unlikely to survive. In periods of stable growth it has demonstrated its superiority by striking an even balance between the human aspects of the work environment and productivity. But so far it does not seem capable of adjusting fast enough to internationalisation, as exemplified by the Japanese challenge. The bureaucratic distinctions and demarcations between "industrial policy issues", "bargaining" and "cooperation" made by trade unions and employers' federations render them incapable of dealing with such issues in a holistic framework.

The situation today

Currently it seems that labour organisations throughout Scandinavia accept and support the idea of promoting direct worker participation as well as commitment, learning and efficient utilisation of human resources. But when these ideas are put to the test, as in the SBA programme, it seems that the consequences of these ideas have still to filter through these institutions

Generally speaking, current management philosophy in the West supports the idea of a link between direct participation and human resources utilisation. Practical discussions today in Sweden and Norway tend to be concerned with how to improve development of direct participation and how to create links between general company and union strategies and how to achieve these same changes in the public sector. Commonly discussed issues at company level include what the conditions for development beyond the shop-floor might be, how to involve central unions and other institutions and how to work with educational and research institutions and gain their support for development in the workplace.

So far we have mainly looked at strategies that depart from a discussion of industrial democracy, participation, human values and the rights of workers. This debate has gone on for a long time in Scandinavia and is still very much alive. The national programmes discussed above have shown that participation should be a key component of company philosophy given that competitiveness relies increasingly on human resource utilisation.

Over the last ten years new, less visible new managerial concepts have been introduced such as total quality management, "just in time", high commitment systems, high performance systems, lean organisation, team-based organisation and so on. These concepts have found their way into relatively innovative companies, inspired by Japan and the United States. Success has generally depended on the implementation of participation. "Empowered" workers have to be an essential part of any new solutions. There is a clear parallel with socio-technical thinking and techniques - "focusing on the tasks" (most clearly expressed in total quality management) and "setting up conditions for self-management" at individual and work group levels.

These developments have tended to be fairly low-key management initiatives in which local unions have been invited to participate. The impact of these approaches on productivity and participation is already considerable and is growing fast in Scandinavia. The most successful SBA projects (e.g. those in the public sector such as the postal system, the railways and road construction), have been linked to total quality initiatives which SBA has helped to make more systematic.

With a weaker economy and rising unemployment, first in Denmark and then in Norway, Sweden and Finland, employee ownership schemes have frequently been proposed as a possible means of achieving financial stability. But a political swing to the centre-right in all four countries has meant that legislation, which would have meant increased State ownership, State financing or new ownership schemes is now unlikely. In all four countries privatisation of State-owned companies and the decentralisation of public services such as the postal system, telecommunications and the railways is now underway.

In Denmark, developments in the workplace over the last decade have not been linked to large-scale action research or programmes for democratisation but have generally been promoted either through technological research and development initiatives (some linked to EU programmes) or have been the product of company/local union-level cooperation with technological centres (e.g. Graversen, 1984) or university departments (Handberg, 1993). These projects have frequently had important links to environmental issues.

Until relatively recently Finland had not kept pace with the rest of Scandinavia in terms of workplace reform. However in 1988 the Finnish government, in cooperation with labour partners, launched an action research project on workplace development (Kauppinen, 1993). This programme is developing rapidly and spans all sectors of working life. It involves a number of university and scientific centres and has already achieved considerable penetration. The serious recession which hit the Finnish economy following the collapse of its most important market, the Soviet Union, seems to have strengthened national commitment to pursuing this programme.

Concluding remarks

The slow shift in management thinking from seeing direct participation as a purely ideological issue or a workers' rights issue, to seeing it as a means of promoting productivity and organisational flexibility is still continuing and indeed is spreading at company level. New theories on organisational development lend support to the idea that participation is a common vision and can mobilise worker understanding and competence to develop and implement company strategies (see e.g. Parker, 1990; Beckhard & Pritchard, 1992).

There has been a simultaneous shift in thinking at local union level and amongst workers to regarding direct participation as the key to raising productivity and thus guaranteeing job security. This kind of change in thinking normally follows personal and practical experience with direct participation. However, fostering this kind of thinking so that it penetrates labour organisations, their policies and their practices is a much slower process. It may eventually mean that they will lose at least part of their present role in society and industrial relations.

There are signs in Scandinavia, at the national, political level, that the concept of "human resources" has developed even further, as exemplified by the current proposals in Finland for a programme of inter-disciplinary research and development projects. In work situations in which highly-educated professionals are involved in creative tasks, participative forms of management and organisation seem to be seen as an accepted necessity, as exemplified by projects on offshore production systems (Qvale & Hanssen-Bauer, 1989).

Of course if productivity and hence employment are to be sustained, labour organisations are only some of many actors or institutions within the company environment or "ecology" which need to be changed. To encourage or facilitate changes in work there must be a systematic attempt to change the curricula and teaching methods of educational institutions, research and development institutes and local, regional and national industrial policy. In Norway systematic efforts to get schools to adopt participative methods of teaching (in parallel with changes in industry) began in 1968 (Blichfeldt, 1973, 1975). Work in specific sectors of industry and their institutional frameworks began in the Norwegian shipping industry at about the same time and in the offshore oil industry in 1978 (Qvale, 1985, 1993). These programmes have proved successful but did not create a basis for widespread application of this idea.

Mechanisms for obtaining coordinated or "directly correlated" (Sommerhof, 1981) change across companies, institutions and sectors of industry have to be found. The kind of coordination which national legislation and political/administration decisions provide is not enough. One methodological breakthrough has come with the discovery that company networks represent a new, non-hierarchical form of organisation which could, through joint effort, grow to provide coordinated input or demands to the external environment. Inspiration has come largely from the now famous networks in northern Italy (see e.g., Sable & Pierce, 1984). The nuclei for this kind of systematic development can be found in all Scandinavian countries. The aim of Sweden's LOM programme was to set up networks between companies so that they might learn from each other about company development. In the SBA programme help has been provided to generate several regionally-based networks or develop them into stable economic (business) systems (see e.g. Snow & Hanssen-Bauer, 1993).

Network development may also provide a solution to the problem of what to do for workers in small companies. In large companies attempts at democratisation have usually sprung from the need to reduce or eliminate the negative effects that excessively bureaucratic forms of work organisation have on human development and involvement. In smaller companies the problems may be just the opposite - too little formalisation, frequently combined with limited available expertise. Increased participation in these companies may mean linking up with external resources and envisaging cooperation with other companies.

The fifth phase: productive participative structures - working across institutions - linking company democratisation to the democratisation of society

Researchers involved in action research in Scandinavia now tend to talk of a fifth phase which centres on improving strategies for institutional change to support local development (Gustavsen, 1989) and at the same time contribute to a more general development in society, away from bureaucratic, representative forms of political democracy towards a participative one (Emery, 1989).

Attempts at encouraging direct participation have varied since the first researcherdominated experiments in Norway. Early approaches sought to demonstrate to the central labour organisations that it was possible to increase direct participation in industry without sacrificing productivity. While the next phase in Norway concentrated on democratising the process of change, a number of managementinitiated programmes dominated by experts in the field were being conducted in other countries. Van Beinum (1990) uses the term "social engineering" to describe this approach. This first appeared in Sweden in the production engineering department of the Employers' Confederation and as a result new forms of work quickly spread. Joint management-union programmes for democratisation began at the same time. In Germany the important and lengthy "*Humanizierungsprogramm*" tended, in its initial phases, to be dominated by external specialists. The futility of this approach in obtaining any sustained changes led to a change in programme strategy. These programmes began to press for securing participation in the research and design processes.

The American "Quality of Working Life" movement, which also began in about 1980, was largely triggered by Scandinavian experiences, but was certainly also inspired by Japanese joint-problem solving techniques such as quality circles. This American movement was quite varied. In some cases it was democratic both in terms of process, structures and union involvement. In others, in clearly fell into the category of social engineering with the aim of keeping the unions out. Other examples highlighted local union participation in development without attempting more participative forms of work organisation and hence led only to increased bureaucracy and cooptation.

The participative approach to industrial democracy has always been criticised from a Marxist standpoint (e.g. Braverman, 1974) for being reformist, inefficient in promoting workers' rights and sometimes for being manipulative. In Sweden and Norway these points have never been central to debate and are even less so today than 20 years ago. Danish researchers and trade unions have, however, tended to espouse the view that control over what they see as more important decisions at the top levels of a company should precede what they see as relatively minor shop-floor modifications. Hence discussions of alternative forms of ownership have been more dominant in debate in Denmark.

But discussion in Norway and Sweden changed in the 1970s with the reforms which gave workers/local unions in Denmark, Norway and Sweden one third of all seats on company boards of directors (Qvale, 1979; IDE 1981b), gave them greater influence in legislative support in work environment issues and (in Sweden) expanded bargaining rights and offered the potential for increased influence through changes in ownership (wage earner funds). The belief that there is a need for more general changes in legislation as a prerequisite for increased direct participation has waned. Further, the belief that legislation and government agencies under general or new (community or employee) ownership will automatically promote direct worker participation, or improve productivity for that matter, has largely disappeared.

Debate among academics about the significance of promoting direct participation still goes on. Behavioural scientists who claim that improvements in job satisfaction, productivity, labour stability etc. cannot be substantiated, may be right when these are viewed as isolated, specialist-induced modifications of technology, of administrative systems and of work organisation (IDE, 1981a). On the other hand, short-term job satisfaction (as measured through surveys), productivity gains or labour stability may not be seen by those involved as the

147

aim. What is more, not all participative approaches may necessarily expand the scope of jobs despite declarations to the contrary from, for example, management, as shown by Klein (1990) in her studies of different ways of applying just-in-time techniques in Japanese-owned companies.

The main split among academics, however, both in Scandinavia and elsewhere, is between empirical, single-discipline oriented researchers with a positivist tradition and multi-disciplinary action researchers. The latter group is the one which tends to be involved in strategies for promoting direct participation but it fails to satisfy the scientific research criteria set up by the former. On the other hand, action researchers claim that the kind of real-life, real-time projects they are working on are based on a different research paradigm, so a positivist critique fails (Gustavsen, 1989; Stjernberg & Philips, 1989).

Today, however, the critical issue is not whether direct worker participation will develop further. It is difficult to imagine any other scenario given the advances in technology (see e.g. de Keyser et al, 1988), rising educational levels among the working population and growing criticism of the inefficiency of overly bureaucratic forms of work organisation.

Whether the more far-reaching consequences of democratic participation in society will be achieved is, however, still a very open question. One essential prerequisite is the unions' capacity to change and take an active role in supporting their members in this process. Another is changes in research and education to more participative methods, so as to avoid current specialisation and domination by experts. Recent debate in Scandinavia on the relevance of democratisation programmes for national competitiveness indicate a potentially powerful alliance between economic needs on the one hand and human development in work and society in general on the other. But increasingly successful efforts to raise productivity through participation and new allegiance to national industrial policies and technological R & D programmes will further exacerbate the problem of unemployment which is spreading through every sector of industry. Unless these problems can be dealt with in parallel, it is difficult to see how human aspects of the work environment can be guaranteed in society in general.

Whether the Scandinavian system of industrial relations will develop sufficient flexibility to take an active role in these potentially very important developments is an open question.

13 Participation and social Europe

Janine Goetschy

What role can direct and indirect participation play in the construction of social Europe? The question takes a new dimension with the very recent adoption of a directive on European Works Councils, in September 1994. To answer the question of what role direct and indirect participation can today play in a social Europe, it is essential to take a look back at the past and trace the development of various European drafts on participation, to try and see how the attitudes of politicians and other social actors have changed over the years. In doing so we will try to see the extent to which the contentious history of indirect participation over the last 20 years, as illustrated by the dangerous drift of successive failed draft directives, has for years obscured the very question of direct participation .

To appreciate the present relevance of worker participation it must be ranked once again amongst the essential demands made in the construction of a Social Europe. Together these demands must be evaluated in terms of urgency, negotiability and their capacity to check some of the drift evident in economic integration. In the light of the institutional reforms outlined by the Maastricht Treaty, the future of Economic and Monetary Union, the urgency with which unemployment and social exclusion should be fought, forms of participation will be called upon to play new roles in the future. But what will these roles be?

A historical review

Institutionalised (or indirect) worker participation in company decision-making will probably prove to have been the most debated subject of the last 20 years as a European social policy has gradually taken shape. In other words, participation has an important and sizeable past. In 1974 it was already high on the agenda of EC Commission programmes. In 1977 it was taken up again and more recently, in 1990, was again included in a programme concerning a Community charter of social rights. Thus participation has been a constant preoccupation in Europe.

149

From 1975 onwards, participation was at the centre of numerous, ambitious, complex and extremely divisive European Draft Directives. Most of these drafts have, to date, not been completed.

Two of these drafts proved to be successful.

- The February 1975 directive concerning the protection of workers in mass lay-offs. Employers were obliged to hold talks with worker representatives "with the aim of reaching an agreement" so as to avoid the lay-offs. The directive also dealt with the handling of the social consequences. It was revised in June 1992 by unanimous agreement and without too much difficulty. The revision strengthens legal provisions, especially existing provisions for information and consultation of workers. These provisions must be respected at international level by companies and groups of companies during mass lay-offs.
- Similar provisions are to be found in a second directive, that of February 1977 on company transfers, in other words, company restructuring which results in the fusion or transfer of companies.

These two directives were successfully completed because they dealt with specifics within a company and did not rock the institutional balance within the system of industrial relations at national level.

There then followed four series of directives which proved to be long and arduous. These included the 1972 5th Draft Directive, the 1980 "Vredeling" Draft Directive, the 1975 Draft Directive on worker participation related to the draft to establish a European joint-stock company and the 1990 Draft Directive on the European works council.

The 1972 5th Draft Directive

Briefly, its initial aims were to establish in companies of a certain size, within one member state, the principle of worker participation at the very highest level of company decision-making and to introduce a dual decision-making structure within the top managerial ranks. This draft was largely based on the German model of co-determination and was intended to have a direct effect on industrial relations at national level.

Opponents from the very start included employers from many countries who did not want to duplicate the decision-making hierarchies in their top management ranks nor introduce the principle of worker participation. In addition, trade unions in certain countries such as Britain, France and Italy expressed serious doubts about co-determination participation. Of course union positions were to change over the years.

Given these obstacles the EC Commission attempted to find a solution by publishing a Green Paper in 1975 to stimulate debate within each country. Great Britain, for example, launched a national debate with the aim of demonstrating its ability to put forward propositions. A committee of experts was set up (the

Bullock Committee) to study the question. The committee finally published a Minority Report (employers) and a Majority Report (unions and experts). The employers' report proposed a dual system with ternary representation (1/3, 1/3, 1/3) on the monitoring council while the unions and experts favoured a monistic composition with equal weight given to share-holders' and workers' representatives, added to which there would be a handful of outside figures. While the Bullock Report (majority) indicated union approval for co-determination, it has to be said that the report went considerably further than the TUC wanted to. For the TUC, traditionally in favour of collective bargaining, remained divided on the issue of worker participation on management bodies. Resolution 10 at the 1977 TUC congress made this clear, stating that this was just one of many forms of participation. As for the employers' report, which had boldly put forward the idea of ternary representation on the monitoring council, it met with resistance in the Conservative party which wanted nothing to do with it. In fact both of these reports put forward propositions which were quite avant-garde given what and whom they actually represented.

In addition to the debates at national level, decisions and amendments passed at the European Parliament (EP) contributed to making the Commission's initial draft less ambitious and more flexible. In fact the EP's 1982 proposals considerably watered down the Commission's initial draft by proposing a choice between four participative models - two different kinds of co-determination, one works council model and one model derived from a bargaining agreement. (These models are to be found today in another draft directive, the 1989 European joint-stock company draft).

By 1984, the British TUC, one of the most important members of the European Trade Unions Congress (ETUC) had changed its position as regards participation and now accepted the principle of the 5th directive (and later the Vredeling draft). However, the ETUC remained critical of the Commission's revised 1983 draft. It cited the problem of the functional non-equivalence between the four models. This was a problem which was to reappear and cause even greater problems in 1989 during discussions of the draft statutes of the European joint-stock company.

Thus despite being made less rigid by the Commission in 1983, the 5th draft directive was nevertheless rejected by the Council of Ministers and shelved for a number of years. As a result, another slightly different Draft Directive on participation, the Vredeling Draft, named after the commissioner, appeared in 1982. It was to prove as drawn-out and divisive as the 5th draft directive.

To conclude, the reasons behind the failure of the 5th Draft Directive, whose 12 years of debate reflected the degree of disagreement, were the following.

The draft rocked the institutional balance of national systems of industrial relations and met with resistance because it initially tried to impose the German model. Beyond the refusal to accept any given national model, it has to be said that this model was extremely nation-specific and that German co-determination was far-removed from practice in other countries.

Union conceptions of participation were splintered and there was increasingly fierce opposition to the German model of co-determination. Amongst the opponents were the French and Italian unions who shared a similar outlook, based on the idea of works councils, and the British with their preference for collective bargaining.

Nevertheless, as the decision-making process of the draft directive continued, the principle initiator, the Commission, finally hit upon a compromise which favoured national debate (which in fact enabled union ideas to develop) and the EP amendments. It should not be forgotten that at the beginning of the 1980s the relationship between the EP and the Commission was not the same as it is today. The EP, whose political majority was not centre-left as it is today, assumed the role of moderator of the Commission's relatively ambitious drafts. By the end of the decade the situation was reversed.

Thus a compromise appeared to have been found but the time, the early 1980s, was not ripe. The weight of the economic crisis, staunch employer resistance and the stubborn position adopted by the British Conservative government in the Council of Ministers were the main reasons behind the draft's failure.

The "Vredeling" Draft Directive (1980)

In the wake of the failure of the 5th Directive, something else had to be found. Unlike the 5th draft directive which had aimed at aligning decision-making and participative bodies throughout the EC, the "Vredeling" Draft (1980) dealt with information and consultation in complex-structure and trans-national companies. The "Vredeling Draft" dealt with a problem which had arisen with the globalisation of the economy and the internationalisation of companies and which had remained unresolved by legislation at national level.

Thus it seemed that there was good reason for Community level intervention. The mother company would be obliged to provide information to worker representatives of the subsidiary companies and to consult them before taking any decisions regarding the group which might have serious consequences for the workers' interests, such as relocation, production cut-backs, introduction of new technology, etc.

From the very start this draft met with strong resistance from the Union of European Community Industries (UNICE - an employers' organisation), the American employers' lobby and employers with links to the Economic and Social Committee. But the ETUC (European Trade Union Confederation) supported the draft.

In 1982 the EP succeeded in re-orienting the Commission's draft by making important modifications of a number of points. Despite being completely overhauled in 1983, the draft was not adopted by the Council. Britain (in favour of economic liberalisation and collective bargaining) together with Denmark (which preferred collective bargaining) refused to legislate on the social aspects. Numerous attempts to save the contents of the draft were made. Some suggested turning it into a simple recommendation and others proposed transferring the essentials to collective agreements while yet others suggested limiting the contents to technological matters only. But finally in 1986 the Council officially decided to freeze the draft until 1989. The Commission, believing that Britain could not be persuaded to change its position, was no longer willing to defend a draft which seemed likely to simply drag on and on. Furthermore, priority was now being given to the question of flexibility.

In 1985 the Commission decided to engage a Social Dialogue centred on a debate on new technologies. Earlier, in 1984, when ruling on a Commission document (technological change and social adjustment) the Council of Ministers had already deemed that it was necessary to adopt guidelines on this subject at European level.

But in 1986-87 several events sparked off new debate of "Vredeling". Unfair practises on the part of multi-nationals (Michelin, Memorex and the transfer of production from Belgium to Holland) led the ETUC, the European Metalworkers' Federation (EMF), the Economic and Social Committee, the European Parliament and especially the Belgian government (Belgium was directly implied) to actively strive for the implementation of measures which would penalise multi-nationals which did not fulfill their social duties. When Michelin closed a factory in Belgium in 1986, it was accused of having flouted Belgian law, a 1975 Community law and the non-compulsory OECD code of conduct for multi-nationals regarding the transfer of production. The joint demands of these various Community protagonists naturally led to "Vredeling" being dusted off. Some French industrial companies such as Thomson GP in 1985 and BSN in 1986 had already set things in motion by creating group councils designed to provide information for and consultation with workers. But apart from these few exceptions, most industrial groups or companies were categorically opposed to promoting worker participation at company level. The ETUC noted a very real and unjustified "anachronism" between existing and relatively well-developed rights regarding participation at national level and an absence of any such rules or regulations at international and European level (cf subject taken up again at the Stockholm Congress in 1988).

To conclude, the Vredeling Draft, like the 5th Directive, was an initially ambitious Commission draft which was considerably amended and rehashed by the EP but never completed. The economic situation and the balance of power had changed While participation remained an essential way of forging consensus within a company, employers at both national and European level refused to implement new legal constraints regarding participation throughout Europe, preferring instead more flexible proposals. Employer lobbies, especially the American ones, were vehemently opposed to the Vredeling draft. Added to this was government resistance, visible in the Council of Ministers and impossible to alter as long as the rule of the unanimous vote remained.

The draft directive on worker participation in the context of the draft for a european joint-stock company (1975)

Jacques Delors made it clear that he was aware of the ETUC demands concerning participation in the numerous propositions put forward at the Hannover Summit (27-28 June 1988). Initial work on the charter and the relaunching of the 1975 draft on the European Joint-Stock Company (EJSC) were proposed. The 1975 draft proposed a choice between three systems for promoting information for and consultation of workers. At that time it had been debated in Council but had not been settled.

In 1988, despite the objections of Britain and the Netherlands, the member states asked the Commission to prepare new measures for the European joint-stock company. The Commission presented a memorandum for discussion (1988) to the social partners and relevant European bodies and presented its European Joint-Stock Company (EJSC) Draft in August 1989. The draft included one ruling and one directive concerning participation.

The statute would permit groups operating in several member states to set up a European joint-stock company if they so wished. This would make things considerably easier for them in terms of accounting and taxation. The creation of such a company would be optional but should a group opt for this solution, it would automatically be obliged to introduce a certain number of measures regarding worker participation, as outlined in the participation directive. This draft differed from others in its flexibility. What was important in it was the function that participation fulfilled and the consequent results rather than the institutional similarity between countries. This kind of flexibility can be seen in the following areas:

- the EJSC model is not obligatory. Nevertheless, if an employer opts for it, he must agree to abide by the rules of participation which it implies.
- the directive provides a choice between three institutionalised models of participation (German co-determination, the French, Italian or Belgian style of works councils or participation in the form of collective bargaining between management and workers or their representatives).
- each country chooses its own form of implementation. Each country, may, should it so wish, limit the choices available to European companies whose head office are within its borders.

In an effort to make passage through the Council of Ministers successful, the Commission opted from the very start for a flexible draft. This was all the more important given the fact that throughout the 1980s an increasing variety of different forms of participation had appeared (cf Dublin studies) and it was thus important not to be limited to a single model.

It is true that many objections were raised to the Commission's draft (by the ETUC, the Economic and Social Committee, the European Parliament). One of the main objections concerned the difficulty in ensuring an equivalence in the models. Professor T. Treu, for example, maintained that in order to ensure equivalence, the different forms of participation should be analogous in terms of the breadth of subjects dealt with, the extent of power wielded and the moment at which participative intervention occurred.

What was implicit in the general debate was that the German model was still the superior form of participation and that the other two forms, especially the one based on collective bargaining, could not hope to match it. Furthermore, if bargaining failed, management or the company administration would have the last word.

Opposition came above all from employers and some countries which regarded this draft as a possible precedent for further advancement of the 5th directive and the Vredeling Draft. By the end of 1990, the situation was a now familiar one. For whenever a draft falls by the wayside, another has to be tried. And this is exactly what happened when, in December 1990, the Commission proposed a new draft directive on European works councils.

Progress in the 1980s and 1990s

Participation in the "Val Duchesse" social dialogue. The possibility of direct participation

In 1985-86 when it became apparent that the three directives concerning institutionalised participation were being blocked by the Council of Ministers, a contractual body, the Social Dialogue, took over. Unions and employers sat in equal numbers on this body with the aim of adopting joint non-binding opinions. Thus on 6 March 1987 "an opinion concerning training, motivation, information and consultation regarding new technology" was published. Agreement on this Opinion was reached as a result of acceptance on the part of the ETUC of new technology in companies in exchange for recognition by the UNICE of the need for provision of information for and consultation with workers when new technology was introduced and appropriate measures for vocational training (initiation, advanced and retraining). These rights would be implemented when the time was right and would respect the rules of confidentiality, with the final decision, nevertheless, lying with the employer. The Opinion adopted aimed to encompass the diversity of existing forms of participation at national level. It should be remembered that the German and Danish unions expressed some reservations about this Opinion since their respective national systems of participation offered much better solutions to this particular problem.

Apart from provisions for information for and consultation with workers and/or their representatives in accordance with national practises already in effect (and in this sense it relied more on existing practises than innovation), the March 1987 Opinion did actually pave the way for direct participation. "The participants stress the need to motivate a sense of staff responsibility at all levels and encourage them to develop their capacity to adapt and change, by means of, amongst other things, thorough information and consultation".

It took 16 months for the Opinion on new technology to be drawn up and it was to take several years for the Opinion which followed and completed it to be finalised. That Opinion concerned "new technology, work organisation and the adaptability of the job market" (January 1991). The Opinion was novel in that it envisaged as yet unprecedented possibilities of direct participation. "The participants agree to seek through legal or contractual channels, new forms of administration or new approaches which would meet both the specific needs of companies to improve organisation and the work environment and the needs of workers to take part in the social and cultural life of the community in which they live. To this end, it is necessary to identify both within each country and at Community level all the provisions which must be adapted to suit new situations." This was indeed a vast undertaking.

Other "Joint Opinions" such as the one regarding the organisation of the job market (February 1990) or the one on youth training (November 1990) naturally specified the participation of the social partners in regional, national and European bodies examining these subjects. The March 1987 Opinion refers to job management at company level.

It is very clear that the large number of European initiatives such as directives, Social Dialogue Opinions and company agreements on group councils all favoured indirect forms of participation over so-called direct means. There are some exceptions in some "Joint Opinions". Amongst the directives there is nevertheless one form of direct participation, on health and safety issues, within the framework of the June 1989 directive.

The lack of any form of direct worker participation in the various issues tackled at European level is mainly the result of years of union preference for institutionalised forms of participation. The German DGB in particular had previously sought to export its model of co-determination and this did in fact find its way into many initial directives. But another reason is the fact that it proved to be so hard a struggle to get European employers to accept that workers should have a legal right to information and consultation. Obviously, before attempting direct participation at European level it was important to win ground on indirect participation as some form of protection against practises such as flexibilisation delocalisation and social dumping unilaterally practised by employers.

It is to be noted, however, that as far as the employers were concerned, despite numerous initiatives for direct worker participation put forward at national confederation level, these never materialised at European level.

Financial participation in the European Community

In the plan of action for the implementation of the Social Agreement, it was stipulated that Community-wide measures should be drawn up. This resulted in the

PEPPER report (Promotion of Employee Participation in Profits and Enterprise Results). It was on the basis of this report that the Commission, in 1991, prepared a recommendation on participation in profits and enterprise results which was adopted by the Council in July 1992. The aim of the PEPPER report was tm provide a comparative look at different experiments in worker financial participation (including share-based profit-sharing and cash-based profit-sharing) throughout the European Community. With the notable exceptions of France and Britain, such experiments have not been widely reported or adopted. The 1992 Community Recommendation aims to do just that - namely, encourage member states to provide mostly fiscal incentives for companies to set up systems of participation in profits.

The advantage of financial participation, as far as human resource and job management is concerned, is that it offers some of the advantages of wage flexibility. As far as democratic management of a company is concerned, financial participation does pose increased risks for workers, in exchange for increased control over a company's general policies (cf economic democracy).

The Directive on the European Works Council in Trans-National Companies

The development and adoption of this Directive have been described in Chapter 2 of this book.

What future for direct and indirect participation in Europe?

As we approach the end of this century, the accelerated speed of European construction and internal changes in our societies have created new economic problems and problems of identity and social integration for employees and citizens. Both indirect and direct participation should provide some solutions.

The possibilities that the Maastricht 11-country social agreement offers for participation

It should be remembered that during the negotiations of the Maastricht Treaty, several criticisms were made of a Social Europe. There was concern about the lack of any concrete achievements on social issues while economic integration was accelerating. This was mainly because directives on social issues depended on a unanimous vote in the Council (except the Directive on health and safety).

More generally, criticism was made of the "democratic deficit" - a reference to the inadequate powers of the European Parliament. The legitimacy of the way in which social legislation was drawn up at European level was questioned in view of the fact that the social partners did not play as important a role as they should in traditional Community legislation processes, despite initial progress made by the Social Dialogue, otherwise known as Val Duchesse. Criticism was also made of the lack of openness and democracy in Community activities and amongst its officials. The recent institutional reforms (The Maastricht Treaty and the 11-country Social Agreement annexed to it) have improved matters somewhat and generated a new situation.

First of all, in the Maastricht Social Agreement the subject of worker information and consultation now requires a qualified majority vote in the Council. This will make adoption of directives much easier, particularly given that Britain will not be voting. This scenario became reality following the adoption of the directive on European Workers' Councils in September 1994. But other failed draft directives, such as the 5th Directive and the Draft on the European Joint-Stock Company might now also have a chance of being adopted. The concept of representation and the common defence of workers' rights falls under Community-level jurisdiction but nevertheless require a unanimous vote.

Secondly, the Maastricht Social Agreement offers the possibility for European social partners (the ETUC, UNICE, ECPSE) to have greater involvement in Community social policy legislation. Procedures for consultation with the social partners during the preparation of directives by the Commission used to be informal. Now they have been formalised and will be carried out in two phases. Also, during the consultation period between the Commission and the social partners, the latter have the right to express their preference for an accord or agreement rather than a directive. In this case discussions between European social partners are limited to nine months so they do not risk becoming bogged down or being used to hinder the European legislators if they wish to take over. Finally, at the joint request of the social partners, a member state can allow them to implement the directives by contractual means. But the most important provision is the right of European social actors to negotiate joint European accords. This provision should make it possible to remove employer obstacles which prevent the adoption of European measures on participation. It should push the UNICE to negotiate European accords on participation. These various aspects reflect the growing role of institutionalised participation of social actors deemed as "representative" (ETUC, UNICE, ECOSC) in the development of Community social policy.

The inclusion of the principle of subsidiarity in the Maastricht Treaty is also likely to encourage participative development and perhaps even direct participation. In areas such as social issues which fall under the joint jurisdiction of both the Community and member states, any action taken by the Commission should now, while respecting the social aims of European Union (stimulating employment and improving living conditions and the work environment, providing adequate social protection, fighting against exclusion, etc) also respect the general principle of subsidiarity which will in future influence all Community policies. This means that the Commission will only be able to be concern itself with the decisions of member states when "the aims of any action envisaged cannot be satisfactorily achieved by the member states and can, by the nature of their scale or the effects of such action, be better achieved at Community level."

Interpretation and use of the concept of subsidiarity will become clearer with use. Its aim is to encourage decision-making at the closest possible level to the problem being examined.

To sum up, the new rules of the game outlined in the 11 -country Social Agreement and the presence of supra-national European social actors seeking above all institutionalised European-level recognition and eager to remain the exclusive and privileged protagonists in this still fragile framework, reflect, as far as Brussels is concerned, preoccupations and concerns far removed from the concept of direct participation. Such a conclusion is valid if one argues in terms of a "a process of decision-making and structuring of European actors." In this case this is a crucial and difficult phase of structuring.

However, if one examines the problem from the point of view of the social and economic problems to be resolved in the wake of accelerated European integration, the conclusions are much less clear-cut.

The context of Economic and Monetary Union

Some believe that Economic and Monetary Union (EMU) will mean that by the end of the 1990s there will be renewed convergence of social issues, especially wage negotiations It is true that EMU and the disappearance of the exchange rate mechanism as a means of maintaining a country's competitiveness, will mean that wages and the work environment will become crucial factors in cutting costs for employers who want to preserve their competitiveness. Furthermore, a single currency will make it far easier for workers to compare wages in different countries within the same industrial sector or same company. Many believe that this, together with employer pressure on wage costs, will inevitably lead to a harmonisation of collective bargaining policies, given that comparative European elements will be taken into account when both trade unions and employers draw up their strategies. Some unions believe that this will require better coordination of union confederation policies in different countries and will probably launch debate on the possibility of tripartite European wage negotiations If this were to be the case, direct participation would immediately become relevant as a means of guaranteeing improved productivity on the one hand and as a bonus in exchange for wage austerity, on the other.

Stimulating community bodies to fight unemployment

Given the alarming rise in unemployment in 1992 and 1993, several policy statements at Community level have been issued citing the urgent need to establish a closer link between the policies of European integration and job creation schemes (see Chapter 2).

Given the employment crisis, direct participation is sometimes seen as a means of obtaining internal, qualitative forms of flexibility (such as multi-skilled work, flexitime and flexible wages). This avoids having to resort to external flexibility and limits the dangers of job loss. The kind of direct participation under discussion here should include varied forms of participation which respect collective and negotiated standards and norms. In view of the dimensions of the present job crisis, it would appear that this kind of solution is not sufficient.

We also believe that the speed at which the economies of the European Community are converging and the measures being taken by governments and companies to fight against the intolerably high levels of unemployment will profoundly change the systems of industrial relations. These must, in turn, offer possibilities other than micro-compromises of which direct and indirect participation are two important forms. Far too often over the last 15 years there has been a tendency to become bogged down in just such compromises.

European construction has highlighted the general crisis in society

Indeed the Maastricht Treaty does provide for a more important role for interest groups and associations representing ecological and consumer concerns and, for example, the victims of social exclusion. These developments lend support to the argument that the trade union movement should widen its concerns to include these social problems or at least try to create privileged alliances with such interest groups. In this sense the role of direct participation should be to maintain the social link in the workplace and contribute to promoting a civic sense outside the company so as to fight against anomy.

14 Financial participation: A new challenge for trade unions

Daniel Vaughan-Whitehead

Introduction

At a time when a considerable part of the economic crisis in the industrialised countries can be attributed to a lack of company competitiveness in world trade and, particularly, to excessively high and rigid wage costs and insufficient levels of productivity[1], particular attention should be paid to the different schemes for the financial participation of wage-earners in their company's profits. It is seen as a means of stimulating wage-earners' collective efforts, gaining increased productivity and easing adaptation to new technologies. Participation also appears to make it possible for wages and employment to be more flexible as cyclical recessions and recoveries succeed one another. The recent development of such schemes can also be explained by the failure of past policies of centralised bargaining which have proved to run counter to the present need for rapid and adequate adaptation of workers and equipment - a phenomenon which requires greater dialogue between the social partners within companies.

It is against this back-drop of decentralisation that various forms of financial participation have gained currency among decision-makers. In many industrialised countries such as France, Britain and the United States, governments have encouraged companies to adopt this form of participation by means of a variety of legal provisions and tax incentives. In July 1991 the European Council adopted a recommendation on the subject, put forward by the European Commission as part of its action programme for implementation of the European Social Charter. The recommendation highlights not only the economic potential but also the social advantages of these new forms of participation. The White Paper prepared by the Commission in 1994 stressed the need to develop new forms of incentive payment in the more general fight for employment[2].

In addition to government action, employers have also encouraged the mushrooming of these profit-participation schemes while trade unions have remained sceptical and sometimes openly opposed to the spread of new forms of remuneration which did not fall within the scope of collective bargaining, at a time when workers found themselves confronted by these new systems. Doubtless the stance adopted by trade unions merely encouraged employers to step up introduction of a model of participative management and direct partnership which involved the employer and the employees only, thereby isolating the trade unions even more and widening the gulf between the trade unions' policy choices and the workers' expectations. Today trade unions must examine this problem closely. How can they win back an active role in bargaining in these systems of profit-participation? What are the risks for the workers' in these new systems? What potential do they have, in economic terms, to improve company competitiveness and the employment situation? These are just a few of the inescapable questions which trade union activists must ask themselves today and which we attempt to answer in this chapter.

The explosion of financial participation agreements

The various schemes in practice

The sheer number and complexity of the different systems of financial participation make the situation somewhat confusing. Under the umbrella term "financial participation" there is a host of diverse systems all with one common denominator, namely that part of workers' remuneration is linked to a company's profits or another index of the company's economic performance. This part of the remuneration takes many forms and is complementary to the fixed, basic wage. There are two essential forms of financial participation which should be distinguished from one another.

Profit-sharing in the strict sense of the term means distributing to the workers a sum of money which is directly dependent on the company's profits or another index of its economic performance. Unlike individual productivity bonuses, profit-sharing is based on collective performance and is supplementary to the basic wage. Profit-sharing can take different forms. It can be paid in cash either immediately or after a set period of time, or it can form the basis of a savings or share-holding scheme. The various forms of immediate profit distribution are generally linked to various indices of a company's performance such as profits, value added, sales, physical productivity, etc. The various types of gain-sharing are designed to link remuneration directly to increased productivity or reductions in specific costs such as absenteeism and not to the profitability of capital.

Profit-sharing can also mean that workers are given a percentage of shares in the company. Generally speaking these shares are placed in a fund for a specific length of time at the end of which the workers can chose to dispose of the shares. In addition to company performance, profit-sharing can also be linked to the performance of a region or a country. This was the case in Sweden which set up salary funds aimed at ensuring a fairer redistribution of the national revenue (the

Meidner Plan).

To promote worker share-holding, the enterprise can either distribute freely or sell under favourable conditions (such as low cost, priority sale, long-term credit) a portion of the company's shares to all or a group of workers.

The ESOP (Employee Share Ownership Plan) is one specific form of share-holding participation with the involvement of a bank which lends money to a trust of workers in order to enable it to acquire company capital. Labour-management buy-outs are another form of ESOP.

Country-specific developments

Although the use of financial participation is a growing trend in all Western countries it often takes very different forms mainly because of differing legal provisions and the distinct nature of industrial relations in each country.

Some countries have bolstered the expansion of various forms of financial participation by introducing and modifying laws. This is the case in France where successive governments have drawn up legislation on optional profit-sharing (1956 ordinance), compulsory participation in profits (1967 ordinance), and share-ownership (1970, 1973, 1980 and 1984 ordinances). France has also increased tax deductions and changed certain taxation parameters in parallel with the most recent legal changes. These legislative changes have proved to be decisive and have led to a mushrooming of different forms of financial participation. Forms of profit-sharing multiplied between 1986 and 1990, increasing in number by more than 500% and affecting 10,717 companies, while compulsory participation in profits affected 16,900 companies and nearly 5 million workers in 1992. There have been similar developments in Britain where a series of new laws on share-holding, most of them introduced during the privatisation of state-owned companies in 1989, led to a spectacular increase in the number of wage earners holding shares and some 4,326 different discretionary share option schemes by March 1991. The 1987 Profit-Related Pay Act also encouraged rapid development of profit-participation schemes and by the beginning of 1994 there were some 6,443 schemes involving 1,570,000 workers.

In Belgium and Italy, however, financial participation developed without government intervention and has expanded as a result of the recent decentralisation of wage bargaining. In actual fact, the automatic wage-indexing which existed in Belgium until 1982 and the wage restraint policies in place between 1982 and 1986 limited employers' possibilities of linking wages to company performance. Performance-related wage systems and particularly share-holding systems only expanded in Belgium following the return to free collective bargaining in 1986.

Similarly in Italy in 1988 total devolution of collective bargaining to company-level led to a rapid increase in novel schemes introduced by employers in order to improve production quality and work organisation. These schemes replaced piece wages, a characteristic of collective agreements in Italy until then. Thus Italian companies became characterised by a multitude of mixed schemes based on calculations which took into account profitability indicators as well as productivity and technological progress parameters. These made up more than 75% of all financial participation agreements in the country in 1991. The aim of these schemes was to help adapt the workers to improved productivity so that they could accept more easily new demands put on them in terms of product quality and technological imperatives. The growth in financial participation in Italy was interrupted at the end of 1990, a date which marked the beginning of a long period of confrontation between trade unions, employer organisations and the government on the subject of wage policies. This was to hinder the conclusion of collective company agreements. The July 1992 and July 1993 national agreements which eradicated all wage indexation were to lead once again to a growth in financial participation schemes in Italy.

In Belgium, however, the beginning of 1994 was marked by a return to a wage austerity policy and it was decided that wages should be frozen until the end of 1996. Companies were forbidden to introduce profit-sharing schemes (van den Bulcke, 1995). Doubtless this policy decision will put a brake on the recent development of the only very limited financial participation schemes being run in Belgium.

Decentralisation of wage negotiations in Great Britain during the 1980s, as in Italy and Belgium, also laid the groundwork for the introduction of decentralised schemes at company level. In Japan these agreements have been even more decentralised because there financial participation is part and parcel of a more comprehensive policy of labour management and was not encouraged by resort to legislative or tax measures. Instead it has been established by the social partners at company level, often alongside other participative practices such as wage-earner participation in management and company decision-making, time-share schemes and internal labour mobility schemes (Hashimoto, 1990). Several different systems have quickly spread throughout Japanese companies. By 1991 ESOP schemes had been introduced in over 90% of companies quoted on the Japanese stock exchange and by 60% of all Japanese companies. In 1988 the average value of shares held by each wage earner was estimated to be about US$14,000. This little-known phenomenon might help explain the success of the Japanese economy (Jones and Kato, 1995). In addition to ESOP schemes, profit-sharing bonuses distributed to workers twice a year represent over 25% of total remuneration and thus ranks Japan as the world leader in financial participation. Nearly 97% of companies which employ 30 workers or more distribute these bonuses to their employees.

At the other extreme are the Scandinavian countries which have privileged a centralised approach to financial participation. This is especially true in Sweden and Denmark which have for some years now been running wage fund schemes, the main aim of which has been to ensure at least in part a redistribution of wealth to the *entire* work force. These schemes were introduced at national level following tripartite negotiations and proved to be radically different from the decentralised schemes preferred by other European countries. Abandoning the welfare state model in the 1990s has, however, also meant that this centralised form of participation has had to be abandoned and under employer pressure has led to new, more decentralised schemes determined by companies themselves.

In the former West Germany, only very minimal tax incentives were introduced to encourage share-holding schemes which in 1990 affected 1.3 million workers. All these schemes were intended to encourage savings. Only very few companies developed profit-participation schemes in parallel and doubtless the lack of enthusiasm for such schemes was at least in part due to the relative success of the German economy which dampened political interest in these flexible remuneration schemes. Indeed, in December 1993 the tax deductions introduced to encourage share-holding schemes were reduced.

In contrast to Germany, the productivity crisis observed in the United States led to considerable interest amongst employers and government in all forms of worker participation and team work and any incentive system which might help improve the labour situation. Numerous different tax incentives were introduced to encourage, among other things, profit participation schemes and ESOP schemes. In the United States profit participation agreements now affect about one fifth of the country's work force and participation bonuses are now paid into pension funds. Profit-sharing schemes have also spread among American companies.

More recently in Greece and Ireland tax incentives have been implemented to encourage companies to develop financial participation schemes and some tax exemptions could prove useful in other countries. To this end, the new Community recommendation on financial participation adopted by the European Council in July 1992 was designed to encourage other countries of the EU to develop further financial participation and to ensure a more harmonized approach to financial participation throughout the Union. The recommendation calls on member states of the EU to note the potential benefits of making increasing used of financial participation schemes, to prepare suitable legislation and to envisage the possibility of granting tax breaks to help the spread of such schemes among companies (CEC 1992).

Thus in December 1993 the Netherlands, while preparing a new social pact for 1994, decided to interrupt its austerity measures and wage freeze and encourage profit participation schemes by introducing tax breaks which had been planned for 1994. In Germany, however, recent decisions to cut back on tax deductions for share-holding schemes and in Belgium where, as part of the country's austerity drive, it was decided in 1995 to put a stop to any further spread of financial participation, it would seem that this recommendation has had little effect.

The role of trade unions and employee participation

Financial participation has developed in parallel with other participative schemes in various countries. The stance adopted by trade unions often explains the lack of involvement of workers and their representatives in the negotiation of financial participation agreements.

Trade union leaders have viewed this new form of remuneration with suspicion, believing that it weakens the role of the unions by encouraging direct cooperation between workers and employers. In order to try and avoid a slide towards paternalistic forms of company culture, the trade unions have chosen to fight for extended collective bargaining and greater "constitutional" decision-making within companies (see Gregg and Machin, 1988; Smith, 1988; Mitchell, 1987).

Trade union resistance can also be traced back to fears that workers might see their wages adjusted downwards under a profit-sharing system. More generally, unions believe that financial participation challenges the principle of employee solidarity (equal pay for equal work) - a principle that unions have always practised and defended. Financial participation reintroduces serious wage differences between companies which can encourage selfishness in companies which are financially better off, for example in high-tech industries or capital-intensive sectors (Stallaerts, 1988).

This opposition adopted on principle can, however, vary depending on whether the trade union concerned has a centralised or decentralised power structure. National trade union leaders are adamantly opposed to this new wage differentiation while sectoral unions or individual companies (hi-tech industries, for example) often support it. Devolution of wage negotiation away from the national or sectoral level to company level, which has increased over the last few years, has eased the implementation of collective forms of financial participation.

Several empirical studies have illustrated the extent of trade union resistance to the introduction of financial participation schemes. Freeman and Kleiner (1986) showed how companies tend to abandon these systems once they have become unionised. In another study conducted in the United States, the same authors noted that trade union presence in a company reduced the likelihood of finding a financial participation scheme running (Freeman and Kleiner, 1988). Fitzroy and Kraft (1987), looking at a sample of 61 companies in the German metallurgy industry noted that the level of unionisation clearly had a negative effect on the chances of such schemes being introduced.

A study by Jones and Pliskin (1988) conducted on the basis of a sample of 313 privately-owned companies in Canada revealed that the greater the extent of unionisation, the less likely a company was to resort to these flexible forms of remuneration, although the link between unionisation and the absence of financial participation schemes varied depending on the type of scheme (profit sharing or share-holding). This negative influence in Canada is above all due to staunch union resistance to financial participation. The two authors suggest that there is another reason for this phenomenon. It would seem that companies with little unionisation are often tempted to introduce financial participation schemes to avoid increased unionisation. This backs up research by Fiorito, Lowman and Nelson (1987) which revealed that companies tended to adopt an active human resource policy in order to avoid an increase in unionisation.

166

Poole (1988) in a survey of 303 British firms, noted that "the weakness of trade unions allows management to promote forms of employee financial involvement at the cost of expanded collective bargaining or excessive union representation on the management board." In contrast to other studies, Gregg and Machin (1988) concluded that unionisation encourages companies to introduce financial participation so as to reduce the role of the trade unions in deciding wage levels. However, the greater union power is in a company, the less likely it is that this will occur. When unions wield considerable power in a company, employers appear to be less inclined to promote financial participation, for two main reasons:

- For fear that, should the unions oppose such schemes, they might seek revenge by putting a brake on productivity, a move which would be felt far more, the stronger the union presence in the company;
- Furthermore, should an agreement be concluded, high unionisation might lead to share schemes being manipulated by the unions to their advantage in the sense that they could control the workers' productivity and so gain considerably more power in the workplace.

Numerous examples of trade union action in different European countries illustrate the extent of trade union resistance to profit-participation schemes. In Italy, opposition by the FIOM-CGIL trade union to Fiat's financial participation scheme revealed how much some unions prefer a wage system which guarantees a fixed wage for workers to one which depends upon fluctuating profits.[3]

In France, too, the CGT and FO trade unions have always been bitterly opposed to the principle of financial participation, clearly as illustrated in the following quote: "there is no question of discussing the criteria underlying financial participation schemes because the workers might find themselves trapped in the 'logic' of profitability and this would have grave consequences for wages, employment and the workers themselves".[4]

It is interesting to note the fear of a direct link between employees and employers and hence exclusion of trade unions apparent in such statements: "We believe that profit-sharing, couched in subtle terms, is a trap designed to eradicate unions or change their natural role as a counter-balance"[5], or "I don't want to see a relationship based on collusion developing between employees and employers and hence the emergence of 'an illegal wage system'".[6] The CGT believes that profit-sharing clearly represents a "drain on wages". It should be noted that this comment is far from unjustified. In many agreements, profit-sharing really has become a substitute for and not complementary to wages. Indeed all French trade unions agree on this point and urge caution. In an attempt to calm the situation an inter-ministerial circular dated December 6, 1988 clearly stated the non-substitutional nature of profit-sharing. The CGT and FO have also expressed concern about the fact that profit-sharing appears to lead to excessive wage differentials among firms within a given sector, or even among different sectors.

In Belgium, systematic union opposition to such schemes has prevented any development of profit-sharing. (Stallaerts, 1988). This can be illustrated by quoting the president of the Belgian socialist unions A. van den Broucke: "rather than providing tax breaks for financial participation, we need to see a general reassessment of wage taxation"[7].

In Germany, Fitzroy and Kraft (1985) who conducted a case study of two companies with financial participation schemes showed that acceptance of such schemes sometimes depended on the relative decentralisation of union presence and on work organisation. Very centralised unions saw the introduction of such schemes as a potential loss of power and influence because companies might thereby develop less conflictual forms of industrial relations.

This kind of union opposition is also visible in other countries such as the Netherlands, Denmark (Uvalic, 1991) and Sweden (Sandberg, 1994). In some cases, however, unions have proved to favour profit-sharing. In the United States, for example, unions in the car industry (United Automobile Workers) have accepted profit-sharing schemes in their work contracts (Weitzman and Kruse, 1990).

What kind of participation for workers and their representatives?

It should be noted that union opposition is sometimes justified by the determination on the part of employers to exclude the trade unions from all negotiations on financial participation schemes. The situation is often aggravated by a lack of legislation. For example, in Great Britain there is no legal obligation to negotiate these schemes. This means that most schemes are simply introduced unilaterally by employers. Only 5% are negotiated with trade unions. It is also significant to note that all these schemes are optional and directly implemented by the financial directors of companies and not by the heads of human resources as is the case in France or Italy, for example. Clearly, concluding non-negotiated agreements of this kind has been simpler in industries where union presence is weak. In such sectors these schemes have come to be seen as an alternative to traditional wage negotiations with trade unions.

In some cases, excluding trade unions has been facilitated by systematic union opposition to these schemes. This clearly was the case in Britain during the privatisations of 1986-87 when this opposition resulted in the marginalisation of trade unions. The best example is perhaps that of British Telecom where, during privatisation, the trade unions waged a campaign to try and persuade employees not to buy shares in the company. In the end, however, more than 90% of employees did actually decide to become share-holders.

In Belgium too, financial participation schemes are only rarely the result of collective agreements, something which reflects both trade union opposition and the determination of employers to separate profit-sharing from wage negotiations and so preserve their prerogatives regarding profit distribution.

Things are very different in France where employers are obliged to negotiate all aspects of a profit-sharing scheme with worker representatives (including the basis on which profit sharing is calculated, profit-sharing criteria, channels of information, monitoring, etc). The Auroux Acts ensure that worker representatives are very much involved in decision-making, mainly as a result of the existence of company councils. More recently, in 1994, the French government decided to introduce new measures on participation in decision-making designed specifically for financial participation schemes. These new changes oblige companies in which employees possess more than 5% of the total capital to appoint one or two employees to sit on the share-holders board.

In Italy, employers, keen to improve the quality of production, have introduced a system of employee consultation together with their financial participation schemes. This has proved successful in solving organisational problems within companies. Other participative schemes, although not compulsory by law, have also been introduced by employers. 38% of financial participation schemes provide for the introduction of joint committees whose task it is to solve organisational problems and improve productivity (Biagioli, 1995).

In Belgium, the fact that collective bargaining is more centralised and that wage negotiations are conducted at sectoral level, has prevented the spread of decentralised schemes. This in turn has led to less worker involvement in decisions regarding financial participation and related matters.

The emergence of a new policy?

The trade union stance does seem to have changed over the last few years. A far more pragmatic approach seems to have been adopted in the wake of the concrete experiences gained within companies. In France, many trade unions are now actively involved in setting up financial participation schemes, thus confirming the theory put forward by Mitchell (1987) which suggested that trade unions could gain a new role in negotiations through financial participation and so compensate for their loss of power in traditional wage negotiations.

Similarly, in Belgium, despite repeated opposition by some union confederations at national level, locally-based unions now seem to be playing a more active role in setting up financial participation schemes.

In Italy, devolution of wage negotiations to company level has encouraged the conclusion of company agreements and has given unions the opportunity to play an active role in the introduction of financial participation schemes. As a result, their role in these new forms of remuneration has become far more positive. The national tripartite agreement on wage policy and industrial relations signed in July 1993 illustrated a national consensus on the need to develop systems of remuneration directly linked to "quality, production and competitiveness".

In Great Britain, however, it is interesting to note that, according to one survey, 70% of wage-earners believe that financial participation is an excellent idea while trade unions remain staunchly opposed to any further spread of such schemes (Poole, 1995). This gulf between the trade unions' position at national level and the wage-earners' aspirations, as well as the divergence of opinions between company unions and national confederations, illustrates clearly that trade unions must quickly change their strategies regarding financial participation and suggest a new, coherent policy.

An assessment of the economic effects

Economists point out numerous advantages of these variable remuneration schemes. These advantages can be grouped into three categories.

The first type of effect is at the micro-economic level. Collective participation in profits stimulates workers' efforts, so increasing their productivity and accelerating their adaptation to new forms of technology. At the same time, profit-sharing could be a way of directly linking pay to fluctuations in the state of the economy, but without any intervention by government, so encouraging the much sought-after cyclical wage flexibility. The economist M. Weitzman (1984) believes that this type of remuneration reduces marginal labour costs and would thus create new jobs while at the same time putting a brake on inflation. This would produce a macro-economic effect, the so-called stagflation effect. Financial participation can also be a major factor in other areas of economic policy. For example it could help stimulate employee consumption or encourage employee savings and hence investments. These are all economic policy options which could prove to have a positive effect on employment. Lastly, financial participation could play a decisive role in privatisation as recent experience in the countries of Central and Eastern Europe has proved.

An unquestionable effect on productivity

These payment schemes are above all aimed at improving employee motivation and encouraging them to increase their productivity. The key mechanism in such a share-economy is that increased productivity is rewarded through higher remuneration which in turn has the effect of encouraging greater productivity in the workplace and reducing absenteeism and turnover.

Unlike piece-work payment which has generally led to individualist forms of behaviour and open conflict with management, payment linked to the collective results of a workshop or a company can stimulate team work. In a sharing scheme, unlike schemes with individual incentives, any individual action such as reduced effort has an external effect on the other members of a team. Thus as long as work organisation and the company's technology do not make "interaction" too difficult, sharing schemes encourage workers to collaborate and work together more closely so that these external effects are "internalised". Thus a form of mutual or horizontal monitoring process or incentive system develops amongst workers.[8]

Similarly, profit-sharing can also encourage workers to cooperate with employers. This is of vital importance for the employer. A system of individual bonuses cannot motivate workers' efforts whereas profit-sharing makes it possible for employers to galvanise the power of pressure exerted on workers to prevent any drop in individual effort while encouraging greater cooperation and productivity. Since the various members of a team are far better informed about their colleagues' work efforts than management - so rarely involved in the same duties - can ever hope to be, profit-sharing makes it possible to cut down on monitoring costs and to obtain considerable gains in efficiency. This state of affairs in turn encourages employers to decentralise production and allocate it amongst autonomous production groups and small work teams, so facilitating productive interaction and cooperation amongst workers.

Hence this new form of remuneration appears to complement the changes taking place in work organisation. By the same token, financial participation should also simplify the introduction of new technologies - which are rendering employer monitoring of employees impossible - and help quicken workers' adaptation to these new technologies.

Lastly, according to the literature, these incentive effects will be far greater if financial participation schemes are developed in conjunction with schemes designed to involve workers in decision-making as this would accentuate the feeling of belonging to a company and increase the workers' possibilities of contributing effectively to the company's success.

Practical experiences in financial participation seem to confirm most of these theories. When one looks at relevant empirical studies one can see that the research results today suggest that these schemes do indeed have a positive effect on productivity. All studies conducted in the European Union, including a summary recently drawn up by the Commission and published as the Pepper Report[9], agree on this point and clearly point at the improvements in performance which financial participation schemes can lead to. Absenteeism and turnover rates have dropped notably in companies using financial participation schemes in Germany, France, the United Kingdom and Italy. Econometric tests have also highlighted the direct effect that such schemes have on productivity.

A second comparative study, conducted by Weitzman and Kruse (1990), looks at the EU and beyond - the United States, Canada and Japan - and provides a systematic and detailed breakdown of the situation including simple statistical analysis and econometric tests as well as company case studies and opinion polls. In the light of this synthesis of the situation, the two American authors of the study conclude that without any doubt financial participation schemes have a positive effect on productivity.

Finally, more recently, a third comparative study was conducted by the International Labour Office (Vaughan-Whitehead, 1995). The survey covered the western world but also looked at the countries of Central and Eastern Europe. It also stressed the motivation factor and provided concrete examples of companies in which these systems of remuneration had made it possible to stimulate economic and industrial performance.

All these studies also underline the fact that the motivation effect is more far-reaching when other participative practices are introduced simultaneously in a company. Studies in Germany show that the development of direct employee participation in decision-making or "co-determination" as it is called, is a decisive factor in determining whether or not profit-participation schemes stimulate workers' motivation and productivity (Cable and Fitzroy, 1980; Cable, 1988).

Similarly, studies in the United States reveal that the introduction of ESOP schemes only has a positive effect on productivity in companies which also introduce schemes for participation in decision-making (Mitchell, 1995).

So the effects of these forms of participation are not isolated. Given that financial participation encourages workers to work for the success of a company, his or her participation in decision-making can but add to the employee's motivation. Furthermore, participation encourages worker acceptance of greater income variations, particularly since it allows workers to better understand the reasons for a possible drop in their profit-linked share. Participation associated with profit-sharing allays workers' fears that their share of profits might be appropriated by the employers and share-holders. Conversely, in the absence of participation, workers perceive their share of profits as unrelated to their own performance. This means that profit-sharing has a less striking effect on their efforts and their concern and eagerness to work together, and consequently, on their productivity. Employees' concerns about appropriation are considerable. Profit-based remuneration without participation can easily be perceived as a strategy to reduce wages rather than a way of involving the worker financially and psychologically in a company. The fact that companies generally introduce such schemes during economic recessions doesn't help allay such suspicions on the part of workers.

This link between participation and profit-sharing runs both ways. It would seem that employees only grudgingly accept participation in decision-making which is aimed at optimising the enterprise's wealth when the residual portion of this wealth, i.e. profits, is only redistributed among the management and the share-holders (Cable and Fitzroy, 1980).

Thus, just as the effect of profit-sharing is increased when accompanied by participation, the effect of participation on company performance can only hope to increase when accompanied by profit-sharing schemes.

Furthermore, it would be difficult to imagine how the horizontal circulation of information, stimulated by financial participation, could hope to be effective without a vertical circulation of information which would not only make it possible for management to facilitate cooperation amongst employees but also make it easier for employees to know exactly what the company's often complex and varied goals are and thereby contribute to achieving them effectively. This is especially true given that company profits can rise or fall on the basis of variables which are totally unrelated to the employees' work efforts - a phenomenon particularly present in international companies.

A useful instrument for stabilizing employment?

The second effect that profit-sharing seems to have is in conceptual terms very different from motivation and concerns the flexibility of our economies under the pressure of external shocks. If remuneration is able to respond more rapidly to market conditions, by means of profits, then profits should in time prove to be less variable, thereby having a stabilizing effect on employment.

According to OECD experts (1986), the lack of reaction noted in wage levels in most industrialised countries was the reason behind the enormous variations in employment during the 1980s. The present form of wage negotiation has led to an absence of any correlation between company productivity levels and the level of average salaries. Wage increases appear to have been far too limited in high productivity industries while the least successful companies have clearly found themselves in difficulties because of wage controls.

Although today there seems to be a general acceptance of the fact that salaries must rise, it also appears equally important that in a context marked by economic crisis, these rises should be linked to increases in productivity and company performance. Salary flexibility would reduce the danger of lay-offs during periods of recession, thereby leading to greater stability in the job market.

Although studies on the effects of financial participation are rapidly increasing in number, there is far less research into its effects on wage flexibility. Nevertheless, empirical results do confirm that the effect of wage flexibility is gradually increasing in certain countries. In the United States an analysis by Kruse (1991) of 2377 firms of which 1,205 used share schemes, mostly in the form of deferred distribution, showed that from 1971 to 1985, employment variations were far fewer in share scheme companies. During periods of reduced activity these companies were only subjected to a 2% modification in employment levels compared to 3% employment variations in other companies.

In Japan Freeman and Weitzman (1986) noted that profit-sharing bonuses reacted far more to changes in the economic situation than salaries and that they had thus played a positive role in maintaining employment levels. Although the results of several studies contest the predominant role of bonuses in the success of the Japanese economy, this form of financial participation has, unarguably, contributed to increasing wage flexibility and to stabilising employment in the country.

In France a survey conducted amongst 116 industrial companies showed that financial participation schemes between 1983 and 1986 more or less followed the ups and downs of the market. Companies using such schemes seem to have reacted differently during periods of economic crisis, maintaining employment by reducing the share of profits distributed to employees while companies without such schemes tried to maintain their profits by cutting back on jobs (Vaughan-Whitehead, 1992). Similar results were found by the Ministry of Labour in 1992-93 following a vast survey conducted amongst 12,000 firms between 1987 to 1991 (Coutrot, 1992). In the light of this survey it would appear that fluctuations in the level of profit-sharing are in direct proportion to the economic climate. This leads to greater salary flexibility amongst companies using such schemes. Similarly, in Great Britain, Estrin and Wilson (1989) arrived at the same conclusions on the basis of a sample of 52 firms. They noted greater variations in remuneration in share-scheme companies. Their conclusions were all the more significant given that they cover the period from 1978 to 1982, marked by a serious recession in Britain, during which a lack of wage flexibility led to several massive waves of redundancies.

On the basis of the argument of wage flexibility, the American economist Weitzman (1984) has attempted to look in closer detail at the macro-economic potential of a generalised introduction of profit-sharing schemes and has talked of the importance of the so-called "stagflation" effect. Apart from providing greater flexibility to wages, share schemes, by reducing marginal labour costs, encourage a substantial increase in employment and a drop in overall prices.

The basic principle is quite simple. In a sharing economy, companies would tend to increase their hiring given that the share of profits destined for employees would be shared by an increasing number of employees, thereby reducing the marginal labour costs, in other words the costs borne by the employer for an additional worker. At the same time, monetary policy would be brought to bare so as to check inflation without any risk of exacerbating unemployment. Although it is true that Weitzman's very original theories have sparked off renewed debate on financial participation and have helped shed light on some of its possible effects on wage flexibility, the fundamental hypotheses on which these theories are based have been severely attacked in most theoretical and empirical studies of the subject (see Nuti, 1986 and 1987; Uvalic, 1991). This is particularly true of his central hypothesis which is that the levels of financial participation are not viewed by employers as part of marginal labour costs. This does not seem to reflect economic reality. Several studies conducted in France (Vaughan-Whitehead, 1992), Britain (Wadhwani, 1988) and Germany (Hart and Hubler, 1992) have shown that employers can only hope to attract new workers if they offer a total remuneration equal to the market level. This means that they consider this total remuneration, and not the basic wage, to be the marginal labour cost.

Finally, one important characteristic of Weitzman's model is the voluntary lack of worker participation in decision-making, a choice aimed at avoiding a restrictive employment policy and thereby preempting any drop in salaries caused by an increase in the number of employees and a drop in their share of profits. Yet profit-sharing schemes encourage workers to demand control. Furthermore, as we have seen, the development of financial participation without any simultaneous expansion of other forms of participation is neither realistic nor desirable in terms of economic efficiency.

Financial participation is also an important source of wage-related savings and in this sense could help rectify a double deficit in Europe, the savings deficit and a deficit of capital stock among companies, a particular problem among SMEs. Several countries have tried to explore this avenue by stimulating employee savings. Employee savings schemes have been developed in the United Kingdom, Germany, the Netherlands, the United States and Japan. We have also seen that financial participation in Germany, the United States and Japan was directly aimed at stimulating savings and developing pension funds.[10] In Sweden, employee funds have been used to finance productive investments or company-internal operations, such as training or job-creation schemes. In France, the October 21, 1986 ordinance made the Plan d'Epargne d'Enterprise (PEE - Enterprise Savings Account) the cornerstone of different forms of financial participation with a compulsory proportion of profits being invested for a minimum of five years and tax breaks offered for additional investment of profits in these savings accounts. These PEEs proved to be very successful and made it possible to generate some 80 billion FF in stock by the end of 1990. The report prepared by Pastre and Moscovici (1991) for the Ministry of Industry suggested that this scheme be continued and that genuine Wage Savings Accounts (PES in French) be created using the PEEs so as to encourage long-term savings by offering large tax credits depending on the amounts placed in savings and the fixed term periods for which they were placed (a choice of either 10 or 20 years being offered to employees). Doubtless these measures would be a good way of encouraging savings capital. Increasing capital stock can directly lead to a drop in debt levels which means savings in financial costs and improved company profitability. Improvements in a company's capital stocks can also have a positive effect on employment. It would first and foremost limit bankruptcy among small companies and cyclical redundancies among larger ones. It could also create new jobs, especially among SMEs. But such a system does have several drawbacks.

First, it must be asked whether an increase in savings might not have a detrimental effect on household spending, so crucial during this present period both for companies and for the general macro-economic balance. It is significant that new provisions drawn up by the French government in 1994, far from encouraging savings, were an attempt to encourage consumer spending and demand, in that they introduced the possibility of releasing the compulsory profit-sharing funds should an employee purchase a new or second-hand car or undertake building or household repair work. Similarly, new regulations debated in the French parliament in May 1994 made it possible to convert profit-sharing bonuses into time-saving accounts, the aim being to encourage employees to take additional time off for at least six months and thereby create more temporary jobs.

The expansion of long-term savings through financial participation also holds numerous risks for employees. First, it represents far too great a concentration of risks for the employee. These risks are all linked to the health of the company and this creates a double dependency on the part of employees, concerning both their job and their savings account. The employees would in some senses be forced to "put all their eggs in one basket". It is true that this risk could be limited by investing a percentage of these savings outside the company and by protecting the amounts saved using insurance schemes, but it could not be entirely avoided. Recent events have furnished a multitude of scenarios in which employees of a company which goes bankrupt lose both their salary and the savings they had accumulated in the company[11]. Against this backdrop, it would seem absolutely essential that the social partners and the employees be involved in making decisions about savings investment. In Italy, the trade unions already play such a role, via committees, and are also involved in deciding where pension funds should be invested.

This kind of system would make it possible for trade unions to participate in the allocation of these funds outside the company, which is not the case at the moment in most countries since investment choices are presently made by outside bodies, either a bank or an insurance or mutual insurance company. Similarly it would seem absolutely essential that employees and their representatives be involved in decision-making regarding investments in their own company. Indeed their role could prove to be decisive in the allocation of money for productive investments or job creation schemes. The role of trade unions seems particularly important in that they could view such savings proposals in a wider context of job market flexibility and employment stability.

Although in some cases wage savings schemes could last 20 years, companies are not always keen to maintain their staff levels over such a long period of time. But these long-term savings funds which come from employees' participation in their company's profits should encourage entrepreneurs to devise long-term policies of partnership with employees and policies to ensure greater job security. The funds themselves could be used to protect jobs during periods of recession or to develop other forms of internal flexibility, such as job-sharing or internal employee mobility.

On the other hand, these kinds of savings schemes could have the effect of demoralising employees if they are not informed and consulted about the use to which the funds are put. Here the unions can play an important role by ensuring that wage savings which stem from financial participation are merely one aspect of much more comprehensive partnership and not simply a tool to be used to increase a company's capital stocks.

Italian trade unions have put forward proposals suggesting the creation of a European Solidarity Fund which could pool all pension and financial participation funds collected by national trade unions in their respective countries and which could then be earmarked for European investment projects designed to create new jobs (Miniutti, 1994). Such a system would make it possible to coordinate the actions of European trade unions and to attract considerable sums of money for the purpose of generating new jobs. But one wonders whether employees in a company might not very quickly find themselves alienated in the face of an investment fund managed at EU level, the effects and results of which they might never actually feel.

This concern is particularly valid given the fact that unions and employees have always preferred direct wages to deferred wages to which wage savings schemes inevitably lead, especially those involving 15 to 20-year periods. This preference is particularly noticeable during slow-downs in economic activity, as at the present time when increasing numbers of wage-earners are having to deal with a variety of social problems such as housing, etc., and want to make immediate use of their income and share of financial participation.

The creation of more short-term savings funds, managed in conjunction with trade unions, might make it easier for funds to be made readily available if need be while at the same time creating a reserve fund which could either be used for job creation schemes or to compensate too rapid a drop in participation shares during periods of recession. It should be remembered that all the studies cited have shown that the immediate payment of a share in profits has a positive and significant effect on workers' motivation whereas deferred participation schemes do not have an effect of the same magnitude. Hence any monies from financial participation which were immediately placed in a savings scheme, either on a compulsory or a voluntary basis, could demoralise employees with the result that the aim of encouraging savings and investments clash directly with the aim of stimulating productivity which lies behind these financial participation schemes.

Doubtless a combination of these different schemes is necessary. Immediate profit-sharing schemes would make it possible to stimulate productivity amongst workers while at the same time encouraging wage flexibility during periods of recession and hence also protecting jobs. At the same time, profit-sharing schemes which involve savings schemes and investments outside and inside the company would make it possible to finance activities such as training or vocational retraining of employees within a company in cases where jobs have to be cut but lay-offs are to be avoided. Trade unions could help find a middle road between the risk of unemployment on the one hand and the risk of a loss of income on the other, depending on the financial, industrial and social circumstances of the company concerned.

What is at stake in the privatisation process in Central and Eastern Europe

Financial participation is presently playing an important role in privatisation in the countries of Central and Eastern Europe. Recent legislation on privatisation illustrates governments' determination to redistribute part of privatised companies' capital to employees in the form of the free distribution of shares or the sale of shares at preferential prices. This is a general trend although there are subtle differences regarding the methods adopted and the percentage of capital redistributed to employees from country to country.

In Poland and Bulgaria 20% of shares in companies to be privatised have been offered to employees at half their market value, while in Hungary the figure is

177

15%.

The percentage of capital destined for employees seems to be higher in those countries with a strong tradition of self-management, such as the republics of the former Yugoslavia where, in the cases of Slovenia and Montenegro 20% and 30% respectively were earmarked for allocation to employees. The percentage is lower in countries such as the Czech Republic (5% of capital) which favoured a larger-scale distribution by means of a system of coupons or ownership certificates available to everyone in the country.

Although coupon privatisation is not, in the strict sense of the term, financial participation in that it is not only for employees, it can in practice encourage the development of employee shareholder schemes as in Ukraine or Poland where the two systems have been combined.

It is interesting to note that the trade union positions regarding these forms of privatisation have changed since the beginning of the reform process when they adopted a very clear stance against financial participation.

Between 1990 and 1992 most governments in Central and Eastern Europe were trying to curb inflation by imposing a wage control policy at the same time as removing controls on prices. This led to a plunge in real wages of more than 60% on average while minimum wages fell well below the poverty threshold (Standing and Vaughan-Whitehead, 1995). Against this backdrop unions have constantly demanded wage increases rather than the sale of shares or other forms of financial participation. In most cases employees simply did not have the cash necessary to buy shares.

During the privatisation process unions changed their stance gradually and eventually came to support the development of share-holding schemes for three main reasons. First, such schemes represented a way of directly involving employees in the privatisation process and so incorporating forms of industrial democracy in the reform process; secondly, the distribution of shares to employees seemed to be an alternative to private capital, especially direct foreign investment. And thirdly, with unemployment rates soaring from 1% to an average of 20% in most countries, employees and their representatives came to realise that this would enable them to become involved in employment decisions and thereby avoid systematic lay-offs in the course of industrial restructuring.

ESOP schemes and especially company buy-outs by employees and management quickly spread through Hungary, Poland and the republics of the former Yugoslavia.

But some countries, for example, Bulgaria and the Czech Republic, in their haste to throw out collectivism and quickly develop towards a market economy, set up share-holding schemes while at the same time getting rid of all forms of participation in decision-making.

Clearly trade union involvement is necessary here, especially given the fact that employees do not seem to be in favour of financial participation unless they are directly involved in company decision-making, above all as it concerns their jobs.

Conclusions

Varied practical experience in the area of financial participation as well as research into the subject has revealed that in the past trade unions tended to refuse to negotiate any form of financial participation, preferring traditional wage negotiations even as companies were resorting massively to this new form of remuneration, often created in a wider context of participative management.

Incontestably, this trend has led to a diminution of the scope of collective bargaining and has left trade unions often out of step with the expectations of employees.

Employers in many countries have turned union opposition to their advantage and have developed flexible payment systems which are totally unrelated to wage negotiations and often do not involve the participation of employees or their representatives.

It is important to note that financial participation schemes are always introduced unilaterally by employers in Britain, Belgium and the United States. But this also illustrates the important role that trade unions could play in countering this policy. This role could be played along several different fronts.

Trade unions must above all else be involved in the planning of financial participation schemes, even if this takes place on the margins of wage negotiation processes.

In France, as we have seen, trade unions at company level play an increasingly important role in the introduction of profit-sharing schemes and they help in implementing those schemes which most benefit the employees, for example by refusing any link with absenteeism or sickness leave, or by rejecting excessive differentiation in the amount of profits shared among different categories of workers.

Similarly, trade unions could be more active in deciding what kind of scheme (profit-sharing or share-holding) a company should adopt and which categories of employees would be involved, by looking closely at what kind of company is involved and what the employees' expectations are.

For example, many countries have financial participation schemes which do not cover fixed-contract workers or part-time workers. This leads to a fragmentation of the work force. Similarly, financial participation is only rarely introduced in response to trade union demands.

It is also essential that such schemes be monitored so that the conditions laid down in the original agreements are respected and employees are well informed about the company's results, especially the reasons for any fall or increase in their share of the profits.

This also means winning the right to monitor strategic company decision-making which could have immediate repercussions on company profits, such as buy-outs, mergers or overseas operations.

The role of the trade unions is equally decisive in ensuring that these various schemes complement rather than replace each other.

In Japan the labour-capital partnership model is based on direct worker involvement at the production unit and workshop level, negotiations with trade unions being conducted almost exclusively at company level. The system is completed with a variety of share-holding schemes and profit participation bonuses as well as in-house training schemes and long-term employment policies. All of which strengthens the sense of belonging among workers in a company but only rarely involves them in strategic decision-making.

This model has shown its limitations. For example, it has led to a fragmentation of the workforce with, on the one hand, lifetime employees and, on the other, an army of temporary workers whose pay is far lower and who do not enjoy the same benefits, such as profit bonuses.

In Germany, however, the co-determination system has not been followed by a parallel and complementary expansion of financial participation schemes. Doubtless the co-determination system will find itself even more weakened in the wake of the government decision at the end of 1993 to reduce even more the tax breaks for share-holding schemes.

Here again, the trade unions could help turn financial participation schemes into genuine tools for human resource management, capable of improving employee motivation - and so their efficiency - but also of improving the atmosphere in the company. Here it is important to ensure that, quite apart from participation in decision-making or co-determination, other more decentralised participative methods are encouraged which will allow workers to discuss the problems they come up against in the workplace and help them to solve them.

These decentralised forms of participation are very often more favourably received by workers. It is equally important to encourage the implementation of all kinds of working conditions which may promote the success of financial participation which has proved, in empirical studies, to be particularly successful when work organisation is decentralised and team work introduced.

This seems to be particularly urgent in the countries of Central and Eastern Europe where financial participation is not as yet part of any specific employer or union strategy aimed at improving productivity, the organisation of work and industrial relations.

It is also essential that trade unions place financial participation fairly and squarely at the heart of a wider economic policy designed, in particular, at improving the employment situation.

Several European companies have illustrated that it is sometimes possible to avoid lay-offs by trying to improve industrial relations in a company on the basis of training, improved work organisation, improved production quality and greater productivity.

Work-sharing schemes have also made it possible for large European companies in financial difficulties to avoid resorting to redundancies.

These, then are the forms of participation which have made it possible for trade unions to suggest alternatives to lay-offs. Financial participation can be a very effective part of this policy of flexibility. It is true that these schemes lead to greater variations in income, which vary as company performance varies, increasing with economic growth and shrinking in times of recession.

But in an era in which unemployment is the major scourge, wage flexibility could surely contribute to avoiding lay-offs during periods of crisis just as shortening the working week can, thereby being part of a "solidarity" or "internal flexibility" model. It is significant to note that over recent years in many companies wage concessions have been accepted in exchange for a promise of no lay-offs.

Doubtless European trade unions will have to reconsider their total rejection of any kind of wage flexibility. At the very least, the subject deserves a debate which would in any case allow the trade unions to seek new solutions.

Thus the trade unions could use financial participation to propose greater wage flexibility in exchange for a non-reducible basic wage, which could vary according to the category of employee involved. This would entirely respect the trade unions' priority of protecting the worst-off employees.

Proposing new ideas and new alternatives to the kinds of flexibility put forward by employers would give new momentum to employees whose major preoccupation today is keeping their jobs. Likewise, trade unions must become involved in arbitrating with government and employer representatives the various macro-economic goals of financial participation, deciding, for example between the need to stimulate consumer spending, or encouraging greater wage savings to stimulate investment. To this end, greater cooperation between trade unions and researchers is essential in order that some of these new avenues for employment can be explored.

Finally, consideration must be given to the scope of such discussions in Central and Eastern Europe, where the spread of financial participation is proving to be decisive in this period of transition - a time when state capital is being redistributed and employer representatives and trade unions are trying to promote a new system of industrial relations.

Notes

1. Growth, Competitiveness and Employment: Challenges and Avenues for the 21st Century, European Commission White Paper, Brussels, CEC. 1994

2. CEC, 1994, P. 18

3. See Le Monde, October 20 1988 "Participation Italian Style", page V

4. CGT point of view, quoted by Semaine Lamy N° 419, P. 440

5.   CGT-FO: statement at the Economic and Social Council, 23-24 May 1989

6.   Interview with Marc Blondel, Secretary General of FO, Tribune de l'Expansion, 21 July 1989

7.   See Stallaerts, 1988, P. 11; the same opinion was given at the Central Industry Council; C.B.R. 1986/500 (13/10/1986, P. 18-19)

8.   This argument, developed by Fitzroy and Kraft (1987) was in response to the "free-rider" argument put forward by Jensen and Meckling (1979) which argued that the employee in a share-based economy would have no incentive to increase his work effort given that he would only have a negligible effect on his company's profits, his own effect being proportionally smaller the bigger the company. Rather, he would be encouraged to reduce his efforts so as to take advantage of non-monetary benefits which he would gain from a reduction in his work time without having to bear a reduction in the variable portion of his salary since productivity losses would be shared by all employees. This objection is not valid when consideration is taken of the beneficial effect that financial participation is likely to have on cooperation and mutual monitoring amongst workers.

9.   Pepper stands for Promotion of Employee Participation in Profits and Enterprise Results. See Uvalic (1991). This report was the basis for the preparation of the Community recommendation adopted by the European Council in July 1992.

10.   Especially ESOP schemes

11.   This led the ILO to propose a new Convention on protection of employees' claims in case of employer bankruptcy (ILO 1991). It was adopted by ILO member states in 1992.

15 Central and Eastern Europe

Jacques Monat

At present, it is very difficult to provide an overview of the general situation and the main issues regarding participation in Central and Eastern Europe. In most of these countries forms of participation which, under the old regimes either really did exist or did so only in name have almost entirely collapsed. In a region crippled by an enormous foreign debt, privatisation and the market economy are the key words and various forms of popular financial participation are now being tested. Although such pilot schemes are a priority, their introduction has been slower than expected in some countries. There are fears that investments are being made by the former nomenclatura or even by organised crime groups.

There is a diversity of trade unions and employer organisations in these countries. But union membership is obviously lower than in the past. This phenomenon is accentuated by fear of unemployment and disinterest in trade union membership. The image of trade unions is now tarnished as a result of previous links with the ruling Communist parties.

The prevailing situation is marked by enormous differences between countries because of the general state of flux throughout the region. This is particularly true in the Republics of the former Soviet Union, despite their frequent contacts with international organisations and non-governmental groups including foreign trade unions and their confederations.

The former German Democratic Republic and Hungary both have a much clearer policy than most other countries, the former due to its merger with the Federal Republic of Germany and the latter as a result of the Hungarian parliament's adoption of a new Labour Code which stipulates the introduction of work councils in all companies above a certain size. There was some initial reluctance on the part of trade unions to lend support to the Labour Code since one of its provisions guarantees non-union members the right to be elected to work councils. There is a lurking fear in trade union circles that these work councils have been established partly in order to by-pass trade unions. This fear is also felt in other countries of the region where there are plans to introduce works councils.

Collective bargaining

For the time being collective bargaining is still the most important form of participation. Despite the constraints of inflation and unemployment it is being extended beyond its traditional company level and now covers a wider range of issues.

A tripartite national conciliation body has been set up in Bulgaria and in Hungary. These bodies represent an important forum for participation at the national level in economic and social issues such as collective bargaining and the fight against inflation. They have gone through difficult times and opinions differ as to the potential role they could play.

Today Poland presents a more difficult economic and social picture. Here Solidarnosc, minority splinter organisations and the former trade union confederation, bearing a new name and having shed its past ideological connotations, all remain active. Indeed strikes have taken place. Inflation and unemployment are high. In spite of some privatisation and joint ventures, (statistics indicate that Hungary has attracted the most foreign investment in the region), state enterprises remain the backbone of the economy together with a recent explosion of micro-enterprises in the informal sector of the economy. This phenomenon is widespread throughout Central and Eastern Europe.

However, changes in the legal status of state enterprises as a result of privatisation will have consequences on participation in management. In Poland this was previously the domain of the workers councils, introduced following the spontaneous 1956 workers' protest movement. Legislation to recognise the councils was quickly introduced in the same year but a law introduced two years later reduced their powers.

Polish legislation on participation adopted in the early 1980s proved difficult to implement because of government measures against Solidarnosc. According to various observers outside trade union circles (politicians, lawyers, economists, sociologists and members of the general public), it was felt that workers councils tended to merge their interests with those of trade union representatives and plant managers.

Poland is the only country in the region with a tradition of industry-wide bargaining. In addition to collective bargaining, which deals with an increasing number of issues and at different levels, but tries to avoid inflation, it is felt that there is an increasing need for new forms of participation that will perhaps be in line with the participatory practices of foreign investors. These new forms of participation include the revival of shop-floor participation which had previously offered one of the rare opportunities for genuine worker participation. Efforts to improve competitiveness, guarantee job security, better terms of employment and a work environment mean tackling major issues such as productivity, quality standards, environmental protection and industrial restructuring.

To a certain extent and in spite of the tensions created by the political division of the country, the Czech and Slovak Republics are, in relative terms, enjoying a better social and economic climate. The trade union movement was until recently far less fragmented than elsewhere. However today neo-liberalism or ultra--capitalism are the declared policies of the governments and industrial restructuring seems inevitable in certain areas of Moravia and Slovakia. For this reason tripartite participation at regional or at meso-level may be particularly appropriate.

In Bulgaria the two major trade union confederations (and a recent off-shoot from Podkrepa) are all active. They are faced with high inflation and rising unemployment in a country which has great economic potential in the tourist industry and agriculture. The Bulgarian government has recently been insisting on a policy of tripartite participation at national level particularly in its fight against inflation. The country also has to cope with serious environmental problems.

The situation in Albania remains very unclear.

To a large extent the situation in Romania is also in a state of flux similar to the description outlined above. Elections did not bring about any major changes. Prior to 1989 Romania was a country with a declared policy of self-management but Ceaucescu's megalomania meant that this principle was virtually never put into practice.

In 1991 a tripartite commission was set up in the Commonwealth of Independent States at national level and new legislation on collective bargaining was introduced. Despite differences in each Republic, it was the Soviet model, dating from 1917 which influenced the entire region. The Soviet model was based on the concept of one trade union and the one-party system, the trade union being seen as the "transmission belt" of the party while society in general was held to be free of any major conflicts of interest.

Worker participation as a counterpart

In principle worker participation was intended to be the counterpart of collective ownership of the means of production. In reality it remained largely superficial in the absence of essential prerequisites such as reliable information, openness etc. According to a survey of 5000 workers and middle managers in Hungary, published in the first issue of *"Allam és Jogtudomány"* in Budapest in 1975 most of those questioned felt it was pointless expressing an opinion on, for example, a draft collective agreement which had practically no influence on wages. They maintained that their comments would never been considered.

Throughout Central and Eastern Europe job security used to be guaranteed for everyone except for "political dissidents". The region was burdened by low wages, a generally low standard of living despite economic planning and heavily subsidised industries. The economy was thus marked by unrealistically low prices, low productivity, poor product quality and occasional shortages.

The entire system mainly survived because of the atmosphere of fear and suspicion which reigned. This atmosphere was cultivated by the party and the State security apparatus. Even workers' protests (in East Germany in 1953, Hungary in 1956, Czechoslovakia in 1968, Poland in 1956, 1970 and 1980) produced no lasting changes. Society was ridden with bureaucracy, bribery was rife, "secondary economies" such as homed-based production (gardening, poultry-raising, etc.) flourished and passive submission reigned everywhere. At one trade union congress Brezhnev even complained about pilfering by workers in State enterprises. Trade union officers concentrated on welfare activities such as providing rest homes and holiday camps, ensuring labour inspection (which also fell within their domain) and the running of social security services. The introduction of new technology was mostly limited to the aerospace industry which was making remarkable strides. The arts, music, theatre and sports also thrived.

From 1968 onwards, especially in Hungary where strict economic planning was abandoned, tentative efforts were made to introduce economic reforms to increase motivation amongst workers and raise productivity. These reforms were based on a limited concept of profit. Hungary also attempted to replace some worker representatives nominated by the official trade union with elected shop-stewards while pilot schemes were introduced in which managers were elected by the employees. These new policies were also adopted in Bulgaria and the Soviet Union. They had been introduced much earlier in Yugoslavia.

In the former Yugoslavia, some experiments in worker self'-management were carried out during the Second World War in liberated areas. But these experiments only gained real momentum when Tito broke with the Stalinist model and found himself faced with a crippling trade blockade. After numerous experiments in self-management the system was finally enshrined in a 1950 law. Later it underwent many reforms. Based on the concept of "social ownership" in which the means of production belonged to everyone in general and no one in particular, the key elements were an elected worker council, the election of enterprise managers, the distribution of income amongst "associated labour" (or workers) and some redistribution of income from the more successful enterprises among less successful ones. The latter group included the public utilities and the national railways. Bankruptcy was virtually unknown. With the exception of craftsmen, farmers and some family businesses in, for example, the hotel and catering industry, the system spread throughout the country and included the service sector, adapting itself to the political situation despite persistent interference by the party (the League of Communists). Tito deliberately chose an intensive development policy based on new technology. The unemployed were able to leave the country at that time as migrant workers. In order to increase the influence of rank-and-file workers, workforce general assemblies and referendums were increasingly introduced along with "self-management" agreements between work units and what were known as "social compacts" at regional level.

After Tito's death, tension between the various components of the Yugoslav Confederation became increasingly acute. The turnover of political leaders throughout the political strata and their limited terms in office made it difficult to develop an all-encompassing economic policy at macro-level, such as an appropriate monetary policy. In the wake of the oil crises this was a time when such policies were urgently needed. Self-management of work units had become so decentralised that rapid price adjustments contributed to pushing up inflation even faster. It was at this point that privatisation began to be introduced and the importance of workers (employees) councils diminished correspondingly. Fixed basic wages with equal pay for equal skills have since been introduced along with repeated wage freezes. Bonuses such as profit-sharing appear to have remained while "renationalisation" has occurred in some areas, particularly in Croatia, with managers being appointed by political authorities. Nevertheless at present the prevailing situation in most of former Yugoslavia (with the exception Slovenia), does not allow an evluation of any forms of participation.

Generally speaking worker share ownership is spreading throughout Central and Eastern Europe in one form or another either through the introduction of vouchers, foundations or investment funds, free or preferential share distribution and privatisation (see, Chapter 14)

An analysis of the impact of financial participation on decision-making, motivation and productivity would be an interesting topic of research. Equally useful would be comparative studies, such as on buy-outs and employee stock-option, or share ownership plans and a look at measures to discourage "hostile take-overs" in the financial sector.

In recent years there seems to have been a trend, even amongst trade unions, to rely on the competence and sympathy of managers conscious of workers' interests in the short, medium and long-term. Specific case studies are badly needed particularly during this period of transition when the countries of Central and Eastern Europe are moving towards market economies. The inefficiency of the previous system and the collapse of some trade relations within the dissolved COMECON or CEMA may well necessitate considerable restructuring. Trade unions and worker participation may prove helpful in finding a middle road between the excessive collectivism of the past and the excessive individualism of the present. In this way a new set of ethics and new values may develop and workers may win significant decision-making powers through financial participation and the introduction of a stabilising employment policy.

16 Beyond Europe

Gérard Kester

It takes considerable nerve to attempt to encapsulate in a few pages the trends and developments in what is still called the Third World (over 100 countries), the industrialised countries in the East (especially Japan) and the West (USA and Canada). The section on Africa will be a bit more extensive than those on other areas as (too) little seems to be known on the rapid changes in this continent.

Asia

With the exception of Japan, Asia has never been a breeding ground for major experiments in effective worker participation. In China, worker participation primarily was and remains a political ploy. India has been nurturing worker participation for almost fifty years, initially inspired by Mahatma Ghandi's concept of trusteeship but killed by a stranglehold of tripartism: statutory forms of worker participation had to result from consensus between the government, trade unions and employers. There is no better recipe for maintaining the status quo. There are a number of far reaching experiments in participation which give important powers and sometimes ownership to workers (e.g. in cooperatives) but these cases remain relatively few and are not expected to reach a critical mass.

Japan constitutes a category of its own in Asia. Labour relations in the country have evolved from "managerial family-ism" to a cooperative pattern and then to an incentive pattern. (Ishikawa, 1988). Trade unions had a major role to play in these developments, moving management away from paternalism and into a partnership with labour. To a great extent Japanese labour unions, organised within companies, are company-based and can be regarded as a representative body of all non-managerial employees in a company, somewhat like the works councils in other countries. The majority of Japanese unions are inclined to solve labour-related issues, with the exception of wages and bonus negotiations, through joint consultation. Judging by statistics it would seem that these negotiations and consultations have become increasingly effective. Industrial disputes have dropped from more than 10,000 in 1974 to less than 2,000 in 1987. But within the trade unions, apathy has increased among members, especially the young, and union density dropped from 34% in 1975 to 26% in 1989 (Ishikawa and Széll, 1992).

The tradition of lifelong employment and its concomitant system of super/subordination by seniority disintegrated as rapid technological changes were introduced in Japan, prompting management to introduce measures to mobilise workers - introducing direct participation among the rank-and-file by means of small shop-floor group activities such as quality circles, shop-floor meetings, suggestion schemes and the like. These ideas spread very widely (80% in large companies) and included such varied issues as business strategy, production management, human relations and human resource development. More recently, however, there has been a trend towards integrating these small group activities into company-wide, total quality control management and placing more emphasis on individual reward systems (Ishikawa and Széll, 1992).

Notwithstanding these recent trends, quality circles and similar schemes are today common in many Asian countries and elsewhere.

The United States, Canada and Australia

Unlike Western Europe, the interest in worker participation appears to be a more recent phenomenon in the U.S., Canada and Australia. But ".....by contrast with Europe, participation in the U.S. is prominently a shop-floor phenomenon ..... primarily introduced by management and with the aim of raising productivity."(Strauss, G, 1992:898). The other forms of participation: joint committees, membership on boards of directors, profit sharing, buy-outs and employee shareholding "remain fascinating exceptions (much studied by academics) rather than the mainstream" (ibid.: 899).

Also the ESOP's which extend to over 10 million American workers, have not (yet) given much rise to worker democracy, not even in ESOP's with a majority employee ownership (D.C. Jones and C. Rock, 1992:972). One major reason for the low interest in forms of participation which gives effective access to power is the reluctance of trade unions to put participation on the agenda - as it also sees participation as a threat to their own powers. There are signs that the trade unions view is undergoing change in that it is believed by an interesting number of union activists that worker participation is a union empowering model (A. Banks and J. Metzgar, 1989:33-38).

Also in Canada profit sharing plans and employee share ownership have greater prospects than empowerment but as one author says, the present wave of privatisation could offer the opportunity to link financial participation and participation in decision making. "The benefits of financial participation to employees and employer are likely to occur and to be sustained in an environment in which there is a meaningful worker participation in decision making and

190

employees have access to all relevant information about the enterprise" (H.C. Jain, 1992:97)

In contrast to the U.S. and Canada, the trade union movement has played a leading role in the development of workers participation in Australia, in the 1970[s] and the 1980[s]. Even to the extent of countering employer strategies that sought to de-link worker participation from trade union action. The trade union movement was supported in these policies by the Labour Party. By the end of the 1980[s] worker participation at the place of work but also at higher levels of (government) administration was developing with great promise but the recent recession and the privatisation drive seem to have brought the movement to a halt (Encel, 1992:35-39)

Latin America

Latin America has a much stronger record of worker participation and took a lead in the 1970s when Allende nationalised the copper industry in Chile and Valesco set in motion a diversified participation and self-management strategy in Peru. These experiments did not survive but they left behind a large group of intellectuals and others familiar with the practice who later applied their own solutions. The result has been that even in regions where worker participation is no longer a guiding principle of industrial relations a relatively strong movement of self-managed cooperatives has developed, inspired by the success of the Mondragon cooperative.

Africa

Perhaps the most puzzling situation is to be found in Africa. Here too, a number of national leaders introduced worker participation as a strategy for development. Examples include Nasser in Egypt, Kaunda in Zambia, Nyerere in Tanzania and Boumedienne in Algeria. These strategies did not succeed. Among the external factors for their failure was the fact that unequal terms of economic exchange between the Third World and industrialised countries did not leave enough economic room for manoeuvre, while political independence did not imply economic independence. Furthermore, problems of implementation were totally underestimated. But most importantly, democratically-won power corrupted those in power. There was a drift from utopia to dogma, from dogma to slogans, slogans to repression, repression to dictatorship and often from dictatorship to military regimes. The deterioration of participation echoed this spiral moving from economic and social liberation to manipulation and from manipulation to exploitation.

Today Africa is undergoing a double facelift. There are "structural adjustments" - privatisation, liberalisation, a shrinking of the public sector - and at the same time, an upsurge of political democracy. Development and democracy must go hand in hand. The introduction of multi-party democracy alone will not suffice. It must be coupled with participatory democracy - in the best of Africa's traditions. But today Africa can boast no charismatic leaders to champion participation. Ownership flows into (foreign) private hands, in many cases the hands of multi-nationals but also frequently into the hands of smaller (colonial) entrepreneurs who can buy property at throwaway prices.

Yet in Africa reactions to the phenomena such as those experienced in Eastern Europe have been different. Participation is not being dismissed with the old generation of leaders, ideologies or systems. Rather it is being used as a guiding principle with which to tackle externally-imposed measures for economic recovery. In this context the most vocal protest was the Conference for Popular Participation held in Arusha in 1990 which brought together hundreds of angry young men and women from throughout Africa, protesting against the ruthlessness of the structural adjustment programmes. Leaders of pan-African organisations and institutions drew up a charter based on the principles of national African leaders who, several decades earlier, had formulated a strategy for participatory development. In the charter participation is seen as an alternative strategy. The charter does not accept the dependent position of workers and citizens in the structure of production and society. Human dignity is its cornerstone.

To get out of the vicious circle of slogans and dogma, the charter must be developed and concrete measures must be drawn up to put its noble principles into practice. In a survey study in Guinea it was found that the majority of trade union representatives favoured participation as the main form of trade union action. Their reasons for supporting participation were virtually identical in all sectors of the economy. For 97% of them participation was seen as a necessary part of socio-economic development at national, provincial and local level and union representatives believed that lack of consultation in the past was one of the main reasons for the present failure of the development programmes. They resented the lack of formal or regular frameworks to enable worker representatives to participative in development. They believed that they could contribute enormously since workers were the artisans of development and without them human resource development, as they were very much aware, made little sense. Moreover they maintained that they would be far more motivated in playing a role in implementing development decisions if they were involved in making them (Diallo a.o., 1992).

Similar studies are underway in a number of African countries (e.g. Mali, Tanzania, Zimbabwe, and Ghana) and interim results suggest a confirmation of the Guinea findings.

In the past few years it has become clear that trade unions in Africa will play a much more important role than they have done in the past and this will have important consequences on union policy options, especially their policies on the development of participation.

In the past African trade unions have had little room for manoeuvre. Either they were more or less integrated into one-party systems or they were marginalised. There was no democratic framework in virtually any country but many unions nevertheless preserved their own internal democracy. It has been estimated that when Africa was mainly a collection of one-party states and military regimes, there were some one million democratically-elected trade union or worker representatives throughout the continent.

It has become clear that this trade union tradition has paid dividends. Today we see that trade unions are playing an important role in the process of political democratisation in Africa. The most obvious example is in Zambia where the national trade union federation was the main instigator in the founding of a political opposition party. The trade union leader successfully contested Kaunda in presidential elections in October 1991. In Tanzania the national trade union federation split from the country's sole political party in August 1991. In Mali the national trade union federation held an extraordinary council in 1990 to condemn the country's one-party system and demand political democracy. Eventually in March 1991 the union was instrumental in the downfall of Moussa Traoré. In the virtual anarchy that followed the trade union federation became the pillar of national reorganisation and the secretary general of the national trade union federation was invited to take up the post of vice-president of the country in the transitional government.

Trade unions do, in the eyes of the people, constitute a more reliable backbone structure than many other organisations, certainly more than the discredited armies, corrupt government bureaucracies and now banned former political parties. Thus calls for trade unions to play a leading role in the process of democratisation are increasing. Trade unions are writing a new page in history.

Work-place democracy must not become a Western European privilege

Privatisation constitutes an overhaul of ownership structures in Eastern Europe and the Third World. The State or public sector may eventually become a minority sector. It is already clear that when a nationalised company is privatised participation is shelved along with all the other legacies of nationalised companies. This process is remorseless. In a case study in Guinea it was found that when workers wanted to be consulted on a number of matters of importance to them the owners of the newly-privatised companies reacted coldly, saying "the time for babble is over, get back to work" (Kester, 1991). In the same case study a list was established of the various phenomena that always seem to accompany structural adjustment programmes:

- inflation
- unemployment
- job insecurity
- loss of training opportunities

- lack of protection
- dis-empowerment
- attempts to weaken trade unions
- limitation of labour relations to wage problems only
- increased seasonal labour
- deregulation
- arbitrary dismissals
- reduced emancipation (especially for women)
- alienation
- pure exploitation
- privileges for the few
- marginalisation of the many
- recolonisation!

What should the response of workers and unions be? As far as the new employers of privatised companies are concerned, private companies need to make a fresh start with capitalism and the odds are against those who might put forward any counter-proposals. Governments try to catch the capitalist flies with large doses of liberal honey and they are all too aware that legal forms of worker participation will send potential investors running to a neighbouring country.

What is more, participation in profits and ownership is an increasingly appealing strategy. It appeals to people's consumerist expectations of capitalism. All forms of worker participation based on labour are rapidly disappearing. Trade unions in a number of former one-party countries or military regimes are going to have to be initiated into the art of collective bargaining and other forms of industrial action, never having practised such activities in nationalised or State companies. In those areas where bargaining does already exist it must be expanded to keep up with the growing private sector. Employers in private or para-statal companies will encourage this form of negotiation as it focuses exclusively on wage contract issues. Conversely they may reduce the sphere of worker influence and reintroduce full and exclusive managerial prerogatives in all other matters regarding production and distribution. This new bargaining role for trade unions will absorb all their energy and any loopholes that exist will be fully exploited to prepare trade unions and workers for taking part in the capital game.

It is very possible that once the privatisation storm is over workers will have to start from scratch their struggle to gain influence in areas of decision-making beyond the limited sphere afforded by bargaining. Workplace democracy may become a Western European privilege.

But can this be allowed to happen? Should we not inform, consult, debate with, convince and assist workers and their representatives in not surrendering to capital but fighting to transform what were manipulative or ineffective forms of participation in the former public sector, into improved forms of influence? Should we not assist in defending a set of general principles regarding the basic human right to take part in decisions affecting oneself, rather than permitting the "participation striptease"? Will worker participation become the exclusive right of Western European workers? If this is the case will it not weaken the lines of defence of participation? Clearly, injecting new enthusiasm into trade unions' stances on worker participation in Western Europe is not only of importance to Europe but is of great importance to the rest of the world as well. A lukewarm reaction to worker participation, especially on the part of trade unions, will only have an adverse effect and will be reflected in the priorities drawn up by international trade union organisations and international trade union cooperation projects.

Part III
TRADE UNION - UNIVERSITY COOPERATION ON DEMOCRATIC PARTICIPATION

Introduction to Part III

Edward Zammit

Worker participation may be viewed as the natural extension of the process of democratisation from the political arena to that of industrial relations. Trade unions, as naturally democratic institutions, have a vested interest in promoting worker participation. But as the process of democratisation continues to threaten to usurp the long-established powers bases in society, it will inevitably be challenged. These challenges may be direct and very explicit or subtle and virtually undetected. As a result, the process of democratisation requires constant support at every stage.

In order to ensure the steady development of democratisation, a systematic programme of both research and education is required. Effective functioning of existing institutions of worker participation at various levels demands constant research and implementation of research results. This is the only way in which structures designed for participation can hope to remain relevant as conditions change. Information on and evaluation of experiences in other countries is also important and should help in drawing practical conclusions for the continued growth of participation both in general and in specific company situations. Such monitoring would be an important stimulus to participation.

Undoubtedly, the most important criterion for effective participation is direct involvement of workers and their representatives in the decision-making processes in the workplace and beyond. This is especially important at crucial moments in a company's development. Appreciation of the level of worker involvement at various levels is only possible by means of periodic research. In order for workers to participate effectively, they need the ability and means to influence decision-making and to play an effective role in guiding, evaluating and controlling the decision-making process, thereby ensuring that their own interests are defended. This is only possible through on-going training and education. Here, I refer, of course, to "*transformative*" adult education as distinct from "*traditional*" conservative education which often only serves to perpetuate the existing balance of power. (Freire, 1972). To ensure that these difficult tasks are achieved the help

199

of independent but committed researchers and educators is needed. Yet in most countries of Western Europe the modest level of cooperation which developed between trade unions and universities until the 1970s has since then suffered serious set-backs.

General observations

Traditionally, universities are regarded as places where knowledge is pursued for its own sake or as the point of entry to a specific profession. Universities have generally tended to reflect the dominant social trends of their time. In the current, conservative social climate of the 1990s, it is accountants, business managers and engineers who dominate the academic scene, rubbing shoulders with lawyers and doctors rather than trade unionists.

Indeed in many countries trade unionists have been consistently losing what limited access to higher education they had in previous decades. The current shortage of funds and waning interest in trade union matters amongst universities is now being felt acutely in many countries. Universities are fast becoming simple training grounds for professionals. As a result, research in and teaching of sociology, economics, psychology and other human sciences at universities is today almost exclusively at the disposal of the managerial professions.

As Einemann puts it, "the study of industrial management is oriented only towards a mono-economic rationality and not towards a social rationality as a result of which, the requirements and problems of the worker are not sufficiently catered for in the development of technologies." In his view, the current "scientification" of society has by-passed the unions. It is no comfort to trade unionists to be told that in this way they may remain faithful to their humble, working-class origins. Their limited access to universities may be perceived simply as another symptom of their social marginalisation.

For the trade unions, however, there are many benefits to be gained from closer association with universities. Access to university facilities by trade unions may include professional training in the specific skills necessary for carrying out trade union functions and administration. A knowledge of economics, for example, is required for effective collective bargaining. It may be argued that many of the skills required by successful business executives are the same as those required by trade unions. The latter, therefore, may benefit from university teaching just as much as businessmen. (ILO, 1974:11-13)

Moreover, university teaching is closely linked to on-going research in the specific areas being taught. Profound changes currently taking place in industry require research from a trade union perspective. These changes include new forms of work organisation, the introduction of new forms of technology such as computers, lean production, part-time contracts, deregulation, rising unemployment, relocation, increasing evasiveness of capital ownership structures and related problems of power and accountability. These changes are linked to changes in society such as increasing individualism, loyalism, and a polarisation of the employed and the unemployed. Of particular importance are the problems of young people, women, migrants, racial discrimination and environmental pollution. An adequate trade union response to such fundamental challenges from industry and society can only be offered with the help of independent research carried out by experts. Research oriented to the needs and interests of trade unions not only helps to train and re-train the key players in trade unions, it also raises fundamental questions and provides some possible answers about the changing role of trade unions and their future. Such trade union-related research at universities and other research establishments can enable a better understanding of the processes which lead to the growth of various forms of democratic expression.

In addition, when scientific research and teaching of trade union-related subjects takes place in universities, it helps raise the level of awareness when discussion of such issues takes place at national level, thereby indirectly contributing to the general acceptance of and well-being of the trade unions.

Closer cooperation with trade unions can also be of benefit to the universities themselves. A new organisational perspective is introduced into the analysis of social, economic and political problems and a new list of research priorities is established. When science is pursued from the perspective of the workers in industry, it concentrates on the social processes of change rather than on preserving the status quo. The natural channels through which such change can be achieved are the institutions representing the workers, in other words, trade unions. Consequently, union officials collaborate with "*action researchers*" and consultants in much the same way as management does.

Worker-oriented research may be carried out in various fields ranging from medical-ecological problems to political, economic and social problems. "The stimuli provided by trade unions for scientific activity are particularly important for the university's own development, e.g. for setting up a Management Environment Technology Centre" (EC/661/EN/987). In this way, scientific research can become more socially relevant to real-life problems. Furthermore, research cooperation with unions on matters regarding democratic processes and worker participation may indirectly provide an incentive for universities to render their own institutions more democratic. If participation can help raise worker productivity in companies by unleashing the full human potential, it may also help universities attain their educational and research goals more effectively.

The value of collaboration between universities and trade unions has been acknowledged in most countries of Western Europe in recent years. A number of sporadic attempts have been made since the 1960s by individual academics to obtain state funding for research into trade union related matters. In 1987, an international conference on this subject was held in Brussels, organised by the EU Commission. This stimulated widespread interest in the subject (EC/661/EN/1987). Subsequently, national conferences have been held in most European countries under the auspices of the Commission and these have generally extolled the virtues of such cooperation (Chouraqui, 1991; Coster, 1990; Szell,

1992).

It was felt that among the main areas of research cooperation, the following in particular should be included:

- the introduction of new technology
- problems of health and safety in the workplace
- environmental issues
- job market policies
- industrial relations
- worker-oriented regional and structural development policies

In all the EC national conferences held, the principle of cooperation and the mutual benefits derived from it were reaffirmed. The need to consolidate and expand existing levels of cooperation was generally recognised. Cooperation between universities and trade unions is now considered as more urgent than ever because collective bargaining has gone beyond traditional areas of concern and unions are assuming greater social responsibilities.

Research and education

One main issue which recurred in several of the national conferences of the EU Commission was that cooperation should not simply be limited to research but should also include education and the production of educational materials. This was underlined in the first conference to follow the Brussels conference, held at the University of Aalborg in Denmark in 1987. There, it was noted that cooperation should include (1) provision for constant reciprocal information (2) the "translation" of information, making knowledge accessible not only to those who understand it but also to the people working at grass-roots level. This "educational" cooperation was necessary because of linguistic differences between researchers and trade unions.

Similarly, at the Manchester and Glasgow Conferences in 1990 it was felt that an important way of improving links between trade unions and research centres was through improving the means by which existing research was disseminated. Education is thus considered as instrumental in maximising the fruits of research. In addition, the establishment of an international network for the exchange of information on joint research has been recommended.

Furthermore, it was pointed out at the conferences that trade union-related research and education are normally interlinked because (a) the roles of researchers and educators are mutually supportive (b) the methodology of collaborative research has developed from trade union education methodology and (c) both are committed to strengthening democracy within trade unions and throughout society in general.

Nevertheless, it ought to be stressed that to a great extent the good intentions

202

expressed at the various conferences of the EU Commission have not yet been translated into action. This is particularly true as far as cooperative research and education for workers and participation at national level is concerned. Precious little has been done in these fields. Indeed in most countries what little progress there has been is mainly the result of local initiatives on the part of individual unions and universities. Scandinavian countries and especially Germany seem to be the only exceptions.

The following are some of the main problems cited which hinder cooperation in research between universities and trade unions in most countries:

- the lack of union resources to fund research. Most State funded research at universities is being channelled into industry
- the continuing, traditional gulf which exists between workers and academics
- a lack of union willingness, under present economic and political circumstances, to accept researchers as competent and objective partners
- the numerous political and institutional obstacles which prevent unions from participating in company exchange of information
- a lack of national policies which would encourage the development of cooperation research.

General interpretation

In this section, a general interpretation and classification of research cooperation now underway will be proposed. The different forms of university-trade union research collaboration are:

Spontaneous academic research by staff and students

Individual academics and postgraduate students interested in carrying out research into trade unions and related matters do exist. Very often, the results of their research are published in scientific journals where they may help to advance the authors' careers. However, because of the language used, such publications are of little practical value to trade unions. The same applies to the work of postgraduate students who may choose such topics for their dissertations or theses.

Nowadays many more students choose subjects related to human resource management. Such subjects are perceived as offering better employment opportunities. Nevertheless, the recent political upheaval in Eastern Europe has attracted the attention of a number of scholars and students and subsequent studies of these events may be particularly useful for those countries.

Union-commissioned or union-employed researchers

Most large unions have their own research departments which employ researchers.

They sometimes commission universities or outside research institutions to carry out research on their behalf. Usually the unions are only interested in specific, ad hoc research which will aid their national officers when engaged in collective bargaining.

Otherwise unions regard commissioned, scientific research as too theoretical and generalised and of little practical relevance to them. As a result, trade unions display little interest in such projects.

Collaborative research

This refers to institutional collaboration on research projects between trade unions and universities (or other scientific institutions) which is the main focus of this paper.

There are several criteria for interpreting this kind of collaboration. These include:

(a) the *level* at which such collaboration takes place. This may be the mega-international level, the macro-national level or the micro-local, union-company level. Ideally, all three levels should be interrelated via institutional networks.

(b) the *intensity* of collaboration. It may vary from being of a very high degree, indicating an equal 50:50 partnership between university and trade union participants, to an unbalanced allocation of tasks, resources and decision-making powers. Given the different backgrounds and preoccupations of the two parties, the relationship may become unevenly matched and personalised. For this reason, a strong educational background is required by the participants and their mutual involvement in trade union education is one of the main conditions for effective collaboration

(c) the *quality* of the collaboration. This may also depend on the problems or subjects being investigated. These may be classified depending on how they are perceived by the trade unions as being related to the workers' interests. Thus, research into technical production may be related to its effects on the workers' wage levels, job security, health and safety, quality of work, employment of women, promotion prospects, environmental issues, etc.
It should be emphasised that the topics of worker participation and trade union education, apart from their individual merit as research subjects, also crop up among all other topics being investigated. Very often successful examples of collaborative research are those done by bodies also involved in workers' and trade union education and the methodology of collaborative research develops from trade union education methodology.

204

The prevailing situation in Europe

A brief look at the prevailing situation in Europe shows that existing funds for collaborative trade union-university research and education projects are less than adequate. In most countries, public funding is being drastically reduced or re-channelled for other purposes. Admittedly, some countries do have other sources apart from State funding, such as institutions or foundations which provide limited funds for such projects. There are also tripartite research institutions where the influence of trade unions can be felt. However, most research efforts currently being made are on issues of economic production and technological change. Today, if participation is considered at all, it is likely to be viewed in terms of its contribution to productivity.

In Italy, for instance, collaborative research has became very important since the 1970s due to the strong influence of the trade unions in left-wing cultural institutions. Such research was made possible thanks to the establishment of research institutes, corporations or cooperatives in which trade unions were represented on the top management councils. In addition, each trade union confederation has its own study centres both at national and local level. Funding for these projects usually comes from the National Research Council (CNR) or from ministerial allocations to universities. At present there is a proposal to centralise existing facilities without, however, destroying their autonomy. The subject of participation in Italy is also sparking considerable interest with regard to its effect on productivity (Guarriello, 1992).

In Germany and Sweden, the system of co-determination has been the subject of extensive research for many decades (Eiger, 1994). Much of the research is carried out by academics working in cooperation with trade unions.

These activities are supported by an extensive programme of trade union education which started more than 100 years ago and was revived and expanded after the Second World War (Eiger, 1994). At the same time other educational organisations for workers were founded in collaboration with the unions, for instance in Dortmund and Hamburg. The unions also founded their own educational organisations with educational centres scattered throughout Germany. It is estimated that within a three-year period, the average works councillor and shop steward has been enrolled in at least four weeks of training (Eiger, 1996:36). Many of these educational and research activities are sponsored by foundations such as the Hans-Böckler or the Friedrich-Ebert Foundations which share the same ideological aims as the trade unions.

In the 1970s several cooperation contracts were signed between several German universities (Frankfurt, Bremen and Dortmund) and the DGB. As a result, some major social science research programmes were launched with federal and/or state (*Land*) funding.

These developments have been hampered by the problems encountered in the move towards closer European integration and the problems of German unification. There are many in Europe who are against any moves towards co-

205

determination and some are keen to relegate unions to the sidelines. In Germany, the problems of unification turned out to be much greater than originally imagined. Unification has now been given national priority by the present government and cooperation with the unions has been side-lined. Significantly, the privatisation of the economy of the former German Democratic Republic is being carried out without any union participation (Kissler, 1989).

German unions have only been able to continue their educational and research activities because of their formidable strength and resources. These have been preserved through foresight on the part of the unions which, over the years, have invested heavily in education and research and have maintained an unwavering commitment to co-determination.

Likewise in Sweden, as Sandberg has noted, there are in the nineties *'few or no national change oriented programmes with an exclusive wage earner and union orientation'* though there are several such examples of regional projects which are usually union sponsored (Sandberg, 1994:5-7; Eiger, 1994:40) This situation is in sharp contrast with the one prevailing in the 1970's. As a result of such policies the Swedish Centre for Working Life has been transformed into a 'pure' research institute and its budget severely cut (Sandberg, 1994).

Perhaps the most interesting aspect of the Swedish experience which ought to be mentioned here concerns the extensive use of *'study circles'* for trade union education purposes and *'research circles'* for collaborative research.

Their basic format is based on the concept of participatory learning (or research) without the traditional teacher. Instead one member of a group of five to fifteen participants acts as circle leader who also participates on the same terms as the other participants. It is reported that about one and a half million Swedes participate in over 200,000 study circles each year, regular weekly meetings of two to four hour sessions, for several weeks (Eiger, 1994:43; Sandberg, 1994:8-9)

Until the early 1980s, the French government, through its ministries, was practically the only source of research funding. This meant great financial independence for researchers but at the same time helped to create an ideological defiance amongst them towards the influence of the social actors. As a result, cooperation between research centres and trade unions (and employers) was infrequent and unstructured. A number of economic and legal studies had been carried out but there were very few sociological studies dealing with trade union matters. The traditional weakness of trade unions and the power of companies demanded political intervention. After the election of the Socialist party in 1981, the Ministry for Research tried to encourage closer collaboration with the social partners. An economic and social research institute (IRES) was created which was financed by the government and run by representatives of the French trade unions. After the Auroux laws were passed - an attempt at an in-depth restructuring of social relations in France, the Ministry of Labour and the Ministry for Research launched several evaluation research programmes, some of which were run jointly with trade unions. But, after a short flurry of research between 1983-85 the subject of worker participation was rapidly abandoned by the government, the employers, the trade unions and most social scientists. Meanwhile, the number of studies on human resource management has been rapidly growing. This subject has attracted considerable funding from both the employers and the State.

In 1989 a major conference on cooperation between trade unions and research institutions was organised in Paris (Couraqui, 1991), by the Laboratoire d'Economie et de Sociologie du Travail (LEST), a branch of the Centre National de la Recherche Scientifique, under the auspices of the Ministry for Research and Technology. This conference was one of the first in a series following the EC initiative of 1987. It was attended by representatives of the main trade unions and other local and foreign experts. Three main points were emphasised in the conference, (1) identifying the shortcomings within cooperation between researchers and trade unions, (2) the need to urge researchers and trade unions to work more closely together, (3) ensuring that national and regional European authorities create the necessary conditions under which such cooperation could flourish. (cf Chouraqui, (ed), 1991). The organisers of the conference emphasised the need for an interdisciplinary approach to research in industrial relations, the need for active research to involve the various parties and the need to analyse the underlying social and economic complexities from an international and, most importantly, from a European perspective. Nevertheless, few of these initiatives were ever put into practice. Today, with the exception of the long-term PAROLES research programme (see below) on direct worker participation, and a handful of studies in private companies, the subject seems to have again lost its appeal and there is little financial support from the scientific community, employers or the government. Indicative of the current state of affairs is the fact that since the termination of PIRTTEM (the French acronym for "Interdisciplinary Programme of Research on Work, Technology, Employment and Lifestyle") in 1992, no other comparable research programme has been launched in its place to continue the ten-year work of the programme organised under the auspices of the Centre National des Recherches Scientifiques.

There are a number of institutions promoting research cooperation between universities and trade unions at European level. The EU Commission has supported a number of initiatives, including the FAST programme in which, since 1987, an assessment of technological change has been carried out on behalf of the unions. Another such institution is the EC European Centre for the Improvement of Living and Working Conditions, in Dublin, Ireland. This centre has carried out extensive surveys in the member states of the EC on matters such as worker and union participation in the introduction of new technology (European Foundation, 1990) and, more recently, on health and safety in the workplace. (Paoli, 1992). Contributions from the European Trade Union Institute to research on union matters has been noted above. This research is often carried out in collaboration with academics.

At a wider, international level, the International Institute of Labour Studies, operating under the auspices of the ILO in Geneva, has made a significant contribution towards research into cooperation. Since the mid-1980s one of the institute's projects has been the "New Industrial Organisation and Labour Institutions". Amongst other things, it has identified a model for small firm development which is most typically found in the industrial regions of northern Italy. The success of this model is due not only to business acumen, but also to the highly developed system of cooperation which exists amongst the companies, active State involvement and, significantly, to the participation of a highly-trained workforce - itself the result of an all-encompassing and effective model of trade unionism (Monat et al, 1992).

There are, of course, several other interesting and instructive examples of research and educational collaboration between trade unions and universities at both international and at national level which should be mentioned. These include Sweden's *"Arbetsliv Centrum"*, which has been mentioned above, Norway's "Work Life Centre", Holland's "Science Shops" and the "small-scale, locally initiated research collaboration by individual unions and universities" in the United Kingdom which are reportedly on the increase despite the government's generally hostile attitude and restrictive legislation (see the respective chapters in Part III).

In spite of all these examples it must be said that in general there has been a significant drop in collaborative research and education, particularly regarding worker participation. Where this has not been the case, as in Germany, the reasons are generally to be found in a reliance on local and grass-roots support rather than national funding or international institutions Almost everywhere, the present, main preoccupations are economic, technological and traditional management issues. There is an increasing trend in universities to turn to human resource management and away from traditional subjects such as labour relations, trade unionism and worker participation. Clearly this trend may have long-term consequences for democratic participation at all levels, as future generations of university graduates are taught in academic circles in which labour is merely viewed from the perspective of capital. Universities and research institutions have a duty to reverse this trend and restore the balance.

For this reason, in the next sections of Part III, the focus will be on three successful experiments in collaboration which have been instituted in various countries with the explicit aim of promoting worker participation. These three, very different cases have been selected in order to illustrate the varied conditions under which trade union-university collaboration can actually flourish. Cooperation between trade unions and universities in Germany, Sweden, Italy, the United Kingdom and the Netherlands will be dealt with in more detail in the following chapters.

17 The PAROLES programme

Henri Pinaud

Until the early 1980s French research into human sciences and society, conducted by universities and the National Centre for Scientific Research (CNRS) was overseen by the State, which financed such research.

This does not mean that there were, previously, no direct links between research institutions and trade unions. But these links were simply varied and informal channels of communication which manifested themselves in seminars and clubs and generated very unstructured relations which evolved according to the needs and interests of the academics or the unions. Thus, a very unfocused network of associations developed to allow communication and exchange between the two groups.

It was only after 1982 that the CNRS officially encouraged its researchers to try and directly respond to the needs of society and that various ministries provided funding for cooperation projects between researchers and universities and the social partners. It should be noted that every time a Conservative majority has taken power since then (in 1986 and in 1993), there has been a marked drop in government support (usually financial), for academic-trade union cooperation. Sometimes we have even witnessed the dismantling of state bodies which manage cooperation projects.

In 1984 the CFDT was the first French trade union organisation to sign an agreement on scientific cooperation with the CNRS. The agreement signed by both parties was to last five years and gave rise to the PAROLES programme (Programme for Analysis, Research and Observation of the Freedom of Expression of Workers). Its aim was to introduce the right to free expression for workers on the basis of trade union experience.

A research committee was set up comprising researchers from three CNRS sections, permanent CFDT representatives from the confederation and four federations. This committee was authorised to draw up and carry out the programme. A scientific follow-up committee was established by the CNRS and constantly kept informed of progress on the research programme. Finance for the project mostly came from public funds, i.e. the Labour and Research Ministries and the CNRS.

PAROLES and the results that it produced made it possible to verify the feasibility of, and define the necessary conditions for a successful joint research programme between academics and one of the social partners. It also made it possible to verify numerous hypotheses regarding the implementation of the right to expression.

A number of conditions necessary for the effective and realistic execution of joint-research were identified. These are:

- a strong commitment on both sides at every stage of research (in the case of PAROLES, five years, including 27 one-day meetings of the research committee which brought together researchers and federal and confederal union representatives in charge of research)
- a strict definition of the roles of the academics and the trade unionists
- opportunities for the trade unionists to make practical use of the results
- a relatively long period of research to enable the participants to get to know each other and define rules to guide their work
- uninterrupted funding over a period of years
- the need for scientific legitimacy for the programme by means of a CNRS-CFDT agreement

The research produced a data-base on 4,300 agreements regarding the implementation of the right to expression. More than 50 research meetings were held, bringing together confederate and federal union representatives and some 100 union activists from companies in all sectors of industry. These meetings proved to be extremely productive.

Around 70 articles were published in the press organs of the CFDT and a brochure and a special issue of *"CFDT Aujourd'hui"* were also published. CFDT national study days on the right to expression were held in April 1986. Trade unionists and academics working on the PAROLES programme took part in over 60 meetings, seminars and trade union events in France and abroad.

The academics working on the programme published over 20 articles in scientific journals and organised an international conference at the International Labour Office in Geneva. The proceedings of this conference were published in 1991. The academics also took part in nearly 20 national and international scientific meetings. It was largely as a result of the PAROLES programme that the "Trade Union- Academic Research Cooperation" seminar was held in Paris in 1989.

At the end of the 1989 evaluation meeting which examined the running and effectiveness of the PAROLES programme, the scientific follow-up committee noted that "...the presence of trade unionists on the research committee, with their natural preoccupation with action, did not prevent the academics from defining specific scientific objectives. It did make the academics more sensitive to the specific nature of the project - the expression of a right, the application of a policy and the intervention of social actors and new social actors. The presence of the trade unionists helped the academics formulate matters in terms of social action and the management of relations in an organisation..."

The committee went on to note that "...as was hoped, the joint running of the programme contributed to its practical value, in other words to its social application. There were also some unexpected results. The fact that the researchers were responding to a specific trade union request rather than a more general social request (such as from a government ministry) forced them to be far more precise and succinct in their research. The very fact that a research request had been made stimulated research and generated the warm reception that its results received. Another more paradoxical consequence was that the significance of the research topic and the close union involvement stimulated a lasting interest in a policy for the right of expression on the part of the CFDT, which the mood of the day and circumstances at that time might otherwise have stifled. The very existence of a research programme on the right to expression helped solidify the policy and protect it during the changeable atmosphere of the day."

On February 6, 1991 a second cooperation agreement lasting a further five years was signed by the CFDT and the CNRS. This was the beginning of PAROLES 2. Its aim was to examine the links between direct democracy, union action and modernisation in private companies and the public sector.

This new programme consists of eight separate research projects. Seven of them involve CFDT federations from both the public and private sectors (agriculture and the food industry, the mining and metalworking industries, the chemical industry the energy industries, the legal sector, health and social services and the Confederate Union of Senior Executive Employees (*Union Conféderale des Cadres*) and an equal number of CNRS or university researcher teams. The eighth is a research project which cuts across the seven others and examines three main themes - the links between direct democracy and union influence, the links between democracy and organisational efficiency and academic and trade union interest in joint research. Each project is jointly directed by academics and trade unionists in the form of a "federal" research committee. A coordination committee, made up of all those involved in the programme, is responsible for ensuring cohesion in the entire programme. The eight projects, which were jointly formulated, were put before a new scientific follow-up committee for approval. This committee, nominated by the CNRS, regularly evaluated the work undertaken. In addition to publications (e.g. 2 special issues of "*CFDT Aujourd'hui*" N° 108, March 1993 and N° 114, June 1995), seminars and training sessions specific to each project, the results of the eighth cross-sectional project will, it is hoped, be the subject of a major academic-trade union colloquium held in June 1995. There are plans to publish the results in book form the same year.

Joint research is the fruit of the labours of many people at many levels. All those involved may have different objectives which can at any one time either be convergent or contradictory. After five years coordinating the first PAROLES programme and five more launching and coordinating PAROLES 2, it is possible to try and identify some general principles for joint research, to help optimise these projects.

17 principles have been drawn up under four headings.

The intended aims

Ideally, such cooperation should take the form of action-research with three aims: (1) research, (2) education and training and (3) help in union policy formulation. Achieving these aims is a cumulative process of constant inter-action.

General organisational principles

(4) A centralised firm willingness and commitment is required by all involved, given the numerous variables at play and different partners involved - unions, universities, public or private financial sponsors - all of them institutions among whom jointly-managed cooperation is neither easily organised pursued over a longer period of time.

(5) post of scientific and union coordinator in necessary. This post may be filled by someone whom Crozier and Friedberg describe in the following manner "an actor involved in several inter-related systems of activity who can, as a result, play the indispensable role of intermediary and interpreter of the different and sometimes contradictory actions of the parties involved."

(6) The running of a joint research programme must be supervised by a centralised, but participative, joint body. Differences between unionists and academics risk splintering the project while an authoritarian centralisation could provoke rejection and abandonment of the project. A form of institutionalisation is also necessary. But given that those involved need to be encouraged rather than dominated, the structure that is set up must be flexible and participative in nature. It will only be able to function satisfactorily and permanently in an atmosphere of mutual trust.

(7) The organisational structure must reflect the diverse responsibilities of trade unions and academics: the prime contractor(s), the architect(s), the coordinator(s) and foreman/men must have clearly defined roles, and their functions in the structures well defined.

(8) The partners involved in the project must preserve their autonomy and the principle of the researcher's freedom, in particular, must be respected. The roles and goals of the academics and the trade unionists must be clearly

212

defined and each person involved must assume responsibility for the results obtained. Cooperation must be an on-going mutual learning and reciprocal education process.

(9) Independent bodies should be set up to carry out periodic evaluations of the project. Their function will be to apply both scientific and union criteria to the cooperation process and its results. These bodies will play an important role in legitimising the cooperation both inside union and academic circles. They should also provide a permanent source of enrichment for the project.

Implementation principles

(10) Overseeing the drawing up of joint research programmes is just as important as implementation. The attention paid to planning union-academic cooperation projects can influence the success of implementation, the quality of both the academic and social results and the use to which the results are put by all involved. Such attention is also vital in recognising that the union partner is both a generator of knowledge and a virtual social researcher. For these reasons, each stage of a research project should be thoroughly discussed and agreed upon by the trade unionists and the academics:
- scientific and union hypotheses must be formulated
- methodology naturally depends on what the project's aims are but nevertheless, the methodology should be clearly presented, explained and discussed by trade unionists and academics
- implementation of research should be regularly discussed by both parties
- the manner in which the research results are compiled and disseminated should be specified by common accord.

Thus the principle of union-academic research and its implications should be clearly laid out, discussed and agreed upon in the form of a moral and formal contract before research begins.

(11) Naturally the researchers must strictly adhere to the rules of scientific objectivity, avoid jeopardising union interests or getting involved in internal union rivalries or disputes. If these particular conditions are respected, trade union-academic research may develop on a lasting, long-term basis.

(12) Helping unions evaluate their policies means that throughout the project, joint evaluation committees and various union decision-making bodies at different levels (confederal, federal, activist level, rank-and-file member level) should be informed about progress and be able to discuss the project with the researchers. These discussions are of great value not only for the research itself but also for the formulation of union policies.

213

(13) Research techniques linked to pedagogic aims and to helping unions formulate their policies must be established by the researchers and the unionists prior to the take-off of the project.

(14) The results of joint research should be made available to employees, unionists and the general public, presented in a form understood by everyone perhaps using a variety of media. This means that pedagogical experts must be involved in the project at the earliest stages. Furthermore, the ways in which the results are to be made available should be discussed during the cooperation project.

Links with outside institutions

(15) Traditional attitudes in research centres and universities do not encourage cooperation with the social partners, especially trade unions. For this reason it is unlikely that any academics who might be involved in such projects might use such a project to advance their academic careers. Nevertheless it is important that they maintain their links with the academic world.

(16) Given the present state of industrial relations, it seems likely that most funding of any joint research between universities and trade unions will come from the State or supra-national public bodies, although company-funding should not be completely excluded. Such funding will be dependent on political changes. Financing and detailed budgeting for every stage of a joint-research project should therefore be carefully examined by the academics and the unionists.

(17) By increasing such forms of research and joint-cooperation, links between trade unions and academic circles will grow and strengthen. Only by encouraging more and more concrete schemes in joint-cooperation between the academic world and trade unions the chances of moving on beyond this initial and innovative stage to tackle social practice cannot but grow.

18 The African Workers' Participation Development Programme (APADEP)

Gérard Kester

APADEP is a programme of education and research activities in the sphere of worker participation, run in a framework of cooperation between trade union organisations and universities. The programme started in 1982 and is expected to become a permanent feature.

The launching of the programme was something of a coincidence. In the 1970s, participation was introduced in Africa (as in many other parts of the Third World) at the initiative of governments and political leaders attempting to transform newly-independent societies into Socialist, Communist or Humanist societies or at the very least trying to create a framework for industrial relations in large-scale public enterprises. In most countries trade unions were specifically left out, marginalised or at best merely tolerated when participation policies were being formulated and implemented. Trade unions started to seek access to participation by means of a variety of strategies. They sought to foster participation for workers, to alter it, to widen its application and even to fight against it in some cases. But whatever their strategy, they wanted to get a grip on the phenomenon. Information, education and training were badly needed and at Pan-African trade union platforms the Organisation of African Trade Union Unity (OATUU) was called upon to try and meet this need.

Throughout this same period the Institute of Social Studies (ISS), based in the Hague, had been working together with universities in many developing countries on educational, research and consultancy projects. These projects were being carried out in countries which had drawn up important participation policies such as Sri Lanka, under the Banderanayke government, India, Turkey (under Ecevit), Malta, Zambia, Tanzania, Peru and Chile (under Allende). The overall results of the institute's work were evaluated in 1981 and it was concluded that it had been a fundamental mistake to offer support essentially to political leaders, governments and their bureaucracies and to have kept the results of the work within the confines of the academic community. It was felt that active and sustained trade union involvement in the development of worker participation was vital for success. That had certainly not been the case!

When OATUU requested assistance in 1981 it received a positive response from the ISS in the form of academic support while the Federation of Dutch Trade Unions (FNV) offered financial assistance. A draft programme was submitted to a pan-African conference of trade union leaders in Nairobi in 1982. APADEP was born. The overall aim of the project was to increase and improve union and worker participation. The project was to assess possibilities, establish priorities and examine concrete mechanisms as well as assisting trade unions in formulating and implementing their own participation policies, taking into account the interests of the workers and society in general.

APADEP has become a far more extensive programme than was originally foreseen. The initial approach was, in retrospect, inadequate. "National programmes" were conducted in a number of countries including Cape Verde, Senegal, Guinea-Bissau, Mali, Guinea-Conakry, Togo, Zambia, Tanzania, Zimbabwe and Mauritius. These programmes lasted for about a month and included a policy seminar for trade union leaders, an instructors' course for trade union instructors and occasionally a modest research project and a public forum to discuss the participation policies of the country concerned. The idea was that afterwards the trade unions would organise seminars and other educational activities on their own and that institutionalised relationships would develop between universities and trade unions to conduct labour-related research. In some countries this happened to a certain extent. In most countries it did not.

The next step was logical. The follow-up became a component of the programme. This was first attempted in Guinea-Conakry which eventually became a reference for other countries in the programme. Over a period of three years, 50 seminars were conducted all over the country including the remotest areas. At this stage, research and seminars were rolled into one. The underlying idea was that the seminars should be a two-way process - participants receiving information and knowledge but providing feed-back in the form of their personal experiences, ideas, wishes, etc. A questionnaire was drawn up and conducted. The resulting data produced a wealth of information. This included data on trade union structures, the economic, social, cultural and political position of the union representatives, participation practices, social norms and values as regards participation, the extent to which workers were willing to work actively to promote participation, what policies were wanted and workers' expectations regarding union action. The results could represent important base-line information for trade union policy-making.

Stepping up research efforts in APADEP

The as yet limited research (the Guinea questionnaire and a few isolated case studies) and the results of the seminars, workshops and round-tables clearly illustrated that the trade unions had failed to respond adequately to the challenge that participation represented. The trade unions had been found lacking in terms of policy, education and support.

Trade union leadership often lacked sufficient information and ability to plan any important role in policy formulation. As a result, they were unable to challenge sometimes manipulative legislation or regulations that help shape participation. At the grass-roots level, elected worker representatives have been acutely aware of the shortcomings in education. There is a strong desire for more education and training. Representatives have often bitterly complained about the fact that they lacked time, a meeting place, secretarial help, means of communication and other facilities which might help them develop effective participation. They had expected the union to fight for such things.

The first phase of APADEP, from 1982 to 1987, was evaluated by the participants and by two independent, external evaluators. It was unanimously agreed that the programme should be continued. The value of integrated research, policy-making, education, training, publication and consultancy work was seen as particularly beneficial for local trade union representatives. As the programme continues, in the form of a number of bilateral projects, and eventually, a second five-year project, ending in 1996, the main aim of the initial programme will be maintained - strengthening African trade unions and helping them win effective and meaningful participation. The chief method remains education. Education for union leaders, workers, instructors and grass-roots representatives. The main focus of educational efforts will be on grass-roots representatives. Pan-African coverage will be maintained and the programme will continue in English-speaking, French-speaking and Portuguese-speaking countries.

There will also be greater emphasis on two other objectives. The production of educational material and teaching aids and the development of research. As far as the educational objectives are concerned, the aim is to train teams of instructors and senior instructors, mainly trade unionists, who will be able to encourage, conduct and monitor education programmes on worker participation in their own country at union leadership level and, most importantly, at the grass-roots level, amongst worker representatives in companies. As a result, the publication of manuals, text-books and audio-visual aids for worker and trade union education will be encouraged and, as a spin-off, texts for university education.

The research objectives are to provide empirical information to the African trade union movement on the conditions necessary for the development of effective and meaningful participation by workers and trade union representatives. Such participation should aim to (a) improve the quality of union participation policies (b) provide realistic and useful data and input for trade union action on participation (c) provide trade union educational material based on African experiences and (d) train teams of researchers in a select number of African countries to conduct quantitative and qualitative research to support union policy and action. An off-shoot of this goal would be the production of research manuals dealing specifically with low-budget research.

Education and research aims are intrinsically related. They both seek to mobilise and improve the professionalism of those working in education and research on worker participation, trade unionism and industrial relations within universities and trade union organisations. They also both seek to institutionalise trade union-university cooperation.

Thus the research efforts have become an important pillar of education and policy-making activities. In the coming four years it is hoped that a total of some 8000 questionnaires may be answered and some 60 to 70 case studies conducted in ten different African countries. On the educational side, 4,500 people have so far taken part in seminars and workshops. 20,000 people are expected to directly benefit from APADEP in the coming four years through "participation circles". A far greater number is expected to benefit indirectly as educational materials are gradually made available on an increasingly wide scale.

Trade union-university cooperation in APADEP

APADEP has become an arena for cooperation between trade union officials (mainly tutors) and university researchers. This cooperation has always been regarded as team-work and it was hoped that as much of the work as possible would be shared, with researchers teaching and trade union teachers conducting research. This was made easier by the fact that many APADEP activities were and still are combined education-research activities. The most important project activities are the grass-roots representatives seminars which consists of lectures and group work but at the same time and in combination with these, questionnaires are administrated and interviews held. It is up to each team (there are at present ten teams in ten countries) to decide on the allocation of tasks and roles. The only pre-agreed condition is that the trade union education coordinator be responsible for content and quality of education, and the research coordinator for the content and quality of the research. Once these responsibilities are defined, the teams are free to organise themselves according to their specific abilities and qualities, as these become apparent. Until now this has proved a viable course of action.

The informal nature of trade union-university cooperation does not mean that it is without problems or conflict. Tensions develop regarding the objectives, criteria, materials and interests of the two parties. These tensions arise from the fact that they come from different professional backgrounds and are trained and informed differently. It also can be traced back to inherent role conflicts in such teams which belong to different sub-cultures. Nevertheless, it has been considered best to formalise things as little as possible, instead encouraging a free process of institutionalisation, by ensuring frequent international exchange amongst the different teams.

This kind of exchange and interaction is encouraged by annual six-week international workshops in which team members participate. The workshops help participants to elaborate theories and methodology for both education and research and real-life application. The workshops are held in a different African country every year. These six weeks of intense cooperation, constant interaction between educational and research activities, the inevitable emergence of each participant's particular strengths and the exchange of experiences between different teams, have proven to be extremely important in forging a team spirit, flexibility and acceptance of others' abilities.

In addition to their importance in terms of group dynamics, these international workshops also serve as a platform for developing a common methodology and a set of agreed research techniques. The presence of trade unionists is of obvious importance since the trade union point of view is represented at every stage of the research process.

In future, the frequency of these international workshops will be increased. Each year there will be one six-week international education/research workshop, two four-week research workshops and one eight-week writing workshop. At the latter a team of trade unionists and researchers write educational materials such as guides and manuals, based on their research results.

19 The workers' participation development centre (Malta)

Edward Zammit

The Workers' Participation Development Centre (Malta) (WPDC) operates as an institute for labour and industrial relations studies at the University of Malta - concentrating on the long-term goal of promoting the development of worker participation. It operates under the general direction of a board made up of representatives of the university, the two main trade unions, the major participative companies and public agencies. It provides a source of documentation and information on the subject and keeps abreast with international developments. The need for an independent, research and support service for the further development of worker participation was recognised as a result of a collaborative research project which evaluated the first decade of worker participation in Malta. Early efforts to promote participation had been inspired "from above" and made in an irregular, arbitrary manner (Kester 1980). In order to make this diffuse task more effective, systematic and politically independent, the values and skills necessary for the implementation of participation have to be mastered by those involved at all levels.

The main activities of the Centre are the following:

(i)   Educational activities which encourage the development of participation in the workplace and in society at large

(ii) Scientific research on labour relations and particularly on issues concerning participatory development locally and abroad

(iii) Consultancy and other services related to participative issues

(iv) Dissemination of information through the publication of books, journals, articles, etc., as well as through other forms of mass communication.

In pursuance of these aims, the Centre also establishes networks among the social actors to provide information and support.

The Centre's workers' educational programme includes the following:

1. Two series of short courses entitled *"Participation at Work and in Society"* and *"Women Participation and Development"*

2. A three-year part-time course leading to a university Diploma in Labour Studies which is aimed at workers and trade unionists involved in participative industrial relations and other forms of representation.

3. Tripartite, weekend, residential seminars aimed at trade union leaders and dealing with a variety of subjects including:

Collective Bargaining - Problems and Prospects
Labour, Technology and Participation
Labour, Trade Unions and the Informal Economy
Labour and the Tourist Industry
Trade Union Education for Worker Participation
Occupational Health and Safety
Inter-Union Relations
Human Resource Management: The Challenge to Trade Unions

4. Regional trade union education. Joint educational programmes are organised involving trade unionists from neighbouring countries.

5. A cooperative development programme. As one important form of implementing worker participation, the Centre is involved in educational and research projects in collaboration with the Central Board of Cooperatives. These activities are particularly aimed at the promotion of worker cooperatives.

6. Media programmes on local radio and television aimed at familiarising the general public with the concept and issues surrounding worker participation.

One of the major challenges for the WPDC is to reach workers and help them develop their understanding of participation. This helps them to develop new roles and to work to set up new structures - thus contributing to the success of their own company. The workers' individual understanding of and attitudes towards participation need to be accompanied by new relations with fellow workers and with managers at all the various levels in companies.

In this way workers are encouraged to feel increasingly that they are in control of their lives and to understand all the responsibilities that these new self-perceptions entail. They need to acquire the ability to articulate their problems and ensure that their proposals are implemented.

This is also an "educational process" which involves not only workers but also worker representatives and trade-union officials, at various levels, in interactive relationships.

Evaluation

The impact of the WPDC on the local scene can be assessed in terms of funds, facilities and personnel. The Centre has managed to make its presence felt through its various diverse initiatives. This much, at least, can be deduced from the opinions expressed by those who have participated in the educational activities.

Qualitatively, the WPDC has been a local pioneer in the field of trade union and worker education. The prolonged educational experience of the Diploma in Labour Studies course has been a process of developing and perfecting participative teaching styles which respect and tap the wide experiences of adult participants. The resulting classroom pedagogy is more interactive and stresses dialogue far more than normal classroom situations. Discussion is a main priority.

Quantitatively, the WPDC makes frequent use of television, radio, the press and its own diverse publications to get its message across. Together with its educational courses, these have helped the Centre to come into contact with thousands of Maltese from various walks of life and with scores of foreign participants. Of those who have participated in the Centre's educational activities, there is now a core group of participants who have gained influential positions in political, educational and trade union circles, imbued with the participative ethic and equipped with some of the skills necessary for effective implementation. This general atmosphere also appears to offer many possibilities and challenges for new participative initiatives in the workplace and in society at large.

20 Cooperation between trade unions and academic institutions in the Federal Republic of Germany

György Széll

In West Germany trade unions have enjoyed a relatively long history of cooperation with universities and research institutions. This is partly due to the fact that a large number of the unions' founding-fathers and guiding spirits were intellectuals, as far back as Karl Marx and Friedrich Engels and later, Friedrich Lasalle, Rosa Luxemburg, Eduard Bernstein and others. Thus it is not surprising that research and learning have been one of the main pursuits of German trade unions from their earliest days.

The *Volkshochschulen* (VHS or people's universities) were founded more than 100 years ago in regions were Social Democrats enjoyed a majority and provided most of the funding. After the First World War, the *Akademie der Arbeit* (Labour Academy) was founded in Frankfurt to train trade union leaders and officials. Many leading academics of the day taught there.

Following the end of the Second World War, the *Akademie der Arbeit* was re-established, along with the *Sozialakademie* (Social Academy) in Dortmund, at the very heart of the industrial Ruhr region. At the same time the *Sozialforschungsstelle* (Social Research Institute) was set up and a review entitled *Sozialwelt* (Social World) was launched, dealing with subjects of interest to the Hamburg-based *Hochschule für Wirtschaft und Politik* (HWP, the University of Economics and Politics).

These three institutions offer study programmes in social sciences. Courses at the *Akademie der Arbeit* last one year, those at the *Sozialakademie* two years and studies at the *Hochschule fiir Wirtschaft und Politik,* four years, having previously lasted three years.

Since 1945, and following British examples, in particular in the British-occupied zone of Germany, extra-mural studies were introduced to the working classes on a large scale in cooperation with the VHS. This was, of course, part of the overall re-education programme but was also a tribute to German social resistance to fascism. The programmes included preparatory classes for special university

225

entrance exams, designed for those who did not have a general certificate of education. A large number of later union leaders attended these programmes and, as a result, gained scientific or academic training and qualifications.

During the post-war years the German DGB unions set up two scientific foundations which merged more than ten years ago into the *Hans Bückler Stiftung* (Hans Bückler Foundation). Funding for the foundation comes partly from the directorship fees of the DGB representatives within the supervisory councils, which exist in the German system of co-determination, and partly from government sources. The Hans Bückler Foundation awards grants to some 2,000 students, provides assistance, organises conferences and symposiums and funds research. Its activities are for the most part on a national scale. The programme is supported by some 220 *Vertrauensdozenten* - lecturers who supervise contact and cooperation and who have previously been fellows of the foundation. They publish a very influential monthly review *"Die Mitbestimmung"* (Co-determination), as well as several series of books and pamphlets. Their headquarters are in Düsseldorf where the DGB is also based.

Other foundations also work in similar fields. The *Friedrich Ebert Stiftung,* a foundation close to the SPD, also supports unionists and union activities. Their activities are on a much more international scale. Although the *Konrad Adenauer Stiftung* is close to the CDU it also has a strong workers' organisation, known as the CDA (Christian Democratic Social Committee). The German Minister for Employment and Social Affairs, Christian Democrat Norbert Blom, a former CDA-president and IGM member, benefited from this social promotion programme and earned his Ph.D thanks to a grant from the foundation.

It should be noted here that in the wake of Germany's experience with fascism, the country's trade union movement learned an important lesson. Namely that past union divisions were partly to blame for the victory of fascism in 1933. As a result, after the Second World War the German trade unions decided to unite into one large confederation, based on the principle of "one enterprise means one union". Thus while SPD members dominate the DGB, the CDU still enjoys a strong and protected minority position and indeed one of the vice-chairmen is traditionally a CDU member.

Other political foundations, such as the *Hans Seidel Stiftung* close to the Bavarian CSU, the *Friedrich Naumnan Stiftung* close to the FDP and the *Buntstift*, the Green Party Foundation, play less prominent roles in relations between trade unions and universities and research institutions. The Catholic and Protestant churches, however, and especially their academic foundations, are often sympathetic to union concerns.

The most important academic organisation in this context is the *Wirtschafts- und Sozialwissenschaftliches Institut* (WSI-Institute for Economic and Social Sciences). It was founded in 1955 by Victor Agartz, who was later accused of Communist conspiracy, excluded from the institute and banned from the DGB. Some 60 academics work at the institute today which is located in the DGB headquarters in Düsseldorf. They publish an excellent monthly review entitled *"WSI-Mitteilungen"* (WSI Reports) as well as a series of books.

After the war the unions also founded their own educational organisation, *Arbeit und Leben* (Labour and Life) at *Länder* or state level. With the exception of the VHS, it is the biggest educational organisation in the FRG.

In addition to these institutions, there also exists a large number of DGB educational centres (around 60 in all) throughout the country. These mostly offer training courses of up to three weeks for members and honorary officials, while also conducting independent research.

Each member of a works council or personnel council has the right to educational leave of up to three weeks a year and this period of leave rises to four weeks for those who have been elected to the councils for the first time. A general education leave of an average of five days a year is granted in all states governed by the Social Democrats. This right will soon be extended throughout the country in accordance with the ILO Convention 140. Unions also offer courses to council members in their institutions.

Paragraph 36 (3) of the Works Constitution Act stipulates that works councils may seek advice and consultation from outside experts which must be paid for by the company. As a result, a network of consultancy offices, both inside and outside the university system, has mushroomed all over the country since the 1970s. Several hundred academics are now active in this field.

In the 1960s the student movement gave birth to a new wave of enthusiasm in Germany. Many academics joined the DGB and became active advisers and counsellors to the organisation.

In 1973, the German Minister for Research and Technology, Hans Matthoffer, a former IGM official, launched the research programme *Humanisierung des Arbeitslebens* (Humanisation of Work Life). Financed with an annual DM100 million, it is today the most important social research programme in Germany and probably the world. The guidelines stipulate parity between the social partners, i.e. between the employers and the unions, in terms of selection and evaluation committees. The works council must approve all projects within the framework of the programme and can also itself apply for funding.

Following the Social Democrats' defeat in federal government elections in 1982, the programme became increasingly technocratic. In order to compensate for this trend, the government of North-Rhine Westphalia (the biggest of the German states with some 17 million inhabitants) launched a new programme entitled "Socially-Acceptable Technology Design".

In 1974 the federal parliament formed a technology assessment commission for the benefit of the IGM - the largest single union in the world, with some 3.5 million members. The commission was called the Commission for Economic and Social Change and as a result some 160 projects were implemented. However, the final report of the commission was not accepted by union representatives and they published their own minority report.

Since 1973 the Ruhr-Universitat in Bochum has developed cooperative links with the nearby IGM Sprockhövel educational centre.

In 1976 a pilot scheme, funded by the German Ministry for Research and Technology, was launched to develop *Kooperationsstellen* (cooperation offices) between the unions and five universities (Oldenburg, Dortmund, Kassel and Tübingen). With the exception of the Tubingen office which was closed by the Conservative state government when federal funding ceased, all the other offices continue to function through state funding. Later an office at the Berlin Technical University was added.

Another similar project is the *Technologie- und Innovationsberatungsstellen* (Technology and Innovation Consultancy Agencies) set up in 1973 by the IGM, initially in Hamburg and Berlin but which have since spread throughout the country, albeit under DGB control.

The city-state of Bremen and the Saarland are both special cases which have a long Social-Democratic tradition. Here, workers chambers and employee chambers have existed since the Second World War. These chambers also undertake scientific research. In Bremen, the founding of the University of Bremen in 1970 resulted in the establishment of a cooperation office between the workers chamber and the university, in which some 30 academics worked. It was recently transformed into the Bremen Academy of Labour.

Since many institutions in Germany are run on a tripartite or parity basis and have their own research centres, the influence of the unions is far greater than was ever previously envisaged. For example, the *Budesansalt für Arbeit* (Federal Employment Agency) has a huge research institute - the *Institut für Arbeit und Beruf* (the Institute for Labour and Professions), based in Nürnberg which employs 100 academics. Other large social security institutions have similar institutes at their disposal. It was for this reason that under the Social-Liberal governments of the 1970s, employers spoke of Germany as a *Gewerkschaftsstaat* (a trade union State). Certainly is was true that a corporatist or neo-corporatist situation existed in Germany until the mid-1970s. But then capital interests cancelled these agreements and re-established a capital-dominated policy, especially in the spheres of economics and social affairs. One of the most blatant indications of this is the fact that following German reunification in 1989, the *Treuhand*, the largest "trust" in the world, set up to supervise the privatisation of the East German economy, was established and operated without any union participation whatsoever.

21 Relations between trade unions and academic institutions in Italy

Fausta Guarriello

Cooperation between trade unions and academic institutions in Italy is very widespread. It can be traced back to the post-war years and the rebirth of free trade unionism. Since then it has grown with support from the diverse ideological leanings in Italian trade unionism (Catholic, Communist or Socialist), each defining its own cultural projects. Cooperation between trade unions and academic establishments grew in importance during the 1970s, reflecting the increasingly powerful influence of trade unions in cultural spheres.

It should not be forgotten that during this time, the condition of Italian industrial relations prompted calls for research in areas such as health, work safety, improvements in the work environment, new products, processing technology and bio-technology. Thus requests for research came from the trade unions themselves seeking to improve the work environment and to become involved in work organisation. It was at this time that the Italian Society for Health in Labour and Industry launched participatory research into the work environment. Their research analysed "four types of harmful factors" and examined the "reproductive health of women". In 1974, at the initiative of the three confederations, the Centre for Research and Documentation of Work Risks and Injuries was set up and the review "Workers' Medicine" was launched.

Close cooperation between trade unions and academic establishments such as universities or research institutes grew when legislation was introduced giving workers the right to "150 hours of training" as specified in collective agreements.

Today, the involvement of intellectuals in the cultural development of trade unions takes place in Italy via numerous research institutes (study centres and foundations) run by academics (lecturers and researchers). This form of involvement or participation is fairly widespread and for the most part concerns sociological, economic and legal domains. These institutions exist either in the form of foundations, public companies or cooperatives. But whatever their form, high-ranking representatives of trade union confederations or federations normally sit on the board and provide support for the core programmes run by the research centre. As a result, each confederation has its own foundations and study centres at both national and regional or local level.

Those centres which are legally recognised as foundations receive government funding and accept private donations. The others are financed by the research that they carry out (for public or private clients), the conferences and seminars that they organise, training (mostly for unions and financed by the unions, local authorities or the EU) and the publication of books and periodicals.

There is a dialectical relationship between these institutions and the trade unions, based on an often high level of reciprocal autonomy, as scientific authority is guaranteed by the university or academic rank of its members. The activities of these centres include research projects in which the trade unions obviously have an interest. Research results are published either by trade union publishers, made available through commercial or scientific channels, or published in essay form in trade union or specialised reviews. A few examples spring to mind such as the 1975 research programme led by T. Treu to measure the extent to which the Workers' Statute (*Statuto dei lavoratori*) had been implemented. Another is the 1988 research undertaking led by B. Veneziani into industrial relations in partially State-owned companies following the IRI protocol. G. Cella's research in 1987 into worker participation in industry is another example.

Research projects are often financed by the CNR (National Research Centre) or funded by ministry funds allocated to academic projects. An example is the CNR's important, strategic project for the 1990s, carried out by a group of universities (Milan and Brodolini) and foundations (Seveso in Milan and the Brodolini Foundation in Rome). The former has ties to the CISL and the latter to the CGIL. The project is examining trends in industrial relations and employment in the coming decade.

The research work of the Economic and Social Council should also be noted. This council includes representatives of social partners who drew up the draft laws on economic and social affairs. Recently the council has undertaken research into conciliation in the wake of the 1991 law on individual redundancies. The large number of study centres sympathetic to trade union organisations has resulted in a fragmentation of research projects which are now totally independent of each other. The only exceptions are a handful of joint, inter-organisational projects (such as historical research into trade union presence in parliament, carried out by IRES (Institute for Economic and Social Research), and CESOS (Centre for Social and Trade Union Research). At its last congress in Rimini, the CGIL, hoping for renewed, *concerted* action, proposed the unification of trade union study centres. This proposition was not well received by the CISL which views autonomous, cultural developments in different trade union centres as fundamentally important.

The trend today in the relationship between trade unions and academic and research establishments is generally speaking similar to that of the past, but a few differences should be mentioned.

Firstly, purely university-based research still favours subjects relating to trade unions, work and participation. Universities regard such subjects as specialist topics for economists, labour sociologists, legal specialists, industrial relations experts and so on. As a result, these subjects are taught at university and are often the subject of student theses. Public or private funding for research in these areas has suffered because of the priority generally given to pure sciences rather than the social sciences. This is a consequence of a drastic drop in public funding for research, itself the result of budget cuts. It also stems from a trend towards funding innovative projects rather than those which deal with traditional subjects. Innovation is often regarded as pertinent to what is happening in Europe or other industrialised countries (such as the United States or Japan) and as a result, priority often goes to international comparative studies which, it is hoped, will provide solutions to domestic problems. As a result of these cuts in public funding academics are increasingly turning to other sources of funding such as the European Union (cf. for example, the research led by B. Veneziani on work flexibility in Europe, jointly funded by the EU and the partly State-owned Trade Union Association of Oil Companies).

As far as union commissioned academic research and jointly run or jointly managed research projects are concerned, unions are obviously keen to be directly involved in the conception of the project, discussion of the results and the final assessment. A recent example of research into participation is the work done by the Institute for Economic and Social Research on the implementation of an agreement by metalworking unions at Fiat in Melfi. Here a new department is to be set up and a large number of young unemployed with bleak job prospects are to be employed. The management agreement calls for strong union participation in decisions concerning work organisation, hours, wages (initially reduced in comparison to traditional wage levels) and shift-work, especially for women.

A large number of sectoral trade unions approach research centres to commission research on the process of institutionalisation in companies, with a view to forming European works councils with rights to information and consultation, as specified in the December 1991 EU Commission directive. Initial work, including meetings amongst worker representatives from the various European establishments of one international company, has over the last two years been financed by money from the European Parliament and overseen by the Commission. In Italy one successful example is the food manufacturing group Ferrero. The CISL sectoral federation commissioned a preparatory study from Sindnova, the CISL's labour institute. Then followed a more detailed conference, organised by Sindnova which brought together academic specialists in the subject and trade unionists from the CISL's national adult training college in Florence. A book was published by the CISL publishing house entitled "European Works Councils - Worker Participation in Trans-National Companies". The book was sold at the CISL congress. There are dozens of such examples, all with varying degrees of success for the trade unions and for the academics. It would seem that the positive aspects of successful union commissioned or jointly run research are the active involvement that trade unions benefit from in developing and running the project and the respect earned for scientific studies and the independence of the academics. As far as the academics themselves are concerned, there is a very real interest in the stakes and challenges facing unions and the appeal of serious and rigorous scientific work. Often, when one of these elements is lacking, there is a visible sense of discontent on both sides, as for example when the research is well done but either insufficiently applied or not used at all, or when research is poorly paid, badly done or lacks union interest.

One new feature on the landscape in Italy has been the creation in February 1993 of a European Institute for Social Studies, set up by the CGIL, the CISL and the UIL to examine both scientifically and from a union point of view various aspects of European economic, institutional and industrial integration. The interesting thing about this institute is that it is a unified institute comprising the three confederations and that it attempts to draw on the work of certain academic groups (the institute's Scientific Committee is made up only of university professors) to examine and study those areas of economic, social and institutional life affected by European unification and to provide relevant information and training programmes for trade unions.

22 Trade union-university relations in the Netherlands from committed cooperation to contract research

Peter Leisink

Developments in Dutch society have been parallelled in the scope and form of trade union - university cooperation. With the upsurge of critical expression of opinion at the end of the 1960s, many students took an interest in trade unions issues, including worker participation which was very topical at the time.

By the end of the 1980s, however, human resource management was the issue which interested many students whereas trade union policies on worker participation attracted only a few students. This change will be examined briefly in this chapter together with the factors pertaining to trade union and university policies which have led to these changes.

1968-1985: Committed cooperation

At the end of the 1960s a group of officials and members of the Dutch trade union movement formed the "Union Group of Social Critics". They criticised capitalist society and the lack of union democracy. Their initiative was welcomed by concerned students and researchers as well as by a growing number of groups involved in more or less autonomous activities.

In all universities and especially social science faculties there was an increase in "project groups" which dealt with labour and trade union studies and established diverse forms of cooperation with trade union groups on a more or less permanent basis. Some of the more well-known groups are mentioned below. Most of them existed throughout the 1970s, with some university staff members forming the permanent backbone and new groups of students coming in every year.

At the University of Groningen the Project Group *Noord Nederland* (North Netherlands) became famous for its support of striking shift workers in the cardboard industry. At the University of Amsterdam a group of students and researchers supported trade union activists at the Hoogovens Steel Company and later supported dockers striking at the port of Rotterdam in protest against their employers and their union officials. At the Catholic University of Tilburg students at the Economics Faculty were well-known for their study of Marx and their popular introductions to political economy. At the University of Utrecht, the Project Group *Arbeid en Bewustzijn* (Labour and Consciousness), managed to establish a formally institutionalised department in which it undertook joint research projects with a number of unions in various branches of industry. One of the most well-known projects concerned a five year participatory action research project with transport workers aimed at developing worker participation and collective bargaining structures at shop-floor and company level (Coenen, 1987).

All these project groups cooperated with the Social-Democratic and Catholic unions which merged during the 1970s to form the Federation of Dutch Trade Unions (FNV). At some universities, such as the Free University of Amsterdam and the Technical University of Twente, staff members carried out research projects in cooperation with the Christian National Trade Union Federation (CNV).

Cooperation between trade unions and universities was based on a strong mutual commitment. Students devoted their time to carrying out research projects on behalf of trade union groups. The curriculum used to offer them "free time" which could total between one and two years. University staff could use their research facilities to research union topics and a considerable number were strongly committed to this type of research. Their commitment was founded on criticism of main-stream science which preferred pure, value-free science to science which was willing to integrate research with the researcher's social responsibility.

As far as the unions were concerned, they were, within certain limits, willing to cooperate with these project groups. The limits concerned the goals and activities of student groups which supported communist or radical groups of workers who were openly opposed to the union leadership. Obstacles to cooperation were also encountered when project groups dared to raise topics that the unions considered to be their own internal affairs, such as criticism of the lack of internal trade union democracy. On the whole, however, most project groups managed to establish a form of cooperation with some unions in particular sectors of industry or particular regions.

Apart from on-going cooperation with particular project groups, unions benefited from university research through the so-called "research shops". These information centres were established in many universities at the end of the 1970s. Social organisations committed to emancipation and democracy and which usually lacked the means to finance research, were to be helped to gain access to university research. Unions proved to be frequent clients, having their short-term research needs, such as those regarding health and safety and the work environment, being mediated by students willing to carry out this research as part of their courses.

Apart from the research on worker participation which university staff and students undertook together with the unions, the government commissioned research as well. During the 1970s, the government, in which the Social-Democrats participated at the time, spent a large amount of money on research into worker participation. Under the auspices of the tripartite Socio-Economic Council the government subsidised a series of experiments in worker participation in 13 companies from 1977 to 1983. Some of the experiments lasted several years. These experiments were intended to increase worker participation in company decision-making by a variety of ways ranging from works councils to self-managed cooperatives. The aim of the research was to support and to evaluate the experiments (De Man 1985). Because of the tripartite structure of supervision under which these experiments and research projects were carried out, a number of them never really got underway. Employers usually felt that the worker participation experiments that were proposed would undermine their managerial prerogative whereas union representatives often felt that the experiments did not go far enough (Leijnse & Van der Varst 1981; Coenen & Hens 1980).

The end of extensive cooperation

While research mediated through the research shops has continued to flourish, research in the form of long-term cooperation between unions and project groups has almost completely disappeared. The reasons for this change are to be found both in trade union policy and in government policy on university teaching and research.

Since the end of the 1970s trade unions have had to face the impact of the economic crisis. Redundancies, a dramatic loss in membership, government cuts in public spending and so on have demanded their full attention. When compared with these core concerns, topics such as research cooperation were regarded as extraneous. Some unions, such as the Union of Metal Workers and the Transport Workers' Union, were involved in internal conflicts over future union policy. The parties in these conflicts were divided broadly speaking between those opting for core action such as collective bargaining and those opting for the continuation of a policy aimed at emancipation and democracy through worker participation. These conflicts affected the conditions necessary for carrying out participatory action research. Moreover, unions' research demands frequently shifted to more functional questions.

A number of project groups also disagreed over research policy. This also contributed to ending existing research networks. The last general research programme published by the FNV dates back to 1983. Research policy has since concentrated on specific topics such as the introduction of new technology and affirmative action. In addition to carrying out its own research projects the FNV concluded an agreement of cooperation with the University of Amsterdam in 1984.

It is indicative of present trends that the FNV's research department has been gradually discontinued as a result of a series of successive reorganisations. Recently the FNV proposed that all affiliated unions should coordinate their research capacities under one umbrella research department (FNV 1992). This proposal has been accepted. Consequently at least an institutional linchpin for university researchers has remained.

At the end of the 1970s times were changing in universities as well. Successive reorganisation of study programmes was introduced with the aim of making university teaching more efficient (Coenen & Valkenburg, 1986). Study programmes were reduced from an average five-and-a-half years to four years, students were allowed only six years of State paid higher education, and so on. These changes seriously reduced the opportunities for students to devote a substantial part of their studies to research on behalf of trade unions.

Government policy on university research was another factor which fundamentally affected cooperation between university staff and unions. Research was no longer to be an individual staff member's activity but had to be accommodated within programmes. These programmes had to be supervised by department professors and had to be accredited by national research boards. This proved to be a disaster for most project groups.

During the 1970s, the research carried out by project groups had been criticised by orthodox researchers as being unscientific because it was politically biased. However, this criticism was not very effective because of the enormous interest expressed by students and staff in this type of research. Now, however, professors had the chance to apply their scientific standards in order to select who was to be admitted to research programmes and, more importantly, who was not. Traditional scientific standards included, for instance, the number of articles published in academic journals. Staff members had often been very productive, writing research reports and articles for trade union journals, but had neglected most traditional scientific journals. Consequently, many staff members were now dependent on their professors' willingness to grant them a place in their programmes.

A number of staff members left universities and found other jobs, some of them launching private research and counselling agencies. Others chose to accept a traditional research career. Those who had the chance to find more liberal professors were lucky enough to continue their research interests on condition that they did not shirk their publication duties. By the end of the 1980s all the "old" project groups, as such, had been discontinued. At a number of universities, such as Amsterdam, Nijmegen, Tilburg and Utrecht, some staff members are still at work, mostly on an individual basis.

Throughout the entire reorganisation of university teaching and research policy the trade union confederations never intervened explicitly with the aim of preserving "union-friendly" research possibilities. No attempt was made by the trade unions to influence research policy at national level.

Although the opportunities for university based participatory action research almost completely disappeared, survey research commissioned by the Ministry of Social Affairs and Employment continued to flourish. During the 1980s the government funded several research projects to examine the way in which works councils operated both in large and small companies in the private and public sector. Most of this research was carried out by independent research institutions like the ITS in Nijmegen (Looise & Heijink 1986; Looise and De Lange 1987) and the IVA in Tilburg (Dekkers et al. 1989). In addition, the State also provided some funding for research projects commissioned by the trade union confederations. These projects were carried out by researchers who were employed by the unions or by outside research institutions. Most of these projects did not focus primarily on worker participation but on issues like new technology and affirmative action. One exception was a research project on the careers and motivations of works council members, commissioned by the Christian National Trade Union Federation (Acampo et al 1987).

The dominance of contract research

Today the conditions for the old form of research cooperation clearly no longer exist. University staff must "publish or perish". Students now have to hurry to finish their studies in time. Moreover, they are concerned about their future in the job market and human resource management is a better bet than worker participation. Those students who are nevertheless interested in doing research on trade union topics can still do so through research shops. Unions at local and national level as well as works councils frequently approach research shops with research questions, knowing that this form of research is usually of mutual interest to students and unions alike.

New forms of cooperation have developed between university staff and trade unions on a smaller scale. Since university research activities have to be accounted for in terms of accredited publications, staff members have only limited opportunities to use their research time for any trade union research which is incompatible with university research programmes. Nevertheless at most universities there are still a number of researchers who are engaged in research with trade unions, albeit on a voluntary basis and without being commissioned. The results of such research projects may be found in academic publications but also in contributions to trade union magazines, shop-steward bulletins and presentations in seminars and workshops.

In addition, a number of unions have now adopted a policy of buying research. Funds are raised to carry out specific research projects and university staff or independent research and consultancy agencies, usually depending on personal contacts, are contracted to carry out the research. One example of a major project of research cooperation is a longitudinal survey of the development of union membership in relation to labour market trends. The research is funded by the Federation of Dutch Trade Unions (FNV), the Christian National Trade Union Federation (CNV) and the Ministry of Social Affairs and Labour. The project is being carried out by researchers of the University of Amsterdam and the Free University of Amsterdam. Another example of contract research is a project commissioned by the Union of Workers in the food industry on working time patterns and a similar project by the public sector union ABVAKABO. Both projects are being carried out by researchers of the University of Utrecht working with an independent research institution. As these examples illustrate, the topics of research are mostly only indirectly related to worker participation. The form in which research results are published is usually specified in the research contract and ranges from research reports to educational materials and contributions to seminars and workshops.

There is nothing wrong with contract research in itself In one sense it is a sign of increased union independence that they are able to buy the research that they feel they need. Yet it is also peculiar that a relationship which was predominantly based on a commitment to worker emancipation is now largely a commodity-based transaction. More specifically, there are a number of drawbacks inherent in the present situation which are worth examining. Firstly, contract research can clearly only be commissioned by those unions which have the financial means to do so. Some unions simply cannot afford to contract university staff and if they are not successful in raising funds they are unable to back up their policy by research. Secondly, the type of research being contracted is mainly orthodox survey research and this is usually commissioned by central union directors. There is no demand for the kind of participatory action research which was carried out by students, university staff, union officials, shop-stewards and union members. Research is therefore no longer a joint learning process between academics and trade unionists. Whether research findings are applied and implemented depends exclusively on the union boards which commission the research. Thirdly, topics selected for research usually reflect short-term, concrete policy problems. Long-term research on the future of trade unions, for example, is not commissioned both because of its cost and because unions do not want external observers to take a look behind the scenes.

Perhaps some of the above considerations may be interpreted as a desire on the part of researchers to indirectly intervene in union policy-making. This is not the intention, however. Clearly, researchers should respect union decision-making structures. But if research is to contribute to furthering the cause of democratic participation, it should be democratic itself. That is, unions and researchers should establish a forum in which they can jointly discuss research agendas and goals. Whenever research projects offer an opportunity for union members to work as coresearchers, the chance to contribute to expanding worker competence should be seized. Lastly, research results should be discussed jointly with the aim of examining the scenarios for action which they offer while also respecting the different responsibilities which union members and researchers have. It is these wider goals of trade union-university cooperation which, it is to be feared, will suffer most from a predominantly financial regulation of research.

It would be unrealistic to want to turn the clock back to the 1970s. Given the present situation, one must look for opportunities for a strategy which will provide new enthusiasm. There are still university staff-members willing to cooperate with trade unions on topics of worker participation and there are still students who take an interest in these issues. The Scenario 21 project may therefore be a good opportunity to discuss new forms of trade union-university cooperation.

23 Educational and research links between trade unions and universities in the United Kingdom

John Holford

Educational and research links between British unions and universities, never particularly strong, have weakened in the last decade for several reasons. Union links were traditionally concentrated in a particular sector of British universities (the extra-mural departments) which have suffered from shifts in government educational policies. Universities' provision of union education centred on the nationalised industries and the manufacturing and extractive sectors which have borne the brunt of privatisation and deindustrialisation. The trade union movement's own educational provision has relied increasingly on further education colleges - outside the university sector, and with little commitment to research.

Through increasingly divorced from the university sector the educational activities of British trade unions have been substantial. Education, for instance, accounts for roughly one-third of the Trades Union Congress (TUC)'s annual expenditure. Their commitment to research, however, has never been strong. For narrowly instrumental purposes (wage bargaining, speech writing for senior officials and so forth), major unions had evolved modest research departments by the 1960s. But the movement has not seen research as a mechanism for setting agendas in social or industrial policy. The main exception was the TUC Economic Department's relatively sophisticated research apparatus of the 1970s, with links with the university research sector developed when unions sought a major role in national economic management. Moreover, despite (or perhaps because of) the weakness of their own research departments, British unions have rarely encouraged, sponsored, or sought a role in research in the university sector

There have, of course, been exceptions to this pattern. There is a long tradition of informal links between university staff and unions, based largely on personal contacts. Strongest at a grass-roots level these have been supported by university staff's involvement in teaching union courses. This is becoming less common. Some university staff, and a few universities have made efforts to maintain links with unions in recent years. These have met with very limited success. Recent government moves to reorganise higher education and to discontinue public funding of union education seem likely to limit still further the space for such contacts.

Background

Until the 1950s British trade unions left the education of their members largely to two semi-independent voluntary bodies, the Workers' Educational Trade Union Committee (WETUC) and the National Council of Labour Colleges (NCLC). Research was also largely sub-contracted to such organisations as the Labour Research Department (LRD) and the Fabian Society These bodies sometimes enlisted support from sympathetic scholars in universities (both as researchers and teachers), but there was little formal involvement from higher education. Little distinction was made between the educational/research agendas appropriate to trade unions, and those applicable to the labour movement as a whole. Courses typically reflected a broad curriculum in the humanities, though with a socialist ethos and a concentration on topics (such as economics and political history) which seemed relevant to the labour movement's aims. The organisations also reflected, directly and sometimes fiercely, some of the movement's political division. For example, the Marxist NCLC saw the WETUC as an agent of the capitalist state.

From the late 1940s the political and industrial agenda was set by the 1945-51 Labour government and the changes it had introduced. Some unionists sought a role as social partners in the new welfare state. This meant training their members, and particularly their unpaid officials, in areas essential to these new roles. Education programmes were introduced which covered topics such as work study and payments systems. To achieve this the TUC and some of the larger unions developed their own education departments, though on a modest scale. The voluntary educational bodies also reflected this shift in outlook, partly because they found the working-class students less interested in liberal academic study (and suspected that, as educational inequality diminished, this trend would intensify), and partly because unions played an important role in their decision-making or finances (WEA 1953, Millar 1979). In the new political environment, several universities in the early 1950s also established educational programmes for trade unionists

Union priorities and the university extra-mural response

In the 1950s and the 1960s unions sensed they had a major role in industrial structures and policies. In the context of the cross-party political commitment to full employment which lasted until the late 1970s, several problems emerged. One was wage-driven inflation - due (so it was argued) mainly to workplace-level bargaining. Nationally-agreed wage deals had become mere base-lines for shop stewards and plant managers to negotiate higher increases, and as inflation became more deeply-rooted, annual wage bargaining (and consequent increases) became institutionalised. Related to this were the increased power of the workplace bargainers relative to national union leaders and an increasingly disorderly pattern of industrial relations

Both for unions and for government, the shop-stewards became a central focus of concern. Long important to union organisation, they were now also powerful. Any effective union strategy needed their allegiance. If unions were to have a new say in national economic policy, many union leaders felt it also meant taking a responsible approach in bargaining. For government, controlling inflation and improving industrial competitiveness meant regularising workplace industrial relations.

The trade union movement was forced to think through a clear strategy on education (though not research) in 1964 when the TUC took over the work of the CLC and the WETUC. By the late 1960s it had done so. With limited resources, union education should be targeted primarily at union workplace representatives (rather then members in general, or full-time officials), who should be entitled to paid release from work for training. (During the 1960s a number of deals were struck with employers along these lines). Such training, the TUC held, was conducive to "good industrial relations", as well as being educationally valuable in its own right. Union students should have access to (subsidised) public sector teaching resources, just as management students did (TUC 1968). But although there was some common ground between government, employers and unions on the aims of unions courses, the TUC was firm in demanding the independence of union courses from outside interference, particularly when, under the 1970-74 Conservative government, the Commission on Industrial Relations (1972, see also Holford, 1993) asserted that training union representatives should be a joint affair between employers and unions.

When the in 1960s and the 1970s the TUC sought to implement its new strategy and to establish and maintain its control, tensions arose with several universities which had already established strong roles in the field. The TUC approach contrasted with theirs. It also sought a standardised structure in which all union workplace representatives could secure adequate training of good quality. University staff resisted what they saw as TUC attempts to interfere in their academic freedom to set curricula. Areas of debate and conflict included the length and content of courses and the extent of employer involvement. University day-release courses tended to last, on a part time basis, for one or even three years. The TUC sought to provide education for many more students, and settled on a pattern of ten-week day-release courses. For the universities, while starting with workplace issues, union courses should lead on to broader study in the social sciences. For the TUC, such ambitions were liberal diversions from the main priority of helping shop-stewards become more effective in representing their members at their workplace, and unachievable in a ten-day time span. Some university programmes had evolved quite close links with particular companies. During the early 1970s the TUC felt some university staff were prepared to work with the Conservative government's approach of dividing "industrial relations training" form "trade union training" and teaching the former on a joint basis with management. (Holford 1993, McIlroy 1998a, 1988b).

The weakness of union's research relationships with the universities reflected their long-standing suspicion of academia and their tensions with the extra-mural departments (in the 1960s the main repositories of union-aligned university staff). They also reflected a failure of vision - a function, perhaps of British union's fear of any dispersal of legitimate authority. With the exception of the TUC Economic Department, which had some impact on economic policy, unions remained at an official level largely aloof from most of the social research developments of the 1960s and 1970s - a time when they could well have established a major role in the direction of social research (through, for instance, winning and using representation on official grant-awarding bodies). In the 1970s unions were object of research - in the work of the Industrial Relations Research Unit at Warwick University , for instance - but rarely the subject. There were limited examples of projects which sought to further broad union aims. These tended, however, to stem from larger government policy ventures and to be the immediate initiative of academics. The Bullock Report, for instance, led to a series of research project linked to questions of industrial democracy as well as some useful research with implications for trade unions (e.g. Gold, Levie and Moore 1979, Schuller and Henderson, 1980, Schuller and Roberston, 1983). Industrial democracy was, however, only briefly on the political agenda. In the 1980s, moreover, industrial relations' reform in any sense which gave unions a positive role quite rapidly disappeared from the policy agenda. So too did such research initiatives.

The impact of funding for union education

Having outlined an educational strategy and worked out much of the details in the struggles over the Donovan and Commission on Industrial Relations proposals, the unions in 1975 successfully pressed the Labour government for direct public funding for union education. Grant-aid amounted to £400,000 in 1976/77 rising to £1,840,000 in 1981/82. It then remained roughly stable in money terms for the next decade. (The unions also won legal rights to paid release for shop stewards to attend union courses). Suddenly, the TUC was able to dispense quite substantial funds to purchase courses in educational institutions It did so in pursuit of its own educational strategy. A curriculum development unit was established at TUC headquarters. The TUC developed still further its own distinctive approach to union education. Syllabi were set and printed course materials and model timetables issued. These were fundamental to what the TUC saw as quality control. A similar (and high) standard of tuition should be available to union representatives throughout the country. The large programme of courses required a new cadre of tutors (in very short supply in the early 1970s, as a government report - Department of Education and Science 1972 - showed). Training courses were organised by the TUC for tutors employed in the public sector colleges.

The new tutors, however, were not typically *university* staff. They were employed chiefly in further education colleges and to a lesser extent in the Workers' Educational Association (WEA - a body related to the defunct WETUC) and the polytechnics. This was due to several factors. Tensions with universities intensified as the TUC pressed for growth. Several disputes occurred as the TUC sought to assert its authority at the expense of long-standing (but in its view outdated) local arrangements between unions and universities. University democracy principles (and bureaucracy) could make decisions slow and contentious. Staff in the university sector were more expensive, with higher salaries and research expectations, than in the colleges. Further education, long used to supplying courses for external clients, had few institutional reservations about working with the TUC. Within the colleges, TUC courses had relatively high status while in the universities and polytechnics they were always seen as low-level and marginal, supported by a band of advocates, but always potentially controversial. It was, therefore, easier, to build up centres of excellence, groups of committed tutors and institutionally-recognised "trade union studies centres" in colleges than in universities or polytechnics.

As a result, not only did the major growth occur outside the universities. The role of the universities in union education actually declined from the late 1970s. According to Campbell and McIlroy (1986, p 214), university industrial studies provision (chiefly trade union courses) "reached a peak in 1977-78, after which it began to decline". This decline was relative as well as absolute. Trade union studies became smaller within universities' overall extra-mural provision, and universities became relatively marginal providers within the TUC's educational scheme. The character of university activity also changed. The universities tended to assume that their role would be in the provision of higher level courses. In the event, however, it was clear by the early 1980s that the "more specialised (and arguably the more academically demanding) courses are not being taught in the universities", but rather in further education colleges (Campbell and McIlroy, 1986 p 222).

The TUC's tendency to build up provision outside the universities would have mattered less if it had not coincided with other developments. First, the universities' own traditional strongholds in the field were lost. The universities' reservations about the TUC scheme were linked to a view that the best union education was conducted in the longer, one or three year courses that they had provided since the 1950s. But the days of such courses were numbered. The TUC now competed for their students. Unions would supply (albeit rather different) courses without charge. More important, however, the 1980s frenzy of deindustrialisation, linked to the Conservatives assault on the nationalised industries and fetishisation of the service sector, destroyed the basis for these courses. They had been based overwhelmingly in traditional manufacturing and extractive industries and in the nationalised corporations - primarily coal-mining. Durham, Leeds, Sheffield and Nottingham universities, for instance, had long-standing (and justly renowned) programmes with the National Union of Mineworkers (Barrat Brown, 1969 and 1991; Croucher and Halstead, 1990; MacFarlane, 1975; Mee, 1984; Stoker, 1983; Williams, 1954). There were also programmes in, for instance, engineering, railways and steel. These were, of course, the very industries which suffered most in the 1980s.

Second, the traditional centres of union education in the universities (the extra-mural departments) found themselves under attack from changing government education policies. Liberal adult education, a category within which union courses had found a somewhat uneasy home, was no longer thought to justify public expenditure. The departments, now funded in line with student numbers, needed to raise even larger fee income. Union courses were more difficult to organise, yet less staff time was available for the purpose. New staff were rarely appointed and existing staff often found themselves having to develop or deploy expertise in other fields (from management to gardening).

Public funds, then, enabled the TUC to build a central role for itself in the provision of trade union education. For a number of reasons, the universities proper were increasingly marginalised. A few continued to cooperate with the TUC, but none were major providers. A few individuals found niches in cooperating with the educational services of individual unions. These provided a workload for the lecturers concerned, and some worthwhile work was done. But the scale was modest and little was really innovative. Perhaps the main exception was the development of certificated distance learning courses in the Transport and General Workers' Union, pioneered by Surrey University (Fisher and Camfield 1986). Surrey's links with the TGWU, from which this initiative sprang, provided the only real exception to the rule of declining university involvement in union education (Fisher, 1989). (The initiative was taken up elsewhere in the union, Spencer, 1989)

If the universities proper were marginalised, the polytechnics (to be recognised as universities in 1992) were also on the decline. The polytechnics traditionally had a mixture of degree and sub-degree work. As they pressed for university status, sub-degree work was at a discount. A few institutions contrived to maintain it, but chiefly by dint of playing astute intra-institutional politics. By 1992, therefore, higher education had a highly marginal role in union education. The TUC, for instance, provided union courses in only thirteen higher education institutions (universities and polytechnics), as compared to eighty further education colleges and fourteen WEA districts. Although a few other universities and polytechnics provided courses for individual unions, the statistics are telling.

The research fringe

Since 1979 trade unions in Britain have increasingly been excluded from major areas of decision-making, political, economic, social and industrial. In the absence of a mainstream role, however, there have been attempts to establish space to support union activity, and to form a basis for influencing political and social agendas. There have also been some particular areas in which universities have been able to provide support to union activity. Four areas deserve mention here.

First, there have been a number of initiatives involving cooperation with local authorities. During the early 1980s, in particular, a number of local authorities under (often left-wing) Labour control, sought to provide a basis for radical change and to involve trade unions actively in this process. The most prominent example was that of Greater London Council, but there were many others. A common technique was the establishment of local authority 'trade union support units'. Policies included industrial regeneration, often through the work of so-called Enterprise Boards, and encouragement for forms of democratic participation, equal opportunity, and so forth. While for a limited period such approaches seemed to hold much promise, they were soon overtaken by the widespread assaults on local democracy (most notably the dissolution of the GLC itself) and ever-closer limitations on the financial autonomy of local councils. However, in their heyday some valuable work was done, involving links between local authorities, unions and universities.

Second, a number of university staff played valuable supportive roles in several major industrials disputes during the 1980s. The chief example was during the Mineworkers' strike of 1984-85. This spawned a veritable industry of research, including studies of economics of the industry and the viability of individual pits, critiques of Coal Board accounting practices, and studies of the strike itself. However, the decline in union militancy in recent years has left little room for this form of linkage between unions and universities.

Third, the advance of unemployment in the 1980s led the unions to develop a number of initiatives in support of the unemployed. These included, most notably, the so-called unemployed workers' centres (UWCs). By 1988 there were some 180 of these around the country, many funded directly or indirectly through various government programmes. According to Forrester and Ward (1990), some 19.5% of these considered education their main emphasis, while a further 28.3% considered it their second emphasis. While by no means all such education was supported by local universities, some universities did put substantial efforts into the work of particular UWCs (Forrester 1986). On a small scale, some valuable work was done but the UWCs could never be expected to provide the kind of institutional basis for major educational developments achieved by the universities. If nothing else, they were continually short of funds and subject to recurrent internal political crises. There were also a number of attempts to use local economic crises to develop research into the local economy. These were a feature of the early, rather than the later 1980s, often linked to local authority initiatives. Their decline may have been due to the overwhelming scale of the economic crisis, which defied local explanation or solution, but also reflected the tendency of local authorities (of right and left) to establish local enterprise units to market themselves. A number of trite slogans (along the lines of "Oldtown Means Business") were recycled around the country.

247

Fourth, following the introduction of new health and safety at work legislation in 1974, and the creation of a new category of union representative (the workplace safety representative) three years later, health and safety began to be seen by many trade unionists as an important aspect of employment conditions and an area for negotiations with employers. A very substantial programme of education was introduced by the TUC and many unions followed suit. Linked to this, a number of health and safety groups grew up around the country, linked in an effective network through publications such as "Hazards Bulletin" and, later, "Hazards". These bodies did very often involve academic staff from universities and polytechnics (although probably rather more from further education and the WEA). Their chief contribution was probably to support the education of the trade union movement in health and safety issues. They provided some technical and research support to workplace union organisations, but this inevitably on a limited scale (they were always voluntary organisations). They often gave union representatives access to some of the technical literature in health and safety (for instance, through access to college libraries), and guidance in its use. Partly because of the general erosion of union bargaining power, however, their early ambitions (of establishing health and safety as a major item for collective bargaining) were rarely realised and they tended to rely on trade union studies staff rather then specialists in health and safety as such.

Recent problems and future prospects

There is little sign that the pattern of declining union-university links which characterised the 1980s will change markedly during the immediate future. If unions in the 1970s seldom sought to shape major research agendas, they were at least in a position to do so. In the 1990s they are not. In the 1960s and 1970s networks of formal and informal links existed between unions and universities based on educational provision. If these had limitations (the extra-mural departments, for instance, often had weak research records, and their educational provision was concentrated in a relatively narrow range of industries), in the 1990s the universities have hardly any role in union education. Trade union studies lecturers have been lost and they are unlikely to be replaced.

Moreover, other areas of university activity which formerly had some union links and commitments are being eroded. The quasi-discipline of industrial relations, a product of the 1950s and 1960s (Clegg 1990), always took union activity as central. Increasingly, industrial relations is now being subsumed as a mere aspect of "human resource management" - itself subordinate to the central concerns of "corporate strategy". The research of the Industrial Relations Research Unit at Warwick University, for instance, concerns itself more and more with management policies. Union activities (studies of union workplace organisation were not a major feature of its work in the 1970s) are no longer central concerns.

There are other grounds for concern. Recent legislation on Further and Higher

Education encourages public sector educational institutions to cooperate with outside bodies, but with a strong emphasis on the purchase of services. Unions' ability to purchase services, whether in teaching or research, is inevitably constrained by financial pressures, yet the institutions are encouraged to seek ever-higher fees. In relation to teaching, the government's decision in 1992 to discontinue grant-aid to trade unions for educational purposes will make it more difficult for them to purchase courses in the colleges and universities. Insofar as union-university cooperation requires foundations in course provision or research, the problems are likely to intensify.

While the overall prospect must be pessimistic, some recent developments suggest positive possibilities. The trade union movement is taking a far more creative approach to the professional education of its full-time officials and this may provide some grounds for collaboration with higher education. A number of academics have attempted to develop a dialogue with unions on the importance of research. An important conference was held, for instance at Ruskin College in Oxford in 1991 (Forrester and Thorne, 1992), which led to the establishment of a Trade Unions and Research Network. However, while encouraging, this conference identified a number of significant problems (as compared, for instance, to the position elsewhere in the European Community), including "the absence of central support or funding for collaborative research with unions" and the "inadequacy of links between unions and research centres" (Winterton, 1991). Finally, there are some signs that the unions' suspicion of academia may be diminishing in part, perhaps, because higher education is less and less confined to the elite.

24 Trade unions and research in Sweden

Åke Sandberg

In the following notes on the links between trade unions and academic research in Sweden, the focus of attention is work organisation, production, participation and industrial relations. The term chosen to refer to these related issues is work environment research. An attempt has been made to provide an overview of the collaboration that has taken place between researchers and trade unions and a description of recent policies affecting cooperation. What follows is a rough outline of the situation with examples and some comments.[1]

The role of trade unions and the outlook for employees in the light of the research conducted into the work environment

During the late 1970s research into the work environment mushroomed. The reasons for this were the radical demands made by workers and reforms of labour laws that were introduced at that time, particularly the Co-determination Act. In universities academics took the initiative to expand critical and applied research and contacts were established with trade unions. The Swedish Centre for Working Life (Arbetslivscentrum) was established and the Work Environment Fund (Arbetsmiljöfonden) gained a greater mandate, able to tackle not only health and safety issues but also matters relating to co-determination and work organisation. The Fund is the most important body financing research in Sweden on work organisation, the work environment and health and safety. Another important public research institute working in the field is the National Institute of Occupational Health (Arbetsmiljöinstitutet)[2].

Research projects which were deliberately dedicated to trade unions and employees developed during the 1970s and 80s at both the Swedish Centre for Working Life as well as at most universities throughout the country. Several projects involving cooperation between researchers and trade unions were set up to examine change. For example at the Royal Institute of Technology in

Stockholm the Work Environment Group (Arbetsmiljögruppen) ran projects on improving the work environment in the workplace of different sectors of industry. In these and similar projects the trade unions were involved at national level while elected union representatives and members took part in the projects in the workplace.

New ideas about "quality" or "good" work, employee influence and co-determination were floated at that time and assessments were made of the role of the unions and management. A common thread running through many of these studies was the importance of developing trade union competence totally independently of management control. This proved to be essential primarily so that union activities guaranteed interaction between union leaders and the grass-roots but also so as to ensure osmosis between the unions and management either when working on projects involving major change or during negotiations. What emerged from these research projects were new ideas about the unions' role in "production problems" (as compared to "distribution problems" such as wages). (For an overview of this situation see Sandberg et al 1992).

Joint union-management coordination of development projects remained a bulwark of traditional industrial relations in Sweden. Some of these programmes which are still being run seek to improve both work and productivity. Traditionally, Swedish trade unions have always supported industrial renewal and it is with that in mind that union participation in such programmes must be viewed (TCO 1993).

Such programmes existed at the end of the 1960s and the early 1970s and resurfaced in the 1980s and 1990s. Examples include the LOM programme (leadership, organisation and co-determination) which encouraged local-level change by creating networks between different workplaces and making use of "dialogue conferences" (inspired by Habermas' theories of freedom of communication) to foster the process of change (see Naschold et al 1993). National trade unions and management were, generally speaking, represented in the steering groups and programme secretariats and the unions were expected to participate actively in the workplace projects.

At the beginning of the 1990s there were very few or no national-level programmes exclusively geared to bringing about change for wage-earners and trade unions. However, as will become apparent later on, projects run at regional level did exist at this time and the specific aims of those projects were and remain the provision of information and knowledge for the unions.

The fund for the improvement of working conditions which, it is true, does not conduct very much research, came into being at the initiative of the Swedish parliament which created it in 1989. It has a budget of 15 billion Swedish crowns and in the spring of 1994 was co-funding some 20,000 workplace projects. Two thirds of these projects concerned changes in work organisation. The financing comes from a special tax levied on company profits and thus has brought in large amounts over recent years. Funding is granted to companies which submit outlines for "workplace programmes" which aim to improve working conditions, the

252

organisation of work and adult vocational training. Recent projects have emphasised productivity. The trade unions and local-level management involved in any given project must agree to request funding from one of the regional work environment funds and this gives the trade unions a certain amount of bargaining power. However, considerable pressure is exerted on the unions to get them to accept any programme whatsoever so that the company can obtain state funding. The Swedish Institute for Research into Working Conditions is carrying out a comprehensive assessment of the projects, looking at a selection of projects on improvements in working conditions which are financed by the fund.

Apart from these programmes which target change, the unions try to ensure that they are kept informed about general research into work and research at sectorial level about union organisations. In some cases it is the unions which have prompted certain research programmes. At the National Institute for Work Health one recent cooperation project involving the trade unions looked at working conditions for middle management employees (working with the SACO confederation). At the University of Lund, studies into changes in union membership levels have been conducted, one in cooperation with TCO.

LO has launched a major research programme into its own history and role in Swedish society. It drew up a general framework programme and researchers, acting individually, submitted requests for funding from various sources. LO has also co-financed the creation of a professorship at Uppsala University.

Following a government initiative in 1991, the Swedish parliament decided to transform the Swedish Centre for Working Life into a "pure research institute" and make savings of 10 million crowns (1.1 million ecus) by reducing staff numbers to 35 permanent employees (with a maximum of 10 non-research staff). Some external researchers and doctorate students are still employed by the centre. The total cost of the centre for the financial year 1992-93 was 32.6 million crowns. A new director has been named, new research guidelines drawn up and several members of the staff in administration and the communications department as well as some researchers have been fired. The aims of the centre are to ensure that research results are disseminated by researchers. The researchers maintain that practical use of their work is essential and that they are part of the networks which include companies and trade unions. The institute's areas of research interest are now internationalisation and European policies, the development of competence and productivity in the workplace, job market policies, changes in the social partners and research into women's issues. A great deal of the centre's research concerns trade unions.

Trade unions and research policy

More recently those of the social partners actively involved in the job market have been attending meetings of the boards of directors of the Work Environment Fund and the Swedish Centre for Working Life. However, over the last few years,

Swedish management has come up with a new policy to avoid this type of "corporatist" representation and has decided to abandon most of these board meetings. As a result the present government has decided to put a stop to representation of the social partners and other interested parties on most such boards of directors. Smaller councils have been set up to replace them. These councils are comprised of individuals who do not represent any specific organisations.

This is an example of the waning influence of the social partners in national research policy. As LO has stressed (1993: 43ff), during the 1970s, one government research council commission concluded that employees played virtually no active role whatsoever in research and that this was not a satisfactory state of affairs. Towards the end of the 1980s the influence of the scientific community in research programmes and policy increased whereas the influence of non-researchers decreased. Furthermore, research-related problems do not seem to have been a priority for the trade unions.

But at the same time, as LO stresses, companies and employers, regarded as experts in the field, continue to wield influence over publicly-funded research and they use research to their advantage in public debate. Indeed employers have financial resources at their disposal to commission and fund research and this creates imbalances (Fernvall 1992). Given this state of affairs LO is presently discussing possible action to be taken so that research programmes could be launched by them. Such programmes would examine issues of interest and concern to employees. It is to be hoped that independent university researchers will want to develop these project proposals and try to find funding for them.

TCO insists that the importance of sectorial research into working conditions be recognised and that trade unions play an important part in deliberations on research policy so that they may contribute in ensuring useful and practical research is conducted, thus counter-balancing the emphasis put on scientific research. Furthermore TCO believes that union participation in research projects can help create links between research and practical application in the process of change in the workplace. Cooperation and collaboration between researchers and trade unions is considered to be an integral part of the revitalization of trade union work and example of their active participation in improving work methods and production methods (Danvind and Mörtvik, 1994).

In a recent policy document LO (1993) stressed two areas in which future research should be concentrated. The local level, concentrating on change-oriented projects and the international level, characterised by international and European researcher and trade union cooperation. LO and TCO both regard regional networks as a successful way of organising practical research. LO wants similar networks to develop throughout Europe which could interact with the regional and local networks. Researchers should be encouraged to participate in joint European research projects.

At national level LO has at its disposal the Trade Union Institute for Economic Research (FIEF) which concentrates on long-term research projects with high academic standards. Building on the Swedish tradition of popular education and study circles, LO is now planning to establish a trade union university (LO:s Högskola), which will stress collective and change-oriented research into information and knowledge. Preliminary reports suggest that the main aims of the institution are to provide qualified training courses for leading trade union officials at different levels, to develop better organisation and leadership within the unions, to provide a forum for debate of basic ideas, to support local and regional development work, to influence the direction of research by means of dialogue between union activists and researchers and to foster international networking in these areas. This trade union university may, in institutional terms, be regarded as a network in itself, based on activities in existing universities, especially the newer, regional ones and the existing regional and local networks already mentioned. This vast network will be supported and coordinated by a small, centralised administrative unit and an advisory board. There is also discussion afoot about whether FIEF (with a broader research scope) should become part of such a network. (LO 1993: 46ff and 1994a).

In this discussion of national research policies it is important to mention TAM, the archives and museums of the white collar workers movement and the archives of the labour movement. Both have scientific committees. They organise seminars and conferences where unionists and researchers can meet and this has contributed to the creation of union-relevant research projects.

Regional networks and research circles

Today both LO and TCO regard cooperation with researchers at regional level as a key activity. The feeling is that with union influence on the wane as far as national policies are concerned and with few major research programmes and projects dealing with employee or trade union issues up and running, the importance of regional activities has grown. This is partly due to the fact that since 1986 the trade unions have received public support for some of their research activities conducted at regional level.

Regional networks have been developed linking universities, workplaces and trade unions. The background to this development is the initial contact between local unions and researchers established in the 1970s. From 1986 onwards regional liaison officers were designated to organise the dissemination of research results and stimulate new ideas about new projects. A variety of activities has grown up including seminars, union-oriented university courses and research projects. Several examples are cited below.

Networks which possess liaison officers include the universities of Uppsala, Karlstad, Umeå and Linköping. In Karlstad cooperation with the regional LO offices has existed since 1979 and there projects have dealt with many issues relating to regional development. Joint development projects have also been organised. In Linköping (at the Teknikcentrum) training courses and projects exist

255

dealing with production technology and trade union influence in work organisation. The University of Lund has a long tradition of cooperation with trade unions. In the mid 1970s university courses for trade unionists were launched and "research circles" were introduced (see below). Several projects have been organised on the subject of union organisation and unionisation. Some of this work has been continued in the new Work Science Centre at the University of Lund (ACLU) but presently there are very few union-oriented projects. Union-oriented university courses are offered at the Unit for Work Science in the history department of the University of Gothenburg. Until 1993 there was also a liaison officer at Gothenburg working with regional LO and TCO organisations. And indeed a researcher-trade union conference on industrial policy was held in western Sweden as a result. At the University of Halmstad joint development projects are regularly organised as is the case in Linköping (either as a component of or along similar lines to the LOM programme). These and other regional networks form the backdrop to the work of the Work Life and Research in Sweden Association, the aims of which are to foster cooperation between trade unions and academics and support research of interest and value to employees.

At this juncture it might be appropriate to explain the concepts behind the term "research circle" cited above. (See LO, TCO, Alfofak and Holmstrand, all 1993 and Fernvall 1992). A research circle is a special type of study circle. The latter has been a familiar concept in the Scandinavian labour movement for decades. In a study circle a group of people, such as workplace union members, study a specific subject. The subject could be anything from French to computer studies, labour in Sweden or the European Union. The circle usually uses written material and one member acts as a group leader. Discussion and mutual learning are important aspects of work in such circles (Brevskolan 1980).

Research circles were first introduced at the University of Lund as a way of formulating research issues by means of cooperation between unionists and academics. The idea was developed in the university and spread to other faculties such as Karlstad where it was expanded to foster research initiation, problem solving, the provision of research results and active participation in research. (Lundberg and Starrin, 1990). The work methods used in research circles are very similar to those employed in "participatory action research". The research circle focuses on a problem clearly defined by the members of the circle. It might be a concrete problem in the workplace. One or two researchers are present in the circle and others may be invited to contribute. The concept of research circles is similar to that behind the union investigation groups developed in the 1970s as a result of trade union-academic cooperation and discussed in Sandberg et al 1992. To summarize, the tasks of the research circles are to provide adult education courses and training for trade union members, to disseminate information about recent, relevant research results and to get employees involved in research and the gathering of information. The common thread running through all these aims is the need to learn in the workplace about new forms of work organisation.

The University of Uppsala has a tradition of research circles. The contacts that have been developed there form the basis for a network of trade unionists and researchers from many different areas of central and eastern Sweden. Seminars, conferences and union reference groups have been built up within the framework of the so-called A Forum (the forum for work and job market research). Experience shows that many of the issues related to information for workers and unionists can be channelled into research projects. Alfofak (Arbetslivsforskning som bygger på fackliga kunskapsbehov - Working life research based on the knowledge needs of the trade unions) was launched in 1991 and now employs three part-time researchers and one part-time union representative. Funding for this and for other research comes from the Work Environment Fund. Alfofak is the result of a long process of research expansion in this region which began with the recognition that unionists needed information and was expanded using the multi-disciplinary team methodology. As for the researchers working on the programme, their ambition is to develop long-term information and researcher competence.

The networks function by means of various kinds of meetings. Joint meetings are held which bring together researchers and members of the reference groups on both the union and academic side. The researchers organise their own seminars while the union reference groups hold their own meetings. The research circles are also seen as meeting places. Several projects are now under development and have received or have requested funding. They cover issues such as:

- new forms of management, new forms of industrial relations and the role of the trade unions
- the restructuring of health care and unemployment / the consequences for nurses
- union training in work environment issues
- changes in workplace health care

These project themes have emerged from seminars and research circles. The common factor is the union need for information. When up and running all these projects will include union reference groups and/or research circles.

In addition to cooperation with academia, Swedish trade union confederations and some of the bigger national unions also have their own research departments. When research into workplace changes is commissioned, the projects are often contracted out to consulting firms. A few such firms specialize in this type of work and are known as "wage earner consultants". In the public sector, national unions receive some 9 million crowns per year to finance these research contracts. In other sectors, workplace unions are obliged to negotiate with management to ensure that the latter pay the fees of union consultants. Studies conducted in the private sector are often short-term studies related to major changes in the companies under study while studies in the public sector sometimes reflect policy or look at longer-term change. Some of the consultants hired to do this research are part-time university researchers hence this form of research can be regarded as a mechanism which links unions and universities (Sandberg 1992).

Some reflections

The aim of this book is to discuss and encourage greater cooperation between researchers and trade unions. Hence in the concluding section of this chapter, attention will be focused on the possibilities which exist while examining some of the union weaknesses in such cooperation.

For decades the Swedish state has supported programmes which examine working conditions and the work environment and which investigate development of technology, competence and work organisation. Several programmes financed by the Work Environment Fund and all of the recent work funded by the Work Life Fund deal with areas and problems which are very relevant to trade unions and their members. This has also been the case more recently for Nutek (and its predecessor STU), a body responsible for providing state support for industrial and technological development and which works hand in hand with the Work Environment Fund on programmes dealing with computers and work. Nutek now also runs a programme on technology and work in specific industries.

At regional level, networks of university-trade union cooperation have expanded over the last ten years to incorporate both new universities and some of the older, traditional ones. Research circles involving direct cooperation and mutual learning between wage-earners and researchers are now very common. The national unions support these regional networks. But when compared to the larger development programmes discussed above, the 150 research circles now in existence have very little funding available.

Both LO and TCP are considering the possibility of a more active role in national research policy formulation and programme definition. Current discussions about the creation of an LO university reflect the growing trend within trade unions to stress dialogue and networking with research bodies in an effort to gain greater understanding about issues of importance and relevance to unions and their members.

Turning now to change-oriented research, national trade unions' difficulties in defending the employees' interests when national research policies are defined should perhaps be regarded not so much as a problem of programme methodology, but rather as a problem linked to the results of many programme projects. One possible explanation is that although there are many successful projects, local union organisations have not always succeeded in exploiting the potential that employee-relevant programmes can offer. In some instances the local unions may lack insight or understanding but more often than not they lack experience and knowledge of research and development activities and the ability to offer counter-proposals to management's solutions. National unions, while sitting on programme boards and being present in programme secretariats, have perhaps not always been capable of providing the necessary support to local unions in the form of expert knowledge nor have they been able to develop networks to provide mutual support among union members participating in the various workplace projects.

Above all, this is a funding and organisational problem. It is essential that the fruits of public research into issues of interest to employees be disseminated and shared by all those concerned (see discussion in Sandberg et al 1992: 83ff, 98ff and 235ff. See also similar reflections in an LO assessment of the role of unions in Work Life Fund projects, LO 1994b). If trade unions are to assume an active and decisive role in research and development programmes, it may be necessary to guarantee trade unions a share of state funding allocated to such projects.

The Swedish employers' confederation (SAF) and its members and sectorial associations have for many years had networks for development projects. There has been very effective dissemination of innovative solutions in different companies. Experience is shared and passed on at national level. (See, for example the pioneering SAF "new factories" programme from the early 1970s).

But the linchpin for central union support and union networks of the kind discussed above must be workplace and corporate-level union organisations. It is their activities and their access to talent within companies and their regions which really matter. An important measure in this regard might be a modification of the Co-determination Act and relevant agreements so that independent and continuous development of information and know-how in unions and among union members is actually rendered feasible. The Co-determination Act is based on one model of change. It focuses on the "decision" at a single point in time when a choice is made between clearly stated alternatives.

Another model of the process of change emphasizes the on-going fight for funding and the struggle against "hegemonistic views" in companies and the working environment. Ideas about change and efforts to bring about change never cease to emerge and under certain circumstances change may occur (see Danielsson 1987). Within companies, management is constantly striving for greater knowledge and understanding and looking at new ideas for action and indeed in this era of increasingly knowledge-based production, that is an essential management activity. If this model of change is to be accepted and if trade unions are to play a role, there must be constant generation of union-relevant information and knowledge. A prerequisite for this is that sufficient funding and time is available for union activities independent of company decisions. This means, among other things, that unions should have the right to consult in-house experts or turn to external ("wage-earner") consultants whenever necessary, irrespective of whether management announces an imminent "decision" to be taken. This form of union access to information and knowledge could be enshrined in law or stipulated in agreements. As has been illustrated, in the state sector an agreement on wage-earner consultation already exists and this gives unions the right to make use of specific, small sums of money for investigations and consultants of their own choice.

Research into work and the work environment unfolds in a field dominated by strong players. It is management which wields ultimate control over researcher access to the workplace and information. Union efforts to build up networks and national support so as to give themselves an active role in research and development projects may inject greater pluralism into such research, generating an abundance of data, honing arguments and brightening the future for those involved. Effective, broad-based employee and union participation could therefore improve the quality of such projects both in terms of scientific content and practical consequences such as technical and organisational change (cf Ehn and Sandberg 1979). To improve the quality of research it may also be necessary to intensify independent academic research into work issues and industrial relations to complement the many large institutes which concern themselves with business administration.

Appendix

Swedish union organisations

Swedish trade union organisations function at three different levels. At national level there are three confederations which cover different wage-earner groups. Traditionally LO represents blue-collar workers and TCO white-collar workers. SACO represents the professional classes and is divided into a union for psychologists, doctors etc. while LO and TCO are confederations of industrial workers. Regional organisations also exist within these two confederations, known as "districts" and each union has a sectorial level organisation. In the case of large companies there is a fourth level at which cooperation takes place, among different shop-floor unions of the same company.

Abbreviations

LO   Landsorganisationnen (Swedish Trade Union Confederation)
SACO   Sveriges Akademikers Centralorganisation (Swedish Confederation of Professionals Associations)
TCO   Tjänstemännens centralorganisation (Swedish Confederation of Professional Employees)

Notes

1.   At the end of the chapter one may find an appendix on Swedish Trade Union Organisations.

2.   The names of the institutes I have cited have changed since the 1970s or are to change soon. The National Institute of Occupational Health was formerly the research department of the National Board of Occupational Health and Safety (Arbetarskyddstyrelsen). The Work Environment Fund

(Arbetsmiljöfonden) was previously known as the Arbetarskyddsfonden. The Swedish Centre for Working Life is known since July 1994, as the Swedish Institute for Work Life Research (Institutet för arbetslivsforskning).

Conclusion
For a re-investment in democratic participation

Gérard Kester and Henri Pinaud

In this book we have outlined the principles behind the policies and strategies which trade unions need to implement in order to claim back participation and render it democratic. We realise that this book does not propose any concrete solutions to the numerous problems and challenges cited. But it would have been unrealistic to attempt to do so. Opting for Scenario 21 means a lot of hard work in the search for practical answers. If Scenario 21 is adopted, this hard work will be the logical next step.

The long-term aim of the Scenario 21 project is to create a lasting framework for purposeful and consistent cooperation in policy formulation, policy implementation, education and research, on democratic participation.

On the long road to European integration, regulating labour relations at European level is becoming increasingly necessary. Participation, the right to information, consultation and codetermination, training and education are all at stake just at a moment in history when Europe is confronted by enormous challenges.

The Green Paper on European Social Policy mentions several critical areas of social policy where changes in the EU are most evident a.o:

- employment, where pressure from technological and structural change is changing patterns of employment and the role of work in society;

- demographic changes; ageing of the population; changing of traditional family solidarity; migration (which strains the labour market and provokes serious problems of ethnic conflict and racism);

- the development of technology which has deeply altered the organisation and even the concept of work; this has affected relationships in the workplace; new challenges for methods of negotiation and collective bargaining between firms and their partners; growing numbers of people excluded from the labour market.

Thus the present situation of the EU on the terrain of industrial relations can be more and more characterised by a growing social rift with on the one hand the socially-integrated, gainfully employed, earning a salary and, on the other hand, the socially excluded, the growing number of non-active people ('dual' society). "Such a [dual] society would not only become increasingly less cohesive, it would also run counter to the need for the maximum mobilisation of Europe's human resource wealth in order to remain competitive" (The Green Paper on European Social Policy).

According to the Green Paper, the combination of these factors will lead to a search for:

- new approaches to responsibility

- new roles for various bodies (a.o social partners)

- new forms of solidarity leading to new partnerships between all the relevant actors in the field of social policy.

- In the face of these developments, Europe is now entering 'upon a period of development where its capacity to build an active and open society and to combine economic dynamism and social progress will be more important than ever' (The Green Paper).

It is especially this area of linking economic and social policy in a time of rising unemployment and social division where the Scenario 21 project will be of strategic importance. The overall aim of such a project is to involve the European Unions through the European Trade Union Confederation so as to assure that democratic participation should become a major component of European industrial relations. The aim is also to commit the European Union, by requesting it to make funds available as a sign of its commitment to the development of democratic participation. The aim is to eventually claim a special budget line for this purpose.

It is important to invest all efforts in the creation of democratic institutions which can express the interdependence of the different groups in society. Participation must be institutionalised in such a way that it promotes solidarity. This can be achieved by developing more effective and meaningful forms of supra-company participation (local, regional, national and international participation) in which less privileged groups can express themselves, can exert influence, can share in the fruits of economic success and above all, can co-determine their future (as explained in part I of this book). Democratic participation as an essential part of the trade union heritage can, if remodelled, shape industrial relations in the EU of tomorrow. For democratic participation will be an indispensable ingredient if social cohesion is to be regained. People are both the ends to and the means of development and thus independent, representative, democratic organisations, especially in these turbulent times, must be given a forceful role.

Simply drawing up a trade union policy for participation, at company level or beyond, is not enough. The implementation of such a policy needs to be constantly monitored and evaluated and those involved must be educated and trained. Democracy is a learning process and democracy can only be achieved if we learn lessons from this process so that the next steps forward can be taken. Participation is a dynamic phenomenon which requires a permanent support structure. Perhaps the greatest weakness in the development of democratic participation over the past decades has not been the absence of policy but rather the absence of sustained support for implementation. The Green Paper states: 'There need to be high levels of investment in infrastructures, research and development and, above all, people. People themselves need to feel involved in the process of continuing change which must be sustained over the medium term; there needs to be a balance between physical and human capital'.

Opting for scenario 21 means opting for the creation of the necessary investment for its implementation. This can be seen as a long term investment: getting ready for the 21st century by adequately strengthening the trade union movement in the development of democratic participation:

(a)   consolidating existing forms of participation

(b)   search for new forms of trade union and worker influence

- deliberately combining the five main forms of participation: collective bargaining, co-management, co-determination, organisational and financial participation

- elaborate this 'comprehensive hold' at the place of work but also at local, regional, national and international levels.

In fact the project should particularly contribute to policy formulation and implementation in innovative forms of trade union action and labour relations.

In order to launch this process of revitalisation, a new initiative must be taken at international European level. A coordinated network must be established which will provide the necessary means to mobilise resources, energy and potential within each country which are presently in limbo.

A specifically designed support base for democratic participation should be created, together with a permanent trade union-university cooperation project with a jointly drawn-up agenda of research, education and training and policy and action development.

One important means of achieving these aims is to continue and increase the kind of cooperation between trade union organisations, research institutes and universities which began several years ago within the framework of this project.

The conclusions of the 1994 colloquium on democratic participation in Paris

In February 1994, CFDT held in Paris, under auspices of ETUC, a colloquium on "Trade Unions and democratic participation". About 80 persons - including representatives of 15 trade union confederations, from 10 countries of the European Union, from Poland and Hungary, academics and representatives of European research centres, of the French government and European institutions as well as of the employers' (UNICE and Human Resources Directors) attended the colloquium.

The colloquium had three objectives:

1 to check the importance of the theme "democratic participation" among the European trade union organisations;

2 to appreciate their reactions to the researchers' analysis and proposals;

3 to elaborate a trade union work programme at European level, with an important trade union - university cooperation dimension.

The conclusions of the colloquium adopted by most of the participants correspond to the bulk of the Scenario 21 proposals (see Chapter 4). They underline insufficient democracy in tomorrow's Europe. They repeat that participation is a fundamental right of citizens and workers in a democratic society of the 21st century....., that participation is an individual and collective right of workers based on his or her work and his or her status as a member and citizen in a company..." They insist on the fact that an independent trade union is "the foremost platform and the basic guarantee of free, individual participation..."

There is no standard model of participation suitable for everyone and every situation but there exists a multitude of different forms, different methods and different instruments of trade union intervention. Democratic participation is an essential factor of the European pattern of social relations. With the possible adoption of a European constitution the right to democratic participation and to citizens' collective social rights must feature as priorities.

The conclusions of the colloquium assert that the "adoption of a work programme on questions of democratic participation and specific aspects such as information, training, research, analysis and particularly, cooperation between trade unions and researchers, should be a way to forward a new investment in this area by the trade union movement".

266

Proposal for a new initiative

One important means of achieving these aims is to continue and increase the kind of cooperation between trade union organisations, research institutions and universities which began several years ago within the framework of this project. Without going into details, we would like to sketch the major goals and methodology of the kind of cooperation which should be implemented.

A methodology adapted to the aims.

On the basis of several long-term cooperation projects between trade unions and universities, (see Part III), we are now able to put forward several proposals regarding general methodology and research principles. Naturally these propositions will need to be adapted to the specific context in each country and depending on the trade unions and academic institutions involved.

The first principle is to ensure that trade union priorities are borne in mind. Consequently, a general framework for cooperation should be designed by the ETUC and trade union organisations in the various countries of Europe so that strategic choices can be made regarding research subjects and a general joint research programme

The second principle concerns the joint running of research projects. Every stage of a research project must be decided jointly by a scientific team and trade union representatives, each party preserving its specific role. These joint decisions must cover the various hypotheses to be examined, research methodology, implementation, and the ways in which the results are to be made available to the trade unions. It goes without saying that the academic researchers should be completely free to publish any direct or indirect results of their research outside trade union circles. The principle of joint management and its implications must be clearly stated, discussed and put down on paper before the research commences.

The third principle regards optimum utility research. This is especially important for the trade unions. Implementation of this principle can take various different forms:

- help with formulating trade union policies and strategies: regular meetings throughout the research project between the researchers and representatives of trade union policy committees at all relevant levels

- comprehensive distribution by the scientific and/or trade union teams of research results (suitably adapted to the varied trade union readership) in the form of articles, communiqués, etc., published in trade union reviews or presented at trade union colloquiums, seminars, etc. Research results should be adapted and used in trade union training programmes. A data-bank should be set up to store and process the material produced by the research. A documentation centre should be made available to the trade unionists and the researchers. Other methods of distributing the research results should also be considered.

· The principle of optimum utility and its implications should be clearly stated, discussed and put down on paper before the research commences.

The organisation must be adapted to the aims and the methods.

Experience has taught us that in multiple joint research there is one major risk which must be avoided at national level and consequently in bilateral or multilateral studies. That risk is that the research, comprised of individually organised projects drawn up by different parties, may be too diffuse and not sufficiently homogeneous to enable proper evaluation or adequate trade union or academic exploitation.

Consequently, adequate measures for regulating and coordinating the work are required. Three major principles may be proposed for obtaining research coherence without affecting the originality of each joint research project.

- Organisational coordination. We have already made it clear that the academics involved in these projects do not want to see the creation of an unwieldy and cumbersome coordination framework. One should want to see the creation of a European network of academics and researchers who have experience in the field of participation and who are used to working together with trade union organisations. The contributing authors in the Scenario 21 documents represent the embryo of such a network. This network of academics would, through the academic institutions in which they work, be available to conduct field research or supervise scientific coordination together with trade union coordination committees at all levels; sectoral, national and European. The form that this kind of coordination might take should be jointly discussed and adopted at each different level.

- Thematic coordination. In order to improve organisational coordination, it is proposed that the academic and trade union coordination committees draw up research subjects which embrace several different research projects. These common subjects could be researched in the field by the scientific and trade union teams at the same time as their own specific research topics. This would considerably facilitate evaluation and exploitation of research results at sectoral, national and European level.

- The creation of independent scientific and trade union committees to evaluate the scientific quality of the research and its usefulness for trade unions and society. This would lend legitimacy to the research and would also provide added coherence to the project.

It has to be realised that involving social actors in all phases of the research process, as well as in the dissemination of the results, is a time consuming affair. It necessitates a well coordinated partnership between trade unionists and researchers, demanding considerable investment in continuous interaction and frequent meetings - all the more so if research extends to multiple levels and to more than one country. Such a heavy investment is a necessary condition for making trade union - researcher cooperation effective and truly democratic, and for avoiding the double trap of laxity and authoritarianism.

Moreover and in general, it should be stressed that one of the major problems encountered in long term cooperative research is the eventual lack of continuity in commitment and availability of all persons and organisations involved. In this respect, the fact has to be taken into account that universities or research institutions normally have a much more stable body of personnel and policy than trade unions, most of whose officers hold elected positions and are therefore more susceptible to turnover. Also, trade union policy and strategy are prone to movement, and shifts in priority may substantially alter the trade union's commitment to, or involvement in, the research process.

Another snag in the process of long term projects is of a more technical nature: more often than not, funds are granted on an annual basis so that no guarantees for continuity exist, putting excessive strain on the coordinators who have to operate in a climate of uncertainty, constantly investing time in fund raising. Moreover, the priorities and criteria of public funding agencies with respect to requests for research projects are often subject to political change.

The programme of trade union - researcher cooperation in the Scenario 21 project has had its full share of the difficulties just described, all the more so as it had been seen as a long term programme from its beginning. But at the same time, it should be pointed out that a major advantage of the continuous involvement of trade unionists has been the fostering of a sustainable and structured common research process, which has already left its mark on trade union policy formulation. Conversely, stability in trade union involvement and commitment would be an invaluable contribution to the creation of greater stability in the long term research orientation of public funding agencies.

Long-term perspective

Given the stakes involved for the development of democracy the proposed work must be programmed in a long-term perspective.

The internationalisation and the globalisation of the economy means that we can no longer think in terms of Europe alone. The challenge that democratic participation represents is not unique to the EU. The EU is committed to the socio-economic development of Central and Eastern Europe and the Third World, in particular the ACP countries. EU social policy and indeed EU participation policy may well prove to be points of reference for other countries and continents.

The Green Paper argues, "the greatest threat to peaceful competition is likely to be wide discrepancies in the economic fortunes of the different regions. It is in the enlightened (and even narrow) self-interest of the advanced, industrialized countries to encourage the growth of new markets in other regions. Thus, if a new balance of power has provided the opportunity for peaceful socio-economic competition, then a new balance of development is probably the condition of its survival. This notion of balance is, for example, central to the discussion about the role of Japan vis-à-vis Europe and the United States".

Democratic participation is a global challenge, also !

The Hague/Paris October 1995

Bibliography

Abrahamsson, B., (1977), *Bureaucracy or Participation: the logic of organization.* Sage Publications: Beverly Hills.

Abrahamson, K., (1993), *Fräan arbetarhögskola till forskningscirkeï.* Utbildingsförlaget/Brevskolan: Stockholm.

Acampo, J., et al. (1987), *OR-lidmaatschap: loopbaan en verloop.* Rijksuniversiteit Limburg and the CNV- Research-Department: Utrecht/Maastricht.

Adebayo, A., et al. (1991), *The Challenge of African Economic Recovery and Development.* Cas: London.

Agersnap, F. and F. Junge Jensen (1973), *Samarbeidsforsøg i Jernindustrien.* Handelshøjskolen: København.

Akkermans, M. (1985), *Beleidsradicalisering en Ledendruk.* Instituut voor Toegepaste Sociologie: Nijmegen.

Albert, M. (1991), *Capitalisme contre Capitalisme.* Seuil: Paris.

Alemann, U. von (ed.) (1975), *Partizipation - Demokratisierung - Mitbestimmung.* Westdeutscher Verlag: Opladen.

ALFOFAK (1993), *Ett samarbete mellan forskare och fackliga organisationer i Mellansverige.* Uppsala university: Uppsala.

Amalgated Union of Engineering Workers (1976), *Investigation into the Scope of Industrial Democracy.* London.

Arbetslivfonden (1993), *Information, kunskap och efterfrägan pä arbetslivsomrädet.* Arbetslivfonden: Stockholm.

Arrigo, G., A. Scajola and P. Settimi (1994), *Democrazia Economica - Sindicato e impresa nella nuova contrattazione.* Edizioni Lavoro.

Asplund, C. (1972), *Some Aspects of Workers' Participation.* International Confederation of Free Trade Unions: Brussels.

Assanti, C. (1990:452), *Dallo Statuto Lavoratori allo Spazio Sociale Europeo. I Poteri Nell'Impresa: bilancio e prospettive.*

Baddon, L., L. Hunter, J. Hyman, J. Leopold, and H. Ramsay (1989), *People's Capitalism? A Critical Analysis of Profit-sharing and Employee Share Ownership*. Routledge: London.

Baglioni, G. and C. Crouch (eds.) (1992), *European Industrial Relations*. Sage: London.

Bagnasco, A. (1985), *Societa e Politica Nelle Aree di Piccola Impresa*. F. Angeli: Milan.

Baldacchino, G. (1988), 'Wages Policy at Malta Drydocks: analysis of an ambivalence', in: *Economic and Social Studies*. University of Malta: Msida,1988.

Bank, J. and K. Jones (1977), *Worker Directors Speak*. Gower Press: Farnborough.

Banks, A. and J. Metzgar (1989), *Participating in Management: union organizing on a new terrain*. Labour Research Review no. 14, Midwest Center for Labor Research: Chicago.

Barratt Brown, M. (1969), *Adult Education for Industrial Workers*. National Institute of Adult Education (England and Wales) and the Society of Industrial Tutors: London.

Barratt Brown, M. (1991: 9-15), 'The Demands of New Technology: the Sheffield university programme of day release courses in the 1960s', in: *The Industrial Tutor* 5(4).

Bayat, A. (1991), *Work, Politics and Power*. Zed: London.

Beaupain, T. (1991), Tripartite Consultation and Co-operation in Economy and Social Adjustment Policies. The Case of Belgium. ILO, Working Paper (draft).

Beckhard, R. and W. Pritchard (1992), *Changing the Essence. The Art of Creating and Leading Fundamental Change in Organizations*. Jossey Bass: San Francisco.

Beinum, H. van (1990), Observations on the Development of a New Organizational Paradigm. Paper presented at the seminar on Industrial Democracy in Western Europe, Cologne, 26th February - 2nd March 1990. Swedish Centre for Working Life: Stockholm.

Bellardi, L. (1984: 49), 'Il Processo di Formazione del Contratto Collettivo: l'Accordo del 22-1-1983', in: Giornale Diritto del Lavoro e Relazioni Industriali.

Bellardi, L. (1989), *Instituzioni Bilaterali e Contrattazione Collettiva*. F. Angeli, Milan.

Benello, G.G. and D. Roussopoulos (eds.) (1971/72), *The Case for Participatory Democracy. Some Prospects for a Radical Society*. Viking Press & Grossman Publishers: New York.

Bernoux, P. (1993), 'Quelques Points Relevés dans la Recherche du GLYSI et Pouvant Servir au Projet Transversal de PAROLES 2'. Document Interne, Lyon.

Bernstein, P. (1976), *Workplace Democratisation: its internal dynamics*. Kent State University Press: Kent.

Bertrand, M. (1991-1992), CFDT et Démarches Participatives, in: *Travail* no. 24. Paris.

Beukema, L. (1987), *Kwaliteit van Arbeidstijdverkorting*. Konstapel: Groningen.

Biagi, M. (1990), *Rappresentanza e Democrazia in Azienda. Profili di Diritto Sindicale Comparato*. Maggioli: Rimini.

Biagioli, M. (1995), 'Italy: financial participation and decentralization of wage bargaining', in: D. Vaughan-Whitehead, 'Workers' Financial Participation: East-West experiences'. *Labour Management Series*, No. 50, ILO: Geneva.

Blanpain, R., and J.C. Javillier (1991), *Droit du Travail Communautaire*. Librairie Générale de Jurisprudence: Paris.

Blauner, R. (1964), *Alienation and Freedom*. University of Chicago Press: Chicago.

Blichfeldt, J.F. (1973), *Bakerst i Klassen*. Norli: Oslo.

Blichfeldt, J.F. (1975), 'Relations Between School and the Place of Work', in: *Acta Sociologica*, Vol. 1, no. 4.

Blichfeldt, J.F., R. Haugen and H. Jangård (1979), *Mot en ny Skoleorganisasjon*. Tanum: Oslo.

Blinder, A.S. (ed.) (1990), *Paying for Productivity - A Look at the Evidence*. Brookings Publications: Washington.

Blumberg, P. (1968), *Industrial Democracy: the sociology of participation*. Constable: London.

Bolle de Bal, M. (1993), *The Double Games of Participation. Pay, Performance and Culture*. de Gruyter: Berlin/New York, .

Bonell, M.J. (1983), *Partecipazione Operaia e Diritto dell'Impresa*. Giuffra: Milan.

Bourdet, Y., O. Corpet, J. Duvignaud, G. Gurvitch, J. Pluet and L. Sfez (1978), *Qui A Peur de l'Autogestion? Liberté ou Terreur*. UGE: Paris.

Brannen, P., E. Batstone, D. Fatchett and P. White (1976), *The Worker Directors: a sociology of participation*. Hutchinson, London.

Braverman, H. (1974), *Labor and Monopoly Capital: the degradation of work in the twentieth century*. Monthly Review Press: New York.

Bruijn, G. de (1992), 'SER-Advies Wijziging WOR na 13 keer stemmen vastgesteld', in: *OR-informatie*, 3 juni 1992.

Bulcke van den, F. (1995), 'The Slow Growth of Financial Participation without Legislation, in: D. Vaughan-Whitehead, 'Workers' Financial Participation: East-West experiences'. *Labour Management Series*, No. 50, ILO: Geneva.

Bullock Report (1977), *Report of the Committee of Inquiry on Industrial Democracy*. Cmnd. 6706, HMSO: London.

Cable, J.R. (1988: 121-137), 'Is Profit-sharing Participation? Evidence on alternative firm types from West-Germany', in: *International Journal of Industrial Organization*, Special issue on Employee Share Ownership, Profit-sharing and Participation, vol. 6.

273

Cable, J.R. and F.R. Fitzroy (1980), 'Productive Efficiency, Incentives and Employee Participation: some preliminary results for West-Germany', in: *Kyklos*, vol 33, no. 1.

Campbell, A. and J. McIlroy (1986: 207-40), 'Trade union Studies in British Universities: changing patterns, changing problems', in: *International Journal of Lifelong Education* 5(3).

Carinci, F. (1986: 425), 'Il Protocollo Iri nella Dinamica delle Relazioni Industriali', in: *CESOS, Le Relazioni Sindicali in Italia*, Rapporto 1984/85. Lavoro: Rome.

Cella, G.P. (1988: 459), 'In un Anno dopo l'Accordo del Gennaio 1983: gli esiti dalla nuova tase di confronto sul patto anti-inflazione', in: CESCS, *Le Relazioni Sindacali in Italia*. Rapporto 1984/88. Lavoro: Roma.

Cella, G.P. and T. Treu (1989), *Relazioni Industriali*. Il Mulino: Bologna.

Cernea's, M.M. (1992), *The Building Blocks of Participation: testing a social methodology*. World Bank: Washington D.C.

CFDT (1976), '37ème Congrès: les conditions de travail', in: *Syndicalisme Hebdo CFDT*. Supplément du 4 mars.

Chouraqui, A., (ed.) (1991), *La Cooperation Syndicats-Recherche en Europe*. CNRS: Paris.

Chouraqui, A. and R. Tchobanian (1991), *Le Droit d'Expresssion des Salariés en France*. Institut International d'Etudes Sociales, BIT: Geneva.

Clark, J. (1991), *Democratizing Development: the role of voluntary organisations*. , Earthscan Publications: London.

Clarke, R.O., D.J. Fatchett and B.C. Roberts (1972), *Workers' Participation in Management in Britain*. Heineman: London.

Clegg, H. (1990), The Oxford School of Industrial Relations. Warwick Papers in Industrial Relations No. 31, University of Warwick: Coventry.

CNEL (Consiglio Nazionale Dell'Economia e del Lavoro) (1984), 'Osservazioni e Proposte in Materia di Partecipazione dei Lavoratori e di Democrazia Industriale', *Assemblea* del 31.10.1984, No 199/146. Rome.

CNEL (1986), Disegno di legge recante 'Norme sulla Informazione Consultazione dei Lavorotori' *Assemblea* del 25.3.1986, No. 212/160. Rome.

Coates, K. (ed.) (1976), *The New Worker Co-operatives*. Spokesman: Nottingham.

Coates, K. and A. Topham (1975), 'Shop Stewards and Workers' Control', Vol. II, in: K. Coates and A. Topham (eds.), *Industrial Democracy in Great Britain*. Spokesman: Nottingham.

Coenen, H.M.J. (1987), *Handelingsonderzoek als Exemplarisch leren*. Konstapel: Groningen.

Coenen, H.M.J., and H. Hens (1980: 285-351), 'COB-experimenten en Medezeggenschap', in: *Tijdschrift voor Arbeid en Bewustzijn*, jrg. 4, nr. 3/4.

Coenen, H.M.J., and P. Leisink (eds.) (1993), *Work and Citizenship in the New Europe*. Aldershot: Elgar.

Coenen, H.M.J., and B. Valkenburg (1986: 335-360), 'Sociale Wetenschappen in de Aanbieding?', in: *Tijdschrift voor Arbeid en Bewustzijn*, jrg. 10, nr. 4.

Cole, R.E. (1993), 'The Leadership, Organization and Codetermination Programme and its Evaluation: a comparative perspective', in: F. Naschold, H. van Beinum, R.E. Cole and B. Gustavsen, *Constructing the New Industrial Society*. van Gorcum: Assen/Maastricht.

Commission on Industrial Relations (1972), *Industrial Relations Training*. HMSO: London.

Coninck, P. de and J. Vilrokx (1977: 608-618), 'Een Bedrijfsbezetting: Prestige-Tessenderlo', in: *De Nieuwe Maand*, 20, 10, December.

Cooper, M.R. (1982), *Search for Consensus. The Role of Institutional Dialogue between Government, Labour and Employers: the experience of five countries.* OECD: Paris.

Costers, B. (1991), 'Joint Research of Trade Unions and Universities', Synthesis Report on the Conferences held in Manchester, Paris, Aalbord and Glasgow, Brussels, (mimeo).

Council of Europe/Social Affairs Division (1981), *Worker Participation in the Life of the Firm*. Strasbourg.

Coutrot, T. (1992: 22-39), 'l'Intéressement: vers une nouvelle convention salariale?', in: *Travail et Emploi*, No. 53, Ministère du Travail, de l'Emploi et de la Formation professionnelle.

Cressey, P., 'Employee Participation' in: M.D. Gold (ed.) (1993), *The Social Dimension: employment policy in the European Community*. Basingstoke, Macmillan.

Croucher, R. and J. Halstead (1990: 3-14), 'The Origin of "Liberal" Adult Education for Miners at Sheffield in the Post-War Period: a study in adult education and the working class', in: *Trade Union Studies Journal* 21.

Crusius, R. (ed.) (1978), *Die Betriebsräte in der Weimarer Republik: von der Selbstverwaltung zur Mitbestimmung (Works councils in the Weimar Republic: from self-management to codetermination)*, 2 vols. Olle and Wolter: Berlin.

d'Iribarne, P. (1989), *La Logique de l'Honneur*. Seuil: Paris.

Dachler, H.P. and B. Wilpert (1978: 1-39), 'Conceptual Dimensions and Boundaries of Participation on Organizations: a critical evaluation', in: *Administrative Science Quarterly*, 23.

Dahlström, E. (1978), 'The Role of Social Science in Working Life Policy', in: *Sociology of Work in the Nordic Countries*. Scandinavian Sociological Association: Oslo.

Danielsson, A. (1993), *Samtal om ledning och ledarskap*. Svenska Dagbladets förlag: Stockholm.

Danvind, E.M. and R. Mörtvik (1994), Learning, reorientation and realization - New bases for trade union work. Draft paper (mimeo), TCO: Stockholm.

Daubler, W. and W. Lecher (eds.) (1991), *Die Gewerkschaften in der Zwölf EG-Ländern*. Bund: Köln.

Davies, A., F. Naschold, W. Pritchard and T. Reve (1993), Evaluation Report. Commissioned by the Board of the SBA programme. The Norwegian Work Life Centre/The Work Research Institute: Oslo.

Department of Education and Science (1972), Report of a Working Party on Shop Steward Education and Training [the Gold Report], Circular FECL 9/72 T2003/08 (5 July 1972).

Deppe, F. (1969), *Kritik der Mitbestimmung: partnerschaft oder klassenkampf?* I.M.S.F.: Frankfurt/M.

Derebnancourt, G. (1991), *Le Comité d'Entreprise Européen: evaluation d'une proposition de directive.* Observatoire Social Européen: Bruxelles.

Deutscher Gewerkschaftsbund, Bundesvorstand (ed.) (1978), *Gewerkschaften und Mitbestimmung.* Zentrale für Politische Bildung: Bonn.

Deutscher Gewerkschaftsbund, Wirtschafts- und Sozialwissenschaftliches Institut (WSI des DGB) (1981), *Mitbestimmung in Unternehmen und Betrief.* Bund: Köln.

Di Martino, V. and W. O'Conghaile (1985), *Worker Participation and the Improvement of Working Conditions: a bibliographical analysis.* European Foundation for the Improvement of Living and Working Conditions: Dublin.

Diallo, M., M. Dopavogui and G. Kester (1992), *Guinée: Pour un Nouveau Syndicalisme en Afrique.* l'Harmattan: Paris.

Diefenbacher, H. and H.G. Nutzinger (eds.) (1984-1986), *Konzepte und Formen der Arbeitnehmerpartizipation*, 3 vols. FEST: Heidelberg.

Donovan Report (1968), *Royal Commission on Trade Unions and Employers' Associations* 1965-68. Cmnd. 3623, HMSO: London.

Dorow, W. (ed.) (1987), *The Business Corporation in the Democratic Society.* de Gruyter: Berlin/New York.

Drago, R., and M. Wooden (1991: 177-204), 'The Determinants of Participatory Management' in: *British Journal of Industrial Relations*, June.

Eaton, J. and A. Fletcher (1976), 'Workers' Participation in Management - a survey of post-war organized opinion', in: *Political Quarterly*, Vol.47.

Ehn, P. and A. Sandberg (1979), 'God utredning ' in: *Utreding och förändring i förvaltningen.* Publica/liber förlag: Stockholm.

Einemann, E. (1989), 'Cooperation Between Universities and Unions' in: G. Széll, a.o. (eds.), *The State, Trade Unions and Self-Management.* de Gruyter: Berlin/New York.

Elden, M. (1979), 'Three Generations of Work Democracy Experiments in Norway', in: C. Cooper and E. Mumford (eds.), *The Quality of Working Life in Eastern and Western Europe.* Associated Business Press: London.

Electrical, Electronic, Telecommunications and Plumbing Union (1976), *Evidence to the Committee of Inquiry on Industrial Democracy.* Bromley.

Emery, F.E. (1959), Characteristics of Socio-Technical Systems. London, Tavistock Institute of Human Relations, Doc. no. 527.

Emery, F.E. (1977), *Futures We Are In.* Nijhoff: Leiden.

Emery, F.E. (1989), *Toward Real Democracy*. Ontario Quality of Working Life Centre: Toronto.

Emery, F.E. (1993), 'The Light on the Hill', in: M. Emery, *Participative Design for Participative Democracy*. The Centre for Continuing Education, Australian National University: Canberra.

Emery, F.E. and E. Thorsrud (1969), *Form and Content in Industrial Democracy. Experience from the Board Room Approach*. Tavistock: London.

Emery, F.E. and E. Thorsrud (1976), *Democracy at Work*. Nijhoff: Leiden.

Emery, F.E. and E.L. Trist (1969), 'Sociotechnical Systems', in: F.E. Emery (ed.), *Systems Thinking*. Penguin Books: Baltimore.

Encel, S., 'Australia', in: G. Széll, (ed.) (1992: 35-39), *Concise Encyclopaedia of Participation and Co-Management*. de Gruyter: Berlin/New York.

Estrin, S. and N. Wilson (1989), 'Profit-sharing, the Marginal Cost of Labour and Employment Variability', mimeo, London School of Economics, May.

European Communities, Commission of (1975: 107), Employee Participation and Company Structure in the European Community, (EC Bulletin supplement 8/75), Luxembourg.

European Communities, Commission of (1992), "Recommandation du Conseil sur 'La Promotion de la Participation des Salariés aux Profits et aux Résultats de l'Entreprise'", in: *Journal Officiel des Communautes Européennes*, No. L245, 26, August.

European Communities, Commission of (1994), *Croissance, Compétitivité, Emploi; les défis et les pistes pour entrer dans le XXIè siècle*. Livre Blanc. C.C.E.: Brussels, Luxemburg.

European Communities, European Parliament (1982), Second report drawn up on behalf of the Legal Affairs Committee on the proposal of the Commission of European Communities to the Council for a fifth directive. Bruxelles.

European Foundation for the Improvement of Living and Working Conditions (1981), *Institutionalized Forms of Participation in Companies*. Dublin.

European Foundation for the Improvement of Living and Working Conditions (1990), *Participation in Change - New Technologies and the Role of Employee Involvement*. Dublin.

European Foundation for the Improvement of Living and Working Conditions (1990), *Roads to Participation in Technological Change*. EEC: Luxembourg.

European Foundation for the Improvement of Living and Working Conditions (1991), *P+ European Participation Monitor*. Issue No.1. Dublin.

Fernvall, L. (1992), LO and the research, (mimeo), LO: Stockholm.

Fiorito J., C. Lowman and F.D. Nelson (1987: 113-126), 'The Impact of Human Resource Policies on Union Organizing', in: *Industrial Relations*, 26.

Fisher, J. (1989: 57-66), 'Industrial Studies. An Example of Union/Uuniversity Co-operation', in: *The Industrial Tutor* 4(9).

Fitzroy, F.R. and K. Kraft (1985), 'Participation and Division of Labour: a West German case study', in: *Industrial Relations Journal*, no. 4.

Fitzroy, F.R. and K. Kraft (1987), 'Cooperation, Productivity and Profit-sharing', in: *Quarterly Journal of Economics*, 102, February.

Flanders, A. and A. Fox (1970), 'Collective Bargaining: from Donovan to Durkheim' in: *Management and Unions: the theory and reform of industrial relations*. Faber: London.

FNV (1983), *Onderzoek voor de Vakbeweging: nota onderzoekswensen van de FNV*. FNV: Amsterdam.

FNV (1987), *Werken in 2000*. FNV: Amsterdam.

FNV (1990), *Economische Democratie en Vakbeweging*. FNV: Amsterdam.

FNV (1992), *De Toekomst van "Onderzoek" in de FNV*. FNV: Amsterdam.

Forrester, K. (1986: 18-26), 'Adult Education, Trade Unions and the Unemployed', in: *The Industrial Tutor* 4(3).

Forrester, K. and C. Thorne (1992), *Research as Engagement*. Avebury: Aldershot.

Forrester, K. and K. Ward (1990: 387-95), 'Trade Union Services for the Unemployed: the unemployed workers' centres', in: *British Journal of Industrial relations* 28(3).

France, Ministère du Travail et de la Participation (1981), *Participation une Réalité Vivante*. Documentation Française: Paris.

Freeman, R.B. and M. Kleiner (1986), 'Union Organizing Drive Outcomes from NLRB Elections during a Period of Economic Concessions', Thirty-ninth Industrial Relations Research Association Proceedings Madison, WI: Industrial Relations Research Association.

Freeman, R.B. and M. Kleiner (1988), The Impact of the New Unionization on Wages and Working Conditions: a longitudinal study of establishments under NLRB elections. National Bureau of Economic Research Working paper, no. 2563.

Freeman, R.B. and M. Weitzman (1986), Bonuses and Employment in Japan. N.B.E.R. Working Paper no. 187.

Fricke, W. and W. Schuchardt (eds.) (1984), Beteiligung als Element Gewerkschaftlicher Arbeitspolitik. Erfahrungen aus Norwegen, Italien, Schweden und der Bundesrepublik. Verlag Neue Gesellschaft: Bonn.

Froehlich, D., C. Gill, and H. Krieger, *Roads to Participation in the European Community*. European Foundation for the Improvement of Living and Working Conditions, Shankill.

Gardell, B. (1977), 'Autonomy and Participation at Work', in: *Human Relations*, Vol. 30, No. 6.

George, S. (1986), *How the Other Half Dies*. Penguin: Hammondsworth.

George, S. (1990), *A Fate Worse than Debt*. Penguin: London.

Germany, Federal Republic of (1972), German Works Councils Act 1972. Commerce Clearing House: Chicago.

Ghezzi, G. (1978: 3), 'La Participazione dei Lavoratori alla Gestione delle Imprese ed il Sistema Contrattuale delle Informazioni e della Consultazione del Sindacato', in: *Rivista Giuridica del Lavoro*.

Ghezzi, G. (1993), 'Prime Note sull'Accordo Governo-Sindicati-Confindustria del 3 luglio 1993'. To be published in: *Rivista Critica del Diritto Privato*.

Giannini, M.S. (1986), *Il Potere Pubblico, Stati e Amministrazioni Pubbliche*. Bologna, Il Mulino.

Giugni, G. (1976: 151), 'Ancora una Nota Sulla Democrazia Industriale', in: *Politica del Diritto*.

Giugni, G. (1985: 53), 'Concertazione Sociale e Sistema Politico in Italia', in: *Giornale di Diritto del Lavoro e di Relazioni Industriali*.

Glaser, B.G. and A. Strauss (1967), *The Discovery of Grounded Theory*. Aldine: Chicago.

Glimell, H. (1990), 'Kunskapsutveckling i Svensk Arbetslivsforskning', in: W. Agrell (ed.), *Makten over Forskningspolitiken*. University Press: Lund.

Globerson, A. (1970), 'Spheres and Levels of Employee Participation in Organisations', in: *British Journal of Industrial Relations*, Vol. 8.

Goetschy, J. (1983), *La Participation des Travailleurs aux Décisions dans l'Entreprise. Etude des Stratégies et des Représentations*. Centre de Recherches en Sciences Sociales du Travail: Sceaux.

Goetschy, J. (1991), 'Bilan du Dialogue Social Européen de Val Duchesse', in: *Travail et Emploi*, n.1.

Goetschy, J. (1993), 'L'Europe Sociale à la Croisée des Chemins', in: *Sociologie du Travail*, n.2.

Gold, M.D. (1981), The Democratisation of Investment by Occupational Pension Funds. Discussion Paper, No.24, Trade Union Research Unit, Ruskin College: Oxford.

Gold, M.D. and M. Hall (1992), *European-Level Information and Consultation in Multinational Companies: an evaluation of practice*. Office des Publications Officielles de la CE: Luxembourg.

Gold, M.D., H. Levie and R. Moore (1979), *The Shop Stewards' Guide to the Use of Company Information*. Spokesman: Nottingham.

Goodrich, C.L. (1975), *The Frontier of Control: a study in British workshop politics*. Pluto Press [first published 1920]: London.

Gorz, A. et al. (1973), *Critique de la Division du Travail*. Seuil: Paris.

Grab, W. (1991), 'Dangers of German Nationalism', paper presented at the International Conference on Return of Work, Production and Administration to Capitalism. Chemnitz.

Graversen, G. (1983), *Ny Virksomhed På Åben Mark*, Vol. 1. Teknologisk Institut: København.

Greenwood, G. (1990), *A Study of Fagor Values*. Cornell University Press: New York.

Gregg, P.A. and S.J. Machin (1988: 91-109), "Unions and the Incidence of Performance Linked Pay Schemes in Britain", in: *International Journal of Industrial Organization.*

Guest, D. (1989), 'Human Resource Management: its implications for industrial relations and trade unions' in: J. Storey (ed.) *New Perspectives on Human Resource Management.* Routledge: London and New York.

Guest, D. and D. Fatchett (1974), *Worker Participation: individual control and performance.* Institute of Personnel Management: London.

Gulowsen, J. (1972), 'A Measure of Work-Group Autonomy', in: L.E. Davis and J.L. Taylor (eds.), *Design of Jobs.* Penguin Books: Middlesex.

Gustafsson, R.A. and A. Kjellberg (1987), *Behavioral Scientists and Workers.* The Swedish Work Environment Fund: Stockholm.

Gustavsen, B. (1985), 'Workplace Reform and Democratic Dialogue', in: *Economic and Industrial Democracy,* Vol. 6, No. 4.

Gustavsen, B. (1989a), *Action Research and the Theoretical Foundations for Large-Scale Development Programmes.* Swedish Centre for Working Life: Stockholm.

Gustavsen, B. (1989b), *Creating Broad Change in Working Life, The LOM Programme.* Ontario Quality of Working Life Centre: Toronto.

Gustavsen, B. (1992), *Dialogue and Development.* van Gorcum: Assen/Maastricht.

Gustavsen, B. and G. Hunnius (1981), *New Patterns of Work Reform.* Oslo University Press/Columbia University Press: Oslo/New York.

Habermas, J. (1987), *The Theory of Communicative Action,* Vol. 1-2. Polity Press: London.

Hall, M. (1992), Legislating for Employee Participation: a case study of the European works councils directive. Warwick Research Paper n.39.

Hammerstrøm, O. (1987), 'Swedish Industrial Relations', in: G. Banber and R. Landsbury (eds.), *International and Comparative Industrial Relations.* Allen & Unwin: Sydney.

Handberg, S. (1993), 'Employee Participation Through Experience Learning. A Case from the Fish Processing Industry', in: *Proceedings from the European Conference on the Role of Research for the Social Shaping of New Technologies.* Ravello, Italy, 13-15 Oct. Rome, The Department of Development and Planning, Aalborg University, IRES/Aalborg.

Harlem Brundtland, G. (1989), 'The Scandinavian Challenge: strategies for work and learning', in: C.J. Lammers and G. Széll, *International Handbook of Participation and Organizations,* Vol. 1. Oxford University Press: Oxford.

Hart, R. and O. Hübler (1989), Profit-sharing: individual participation and shares, and effects on wages, labour mobility and working time. Mimeo, University of Stirling and University of Hannover: Hannover.

Hashimoto, M. (1990: 245-93), 'Employment and Wage Systems in Japan and their Implications for Productivity', in: A.S. Blinder (ed.), *Paying for Productivity - a look at the evidence,* Brookings Institution: Washington D.C.

Heller, F., E. Pusic, J.D. Reynaud, G. Strauss, and B. Wilpert (eds.) (1983-1986), *International Yearbook of Organizational Democracy. For the Study of Participation, Cooperation and Power,* 3 vols. Wiley: Chichester.

Henselmans, J. (1984), 'Zelfbestuur ook voor Grote Bedrijven' in: *Zeggenschap,* nr. 114.

Herbst, P.G. (1962), *Autonomous Group Functioning.* Tavistock: London.

Hibbit, A. (1991), 'Employee Involvement: a recent survey', in: *Employment Gazette.* December, HMSO: London.

HMSO (1977), *Report of a Committee of Inquiry on Industrial Democracy,* Cmd. 6706. HMSO: London.

Hoffman, D. (1976), *The German Co-determination Act 1976.* Metzner: Frankfurt/M.

Hofmaier, B. (1993), 'Workplace Development in Sweden: some preliminary findings from the Work Life Fund', in: *Proceedings from the European Conference on the Role of Research for the Social Shaping of New Technologies.* Ravello, Italy, 13-15 Oct.IRES/The Swedish Work Life Centre: Rome/Stockholm.

Holford, J. (1993), *Union Education in Britain: a TUC activity.* Nottingham University: Nottingham.

Holmstrand, L. (1993: 106-114), 'The research circle: a way of cooperating' in: K. Forrester and C. Thorne (eds), *Trade Unions and Social Research,* Avebury: Aldershot.

Holzer, W. and K.G. Kukuk (eds.) (1991), *Bridges Between Science and the World of Work.* Kooperationsstelle Wissenschaft-Arbeitswelt: Dortmund.

Horvat, B. (1982), *The Political Economy of Socialism.* Sharpe, Armonk: New York.

Hövels, B.W.M., and P. Nas (1976), *Ondernemingsraden en Medezeggenschap. Een Vergelijkend Onderzoek naar Structuur en Werkwijze van Ondernemingsraden.* Samson: Alphen a/d Rijn.

Huebner, J.W. (1981), *Worker participation. A Comparative Study between the Systems of the Netherlands, the Federal Republic of Germany and the United States.* Leiden university: Leiden .

Huiskamp, M.J. and P.A. Risseeuw (1988), *Ondernemingsraden in Vakbondsland?* Amsterdam.

IDE - International Research Group (1981a), *Industrial Democracy in Europe.* Clarendon Press: Oxford.

IDE - International Research Group (1981b), *European Industrial Relations.* Clarendon Press: Oxford.

Industrial Democracy (1948), 'Towards Tomorrow' Series No.1. Labour Party: London.

Industrial Democracy (1978), Cmnd. 7231. HMSO: London.

Institute of Directors (1958), *Understanding Labour Relations*. London.

International Institute for Labour Studies (1987), Report of a Round Table held at Laval University, Quebec. ILO: Geneva.

International Labour Office (1985), Workers' Participation in Decisions within Undertakings. Genève, 1981, xi, 224 pp. (Document prepared by J. Monat - third printing).

International Labour Office (1991), Protection des Créances des Travailleurs en Cas d'Insolvabilité de leur Employeur. Report V (1) and V (2), Conférence Internationale du Travail, 78th session, ILO: Geneva.

International Sociological Association, (1992), Report Research Committee X, 'Research on workers' participation and self-management'.

IRES (1992), *Syndicalismes. Dynamique des Relations Professionnelles. Grande Bretagne, Etas-Unis, Allemagne, Italie, France.* Dunod: Paris.

Ishikawa, A. (ed.) (1988), *Sangyo-Shakaigaku.* (Industrial Sociology). Saiensu-Sha: Tokyo.

Ishikawa, A., and G. Széll (1992), 'Participation and Co-management: the Japanese participation formula', Osnabrücker Sozialwissenschaftliche Manuskripte.

Jain, H.C. (1992: 88-98), 'Canada', in: G. Széll, (ed.), *Concise Encyclopaedia of Participation and Co-Management.* De Gruyter: Berlin/New York.

Jain, H.C. and A. Giles (1985: 747-74), 'Workers' Participation in Western Europe. Implications for North America', in: *Rélations Industrielles* 40 (4).

Janérus, I. (1983), 'Lagstiftiningsarbetet på 70-talet', in: A. Broström (ed.), *Arbetsrättens Utveckling.* The Swedish Center for Working Life: Stockholm.

Jenkins, D. (1973), *Job Power.* Penguin: New York.

Jensen, M. and W. Meckling (1979: 469-506), 'Rigths and Production Functions', in: *Journal of Business*, 52.

Jobert, A. (1990), 'La Négociation Collective dans les Entreprises Multinationales en Europe', in: G. Devin (ed.), *Syndicalisme: Dimension Internationales.* Paris.

John Paul II (1991), *Centesimus Annus.* Libreria Editrice Vaticana: Vatican City.

Jones, D.C. and T. Kato (1995), 'Japan: financial participation in the context of human resources and heightened competitiveness', in: D. Vaughan-Whitehead, 'Workers' Financial Participation: East-West experiences'. *Labour Management Series*, No. 50, ILO: Geneva.

Jones, D.C. and J. Pliskin (1988), The Effects of Alternative Arrangements on Employment: preliminary evidence from Britain. Working Paper series no. 88:2, Department of Economics, Hamilton College, Clinton: New-York.

Jones, D.C. and C. Rock (1992: 967-973), 'Workplace Democracy, United States', in: G. Széll, (ed.), *Concise Encyclopaedia of Participation and Co-Management.* de Gruyter: Berlin/New York.

Jones, D.C. and J. Svejnar (eds.) (1981), *Participatory and Self-Managed Firms. Evaluating Economic Performance.* Lexington Books: Lexington/Mass.

282

Jones, D.C. and J. Svejnar (eds.) (1985-1987), *Advances in the Economic Analysis of Participatory and Labor Managed Firms,* 3 vols. Jal Press: Greenwich/Conn.

Judith, R., O. Brenner, E. Loderer and H.O. Vetter (1979), (eds.), *Montanmitbestimmung. Geschichte, Idee, Wirklichkeit.* Bund Verlag: Köln.

Judith, R., F. Kübel, E. Loderer, H. Schröder and H.O. Vetter (eds) (1979), *Montanmitbestimmung. Dokumente ihrer Entstehung.* Bund Verlag: Köln.

Junge, F., A. Westenholz, P. Møldrup and L. Brinch (1974: 34-50), 'Danish Experiments with New Forms of Cooperation on the Shop Floor', in: *Personnel Review* 3 (3).

Karasek, R. (1979), 'Job Demands, Job Decision Latitude and Mental Strain: implications for job design', in: *Administrative Science Quarterly,* June.

Kaspar, J., Discours au CNRS, le 6/2/1991, à l'occasion de la signature de la deuxième convention de cooperation scientifique CNRS-CFDT. Not published.

Katterie, S. and K. Krahn (eds.) (1980), *Wissenschaft und Arbeitsnehmerinteressen.* Bund-Verlag: Köln.

Kauppinen, T. (1993), 'Management of Change and the JOY project', in: *Proceedings from the Conference Workplace Development in Finland.* The Research Unit, Ministry of Labour: Helsinki.

Kester, G. (1973-1974: 68-83), 'Workers' Participation by Surprise', in: *Development and Change,* 5 (3).

Kester, G. (1980), *Transition to Workers' Self-management: its dynamics in the decolonizing economy of Malta.* Institute of Social Studies: The Hague.

Kester, G. (1986), 'Workers Representatives versus Workers Representatives'. Working Paper 31. Institute of Social Studies: The Hague.

Kester, G. (1991a), *Effets de la Privatisation et Lutte Syndicale.* APADEP: The Hague.

Kester, G. (1991b), 'In Defense of Workers' Participation and Self-Management in Africa'. APADEP-paper, APADEP: The Hague.

Kester, G. (1991c), 'The Participation Striptease'. Paper presented to the International Conference on Return of Work, Production and Administration to Capitalism. Chemnitz.

Kester, G. (1992: 234-241), 'Development Strategy', in: G. Széll (ed.), *Concise Encyclopaedia of Participation and Co-Management.* de Gruyter: Berlin/New York.

Kester, G. and H. Pinaud (1992), 'Trade Unions, Democracy, Participation and Development - a brainstorming paper' (first draft). Leusden and Paris.

Kester, G. and E. Zammit, 'Malta', in: G. Széll (ed.) (1992: 506-512), *Concise Encyclopaedia of Participation and Co-Management.* de Gruyter: Berlin/New York.

Keyser, V. de, A. Ruiz Quintanilla and T.U. Qvale (1988), *The Meaning of Work and Technological Options.* Wiley: Chichester.

King, C.D. and M. Van de Vall (1978), *Models of Industrial Democracy: consultation, co-determination and workers' self-management*. Mouton: The Hague/Paris.

Kissler, L. (1989: 74-90), 'Co-Determination in Research in the Federal Republic of Germany: a review' in: C.J. Lammers and G. Széll (eds.), *International Handbook of Participation in Organizations*. Vol I. OUP: Oxford.

Klandermans, B. et al (1992), *Participatie in Vakbonden. Samenvatting van enkele Onderzoeksresultaten*. Amsterdam.

Klein, J. (1990), 'A Reexamination of Autonomy in Light of New Manufacturing Practices', in: *Human Relations*.

Koda, B. (1991), 'Women, Participation and Development' Paper presented to the International Workshop "Trade Unions, Democracy and Development". APADEP: Dar-es-Salaam/Mbeya.

Kolvenbach, W. and P. Hanau (1986), *Handbook on European Employee Co-Management*. Kluwer: Deventer.

Korpi, W. (1978), *The Working Class in Welfare Capitalism*. Routledge and Keagan Paul: London.

Koziara, E.C. (1975), *The Labour Market and Wage Determination in Malta*. Malta University Press: Msida.

Kramer, D.C. (1972), *Participatory Democracy. Developing Ideals of the Political Left*. Schenkman: Cambridge, Mass.

Kruse, D.L. (1991), 'Profit-Sharing and Employment Variability: microeconomic evidence on the Weitzman theory', in: *Industrial and Labor Relations Review*, Vol. 44, April.

La Democrazia Industriale: Il Caso Italiano, AA.VV. (More authors) (1980), Riuniti: Roma.

Laaksonen, O. (1984: 229-318), 'Participation Down and Up the Line. Comparative Industrial Democracy Trends in China and Europe.', in: *International Social Science Journal* 36 (2).

Labbé, D. and M. Croisat (1992), *La Fin des Syndicats*. L'Harmattan: Paris.

Lakshmanna, C. et al. (eds.) (1990), *Workers' Participation and Industrial Democracy, Global Perspectives*. Ajanta: Delhi/India.

Lammers, C.J. and G. Széll (eds.) (1989), *International Handbook of Participation in Organizations. Vol.I: Taking Stock*. Oxford University Press: Oxford.

Lange, P. (1987: 61), 'La Crisi della Concertazione Sociale in Italia', in: *Giornale di Diritto del Lavoro e di Relazioni Industriali*.

Lasserre, R. (1983), 'Concertation Sociale et Cogestion', in: G. Sandoz (ed.), *Les Allemands Sans Miracle*. Armand Colin: Paris.

Le Boterf, G. and P. Lessard (1986), *L'Ingenierie des Projets de Developpement*. INFREP: Paris.

Le Tron, M. and H. Pinaud (1991), 'Projet Conjoint de Recherche Transversale'. Paroles 2: Paris.

Le Tron, M. and H. Pinaud (1992), 'Democratiser l'Entreprise et le Syndicalisme: Le rôle des salariés', in: *CFDT-Aujourd'hui*. Paris.

Leemput, J. van (1992: 66-79), 'Belgium: the historical development of the Belgian participation model', in: G. Széll, *Concise Encyclopaedia of Participation and Co-management*. de Gruyter: Berlin and New York.

Leijnse, F., and M. van der Varst (1981), *Medezeggenschap bij de NZH. Onderzoeksverslag*. Den Haag.

Leisink, P.L.M. (1989a), 'The Ambivalence towards Democratisation'. Paper presented at the International Workshop on "Social Needs, Ownership and Trade Unions". October 1-6, 1989: Sofia.

Leisink, P.L.M. (1989b), *Structurering van Arbeidsverhoudingen. Een Vergelijkende Studie van Medezeggenschap in de Grafische Industrie en in het Streekvervoer*. Van Arkel: Utrecht.

Leisink, P.L.M. and L. Beukema (1993), 'Participation and Autonomy at Work: a segmented privilege', in: H. Coenen and P. Leisink, *Work and Citizenship in the New Europe*. Elgar: Aldershot.

Levinson, C. (ed.) (1974), *Industry's Democratic Revolution*. G. Allen & Unwin: London.

LO (Swedish central union confederation) (1971), *Demokrati i Företagen*. Stockholm.

LO (1990), Det Utvecklande Arbetet, (mimeo). Stockholm.

LO (1994a), Förslag till riktlinjer för LO:skolenhet (mimeo) Stockholm.

LO (1994b), *Utveckling i arbeted med samhällsstöd-nägot för framtiden ?* Stockholm.

Looise, J.C., and J.Z. Heijink (1986), 'De OR en zijn Bevoegdheden'. Interimrapport van het onderzoek naar de praktische uitoefening van wettelijke bevoegdheden door ondernemingsraden en de knelpunten die daarbij optreden. Instituut voor Toegepaste Sociale Wetenschappen: Nijmegen.

Looise, J.C., and F.G.M. de Lange (1987), *Ondernemingsraden, Bestuurders en Besluitvorming*. Instituut voor Toegepaste Sociale Wetenschappen: Nijmegen.

Lundberg, B and B. Starring (1990), 'Forskningscirklar i Värmland' in : Holzhausen (ed.) *Local facklig kunskapsuppbyggnad i samverkan med forskare,* Arbetslivcentrum: Stockholm.

Macfarlane, J. (1975: 81-7), 'Coalminers at University - a second chance in education', in: *Adult Education* 48(2) July.

Macmillan, M. (1973), Preface to: N.A.B. Wilson, On the Quality of Working Life. Department of Employment Manpower Papers No.7, HMSO: London.

Maire, E. (1976), *Demain l'Autogestion*. Seghers: Paris.

Maire, E. (1986), 'Le Droit d'Expression: un levier de changement social', in: *Désormais les Salariés s'Expriment*. Paris.

Maire, E.(1987), *Nouvelles Frontières pour le Syndicalisme*. Syros: Paris.

285

Maley, B.R., D. Dexter and B. Ford (1979), *Industrial Democracy and Worker Participation: a selected annotated and classified bibliography of international citations on the theory and practice of industrial democracy and worker participation and their role in organizational change.* Unit for Industrial Democracy, South Australian Department of Labour and Industry & University of New South Wales: Adelaide.

Man, H. de (1985), *Medezeggenschap, Besluitvorming en Organisatie.* Den Haag.

Marchington, M., P. Ackers, J. Goodman, and A. Wilkinson (1992), *New Developments in Employee Involvement.* Research Series No.2. Employment Department: London.

Marclay, A. (1971), *Workers' Participation in Management. Selected Bibliography, 1950-1970.* ILO: Geneva.

Martin, D. (1994), *Démocratie industrielle - La participation directe dans les entrepises.* PUF: Paris.

Mason, R.M. (1982), *Participatory and Workplace Democracy. A Theoretical Development in Critique of Liberalism.* Southern Illinois Press: Carbondale.

Maurice, F., F. Sellier and J. Silvestre (1982), *Politique d'Education et Organisation Industrielle en France et en Allemagne.* PUF: Paris.

Mcllroy, J. (1988a: 60-73), 'Storm and Stress: the trades union congress and university adult education 1964-1974', in: *Studies in the Education of Adults* 20(1), April.

Mcllroy, J. (1988b: 109-23), 'Unions and Universities: a troubled marriage', in: *Studies in the Education of Adults* 20(2).

Mee, G. (1984), Miners, Adult Education and Community Service 1920-1984. Nottingham Working Papers in the Education of Adults 6, Nottingham.

Meidner, R. (1978), *Employee Investment Funds. An Approach to Collective Capital Formation.* G. Allen & Unwin: London.

Metallarbetareförbundet (1985), *Det Goda Arbetet.* Stockholm.

Metallarbetareförbundet (1989), *Solidarisk Arbetspolitik.* Stockholm.

Micallef, J. (1975), *The European Company: a comparative study with English and Maltese company law.* Rotterdam University Press: Rotterdam.

Millar, J.P.M. (1979), *The Labour College Movement.* NCLC Publishing Society Ltd: London.

Millward, N., W.R. Hawes, D. Smart, and M. Stevens (1992), *Workplace Industrial Relations in Transition.* Darmouth Publishing: Aldershot.

Miniutti, A. (1994), Constitution d'un Fonds Commun d'Investissement au Plan Européen, dénommé 'Fonds Européen de Solidarité'. Text presented at the Colloquium entitled 'Trade Unions and Democratic Participation', organised by the CFDT under the auspices of the ETUC, Paris, 2-4 February.

Mitbestimmungskommission(1970), *Mitbestimmung im Unternehmen. Bericht der Sachverständigenkommission zur Auswertung der bisherigen Erfahrungen bei der Mitbestimmung*, VI/334, Bundestagsdrucksache: Bonn.

286

Mitchell, D.J. (1987: 1-17), 'The Share Economy and Industrial Relations', in: *Industrial Relations*, 26.

Mitchell, D.J. (1995), 'The United States: flexibility first?', in: D. Vaughan-Whitehead, 'Workers' Financial Participation: East-West experiences'. *Labour Management Series*, No. 50, ILO: Geneva.

MLP (1992: 33), Electoral Programme.

Monat, J. and H. Sarfati (1986), *Workers' Participation: a voice in decisions, 1981-85.* ILO: Geneva.

Monat, J., D. Campbell and W. Sengenberger (1992), Trade Unions and the 'New Industrial Organisation and Labour Institutions' Programme of the IILS.

Mothé, D. (1980), *l'Autogestion Goutte à Goutte.* le Centurion: Paris.

Mulder, M. (1971), 'Power Equalization through Participation?', in: *Administrative Science Quarterly* 16, 31-39.

Müller-Jentsch, W. (ed.) (1988), *Zukunft der Gewerkschaften.* Campus: Frankfurt/New York.

Musa, A.E. (1992), Workers Participation Hijacked. APADEP-paper, APADEP: Dar es Salaam/The Hague.

Myrdal, G., *Objektivitetsproblemet i samshällforskningen.* Stockholm, Ráben & Sjörgen (English original: Objectivity in Social Research).

Nagel, B. (1980), *Unternehmensmitbestimmung. Eine Problemorientierte Einführung.* Bund: Köln.

Naisbitt, J. (1982-1984), *Megatrends. Ten New Directions Transforming our Lives.* Warner Books.

Naphtali, F. (1977), *Wirtschaftsdemokratie.* Europäische Verlagsanstalt: Frankfurt/M (1928).

Naschold, F. (1992), Evaluation Report. Commissioned by the Board of the LOM Programme. Science Center: Berlin / Arbetslivcentrum: Stockholm.

Naschold, F. (1993), 'Organization Development: national programmes in the context of international competition', in: F. Naschold, H. van Beinum, R.E. Cole, and B. Gustavsen, *Constructing the New Industrial Society.* van Gorcum: Assen/Maastricht.

Naschold, F., H. van Beinum, R.E. Cole, and B. Gustavsen (1993), *Constructing the New Industrial Society.* van Gorcum: Assen/Maastricht.

Noblecourt, M. (1990), *Les Syndicats en Question.* Les Editions Ouvrières: Paris.

Nuti, M.D. (1986), 'The Share Economy: plausibility and viability of Weitzman's model', in: S. Hedlund, *Incentives and Economic Systems*, Croom helm: Londen.

Nuti, M.D. (1987), 'Profit-Sharing and Employment: claims and overclaims', in: *Industrial Relations*, Winter.

OECD (1986), *Flexibilité sur le Marché du Travail*, edit. La Découverte.

OECD (1991), *Economic Outlook.* Organisation for Economic Co-operation and Development: Paris.

Oswald, R. and W. Doherty (1991), 'Latin American Labor and Structural Adjustments in the 1990s: a union view of open markets and a worker-ownership response', Washington, AFL-CIO, (unpublished paper).

Paenson, I. (1972), *English-French-German-Russian Glossary of Terms Concerning Workers' Participation in Management*. Insternational Institute of Labour Studies: Geneva.

Pandolfo, A., L. Bellardi and F. Guarriello (1987: 94), 'Strategie e Procedure nella Negoziazione dell'Accordo Iri-Sindicati', in: *Prospettiva Sindicale*, No. 66.

Paoli, P. (1992), *First European Survey on the Work Environment 1991-92*. European Foundation: Dublin.

Parker, M. (1990), *Creating Shared Vision*. Norwegian Center for Leadership Development: Oslo.

Pastre, 0. and P. Moscovici (1991), Epargne Salariale et Fonds Propres. Report for the Deputy Secretary of Industry and External Commerce, December.

Pateman, C. (1970), *Participation and Democratic Theory*. Cambridge University Press: London.

Pedrazzoli, M. (1985: 217), 'Sull'Introduzione per via Contrattuale di Comitati Consultivi Paritetici nel Gruppo Iri', in: *Rivista Italiana di Diritto del Lavoro*.

Pedrazzoli, M. (1991: 33), 'Alternative Italiane sulla Partecipazione nel Dialogo Europeo: La Cogestione', in: *Giornale di Diritto del Lavoro e di Relazioni Industriali*.

Pessi, R. (1986: 732), 'Innovazione Technologica e Sistema di Relazioni Industriali: la contrattazione della trasformazione e il protocollo iri', in: *Rivista Italiana di Diritto del Lavoro*.

Pignon, D. (1975), 'Pour une Critique Politique de la Technologie', in: *Les Temps Modernes*, April, Paris.

Pinaud, H. (1988), 'Droit d'Expression et Participatif', in: *CFDT-Aujourd'hui*. May, Paris.

Pinaud, H. (1990), 'Communication entre Syndicats et Recherche et Diffusion Interne', in: *Coopération Syndicats-Recherche*, op. cit.

Pinaud, H. (1991), 'Pratiques Syndicales CFDT et Droit d'Expression', in: A. Chouraqui and A. Tchobanian (eds.), *Le Droit d'Expression en France: un séminaire international*. Institut International d'Etudes Sociales: Geneva.

Pinaud, H. (1992) 'A Trade Union Approach to Quality Management and Workers' Participation', in: P. Cressey (ed.), *International Workshop on Workers' Involvement*. University of Bath: Dublin.

Pinaud, H. (1991/1993), 'Elaboration et Mise en Oeuvre d'une Recherche Conjointe entre CFDT et Recherche Publique: l'exemple de PAROLES 2'. Rapport intermédiaire (1991) et Rapport final (1993). Institut de Recherche Economiques et Sociales: Paris.

PN (1992: 2), Electoral programme.

Ponzellini, A. (1987), 'Contrattazione e Partecipazione nelle Relazioni Industriali a Livello di Impresa', I and II, in: *Prospettiva Sindicale*. No. 64-65: 105 and 125.

Poole, M. (1978), *Workers' Participation in Industry*. Routledge & Kegan Paul: London.

Poole, M. (1988: 21-34), 'Factors Affecting the Development in Employee Financial Participation in Contemporary Britain: evidence from a national survey', in: *British Journal of Industrial Relations*.

Poole, M. (1995), 'The United Kingdom: financial participation: the employers' new productivity instrument?', in:D. Vaughan-Whitehead, 'Workers' Financial Participation: East-West experiences'. *Labour Management Series*, No. 50, ILO: Geneva

Pradervand, P. (1989), *Une Afrique en Marche*. Plon: Paris.

Prasnikar, J. (1991), *Workers'Participation and Self-management in Development Countries*. West View Press: San Francisco.

PSO (Program for Sammenlignende Organisasjonsanalyse) (1992), *Samarbeid om Bedriftsutvikling. Erfaringer og muligheter*. Department of Sociology, Oslo University: Oslo.

Putte, B. van den, et al. (1992), *De FNV Barometer 8*. Amsterdam.

Quattro note sulla democrazia industriale, AA.VV. (More authors) (1976), in: *Politica del Diritto*.

Qvale, T.U. (1976a: 354-369), 'A Norwegian Strategy for the Democratization of Industry', in: *Human Relations*, Vol. 29, No. 5.

Qvale, T.U. (1976b), 'Organisasjonsprinsipper', in: P.G. Herbst (ed.), *Demokratiseringsprosessen i Arbeidslivet*. Universitetsforlaget: Oslo.

Qvale, T.U. (1979), 'Industrial Democracy in Norway: experience from the board room approach', in: *Journal of General Management* 6 (7), Autumn.

Qvale, T.U. (1985), *Safety and Offshore Working Conditions*. Universitetsforlaget: Stavanger/Oslo.

Qvale, T.U. (1989), 'A New Milestone in the Development of Industrial Democracy in Norway?', in: C.J. Lammers and G. Széll, *International Handbook of Participation in Organizations*, Vol. 1. Oxford University Press: Oxford.

Qvale, T.U. (1991), *Participation for Productivity and Change: a multilevel cooperative strategy for improving organizational performance*. Workplace Australia: Melbourne.

Qvale, T.U. (1993), 'Design for Safety and Productivity in Large Scale Industrial Projects. The Case of Norwegian Offshored Development', in: B. Wilpert and T.U. Qvale (eds.), *Reliability and Safety in Hazardous Work Systems*. Lawrence Erlbaum: Hove (in press).

Qvale, T.U. and J. Hanssen-Bauer (1990), 'Implementing QWL in Large Scale Project Organizations: blue water site design in the Norwegian offshore oil industry', in: H.L. Meadow and M.J. Sirgy (eds.), *Quality of Life Studies in Marketing and Management. Proceedings: The Third Quality of Life/Marketing Conference*. Virginia Polytechnic Institute and State University: Blackburg, Virginia.

Ramsay, H. (1977: 381-506), 'Cycles of Control. Worker Participation in Sociological and Historical Perspective', in: *Sociology* 11 (3).

Regini, M. (1992), *The Future of Labour Movements*. International Sociological Association: London.

Regini, M. and C. Sabel (1988: 305), 'Le Strategie di Riaggiustamento Industriale in Italia: il ruolo degli asseti instituzionali', in: *Stato a Mercato*.

Reynaud, J.D. (1978), *Les Syndicats, les Patrons et l'Etat*. Les Editions Ouvrières: Paris.

Ricci, M. and B., Veneziani (1988), *Tra Conflitto e Partecipazione: un'indagine empirica sul protocollo iri e sui diritti di informazione*. Cacucci: Bari.

Richardson, A. (1983), *Participation*. Routledge & K. Paul: London.

Roccella, M. (1990: 485), 'Una Nuova Fase delle Relazioni Industriali in Italia: la stagione dei protocolli', in: *Lavoro e Diritto*.

Rodota, S. (1977), *Il Controllo Sociale della Attivita Private*. Il Mulino: Bologna.

Rodota, S. (1977), 'Diritto all'Informazione e Controlla sull'Impresa', in: AA.VV. (more authors), *Crisi e Riforma dell'Impresa*, Sari.

Roggema, J. and E. Thorsrud (1974), *Et Skip i Utvikling*. Tanum: Oslo.

Romagnoli, U. (1977: 376), 'Dalla Contrattazione Aziendale al Controllo degli Investimenti', in: *Il Mulino*.

Romagnoli, U. (1977: 1055), 'Per una Rilettura delle'Art. 2086', in: *Rivista Rim. Dir. Proc. Civile*.

Rosanvallon, P. (1988), *La Question Syndicale*. Calmann-Lévy: Paris.

Rubanza, Y. (1991), 'Popular Participation - Vehicle for Development'. Paper presented to the International Workshop: "Trade Unions, Democracy and Development". November-December, APADEP: Dar es Salaam/Mbeya.

Rus, V., A. Ishikawa and T. Woodhouse (eds.) (1982), *Employment and Participation. Industrial Democracy in Crisis*. Chuo University Press: Tokyo.

Rusell, R. and V. Rus (eds.) (1991), *International Handbook of Participation in Organisations, Volume II, Ownership and Participation*. Oxford University Press: Oxford.

Sabel, C.F. and M.J. Piore (1984), *The Second Industrial Divide*. Basic Books: New York.

Sandberg, Å. (1981), *Forskning for Forandring*. The Swedish Center for Working Life: Stockholm, (second edition 1985).

Sandberg, Å. (1982), From Satisfaction to Democratisation, (mimeo). The Swedish Center for Working Life: Stockholm.

Sandberg, Å. (1990), Union Responses to "New Management". Paper presented at the ISA XIIth World Congress of Sociology, Madrid.

Sandberg, Å. 'Wage earner consultants', in: G. Széll (ed.) (1992), *Concise Encyclopaedia of Participation and Co-Management*. de Gruyter: Berlin/New York.

Sandberg, Å. (ed.) (1979), *Computers Dividing Man and Work*. The Swedish Center for Working Life: Stockholm.

Sandberg, Å. (ed.) Enriching production. Volvo Uddevalla and Kalmar Plants: The end of the road to a European alternative to lean production? (forthcoming).

Sandberg, Å., G. Broms, A. Grip, J. Steen, L. Sundström and P. Ullmark (1992), *Technological Change and Codetermination in Sweden*. Philadelphia University Press: Philadelphia.

Sandberg, T. (1982), *Work Organisation and Autonomous Groups*. Liber Forlag: Stockholm.

Saturn-UAW Agreement (1985), Labor Trends: Farmington Hill/Mich.

Schuller, T. (1985), *Age and Capital: Employee Participation in the Management of Pension Schemes*. Gower Press: Farnborough.

Schuller, T. and S. Henderson (1980: 49-57), 'Worker Representation and the Articulation of Training Needs', in: *Industrial Relations Journal* 11(2).

Schuller, T. and D. Robertson (1983: 141-53), 'Convenors as Parents, Branches as Homes: influences on adult learning', in: *British Journal of the Sociology of Education* 4(2).

Sciarra, S. (1978), *Democrazia Politica e Democrazia Industriale*. De Donato: Bari.

Segrestin, D. (1992), *Sociologie de l'entreprise,* Armand Colin.

Seyrieix, H. (1984), *L'Entreprise du 3ème Type*. Seuil: Paris.

Shkaraton, O. et al. (eds.) (1990), *Self-Government and Social Protection in the Urban Settlement and at the Enterprise*. Institute of Sociology USSR Academy: Moscow.

Sisson, et al. (1992), The Structure of Capital in the European Community. Warwick Research Paper, n. 38.

Smith, P. (1974), *Worker Participation and Collective Bargaining in Europe*. Her Majesty's Stationary Office: London.

Smith, S.C. (1988: 45-58), 'On the Incidence of Profit and Equity Sharing', in: *Journal of Economic Behaviour and Organization*, Vol 9.

Snow, C.C. and J. Hansen-Bauer (1993), *Norvest Forum Evaluation Study Report*. The Norwegian Work Life Centre/The Work Research Institute: Oslo.

Sommerhof, G. (1981), 'The Abstract Characteristics of Living Systems', in: R.E. Emery (ed.), *Systems Thinking*. Penguin: Harmonsworth.

Stallaerts, R. (1988), 'The HBK System: a Belgian experience in profit-sharing', *Conference for the Economics of Self Management*, July, Vienna.

Standing, G. and D. Vaughan-Whitehead (1995), *Minimum Wages in Central and Eastern Europe: From protection to destitution.* Central European University Press: London Budapest.

Stendenbach, F.J. (1969), *Industrial Democracy. A Contemporary Need.* OECD: Paris.

Stichting van de Arbeid (1990), *Overwegingen en Aanbevelingen inzake Arbeidsverhoudingen en Vakbondswerk in de Onderneming.* 's-Gravenhage.

Stjernberg, T. and A. Philips (1989), The Swedish Case: dilemmas in democratic development - lessons about action research from 15 years at the Skandia Insurance Company. Paper presented at the Academy of Management Meeting, Washington D.C., 16th August 1989. Stockholm School of Economics: Stockholm.

Stoker, S.G.C. (1983: 15-17), 'Durham Miners and the University - an exercise in co-operation', in: *Labour Education* 52.

Strauss, G. (1982: 173-265), 'Workers' Participation in Management. An International Perspective', in: *Research in Organizational Behavior.*

Strauss, G. (1992: 889-899), 'The United States', in: G. Széll, (ed.), *Concise Encyclopaedia of Participation and Co-Management.* de Gruyter: Berlin/New York.

Streeck, W. (1984: 391-422), 'Co-determination: the fourth decade', in: B. Wilpert and A. Sorge (eds), *International Yearbook of Organizational Democracy.* Vol II. Wiley: Chichester.

Sundberg, E. (1991), 'The Powerstructure of Soviet Enterprises'. Preliminary paper. University of Sundsvall.

Susman, G.I. (1979), *Autonomy at Work. A Sociotechnical Analysis for Participative Management.* Praeger: New York.

Széll, G. (1988), 'Participation, Workers' Control and Self-Management' in: *Current Sociology,* 36 # 3/. Trend report and bibliography. Sage: London.

Széll, G. (1990: 17-20), 'In the Year 2000: Democratized and Humanized Work and Society.', in: *IDOC Internazionale,* vol. 21/6 'Envisioning the Possible', Nov.-Dec.

Széll, G. (1992), 'Cooperation between Trade Unions and Science in the Federal Republic of Germany'.

Széll, G. (1992: 173-199), 'The Environmental Crisis at the Turn of the Millenium', in: *Revue Internationale de Sociologie,* 1.

Széll, G. et al. (eds.) (1989), *The State, Trade Unions and Self-management.* de Gruyter: Berlin.

Széll, G. (ed.) (1992), *Concise Encyclopaedia of Participation and Co-Management.* de Gruyter: Berlin/New York.

Széll, G. (ed.) (1992), *Labour Relations in Transition in Eastern Europe.* de Gruyter (Studies in Organization 33): Berlin/New York.

Széll, G. and A. Ishikawa (1992: 37-46), 'Participation and Co-Management - The Japanese Participation Formula', in: Tüsiad (ed.), *Ulusal Katilim ve Uzlasma (Symposium on Participation and National Consensus)*. Ekim: Istanbul.

Széll, G. and L. Nicolaou-Smokoviti (eds.) (1994), *Participation, Organisational Effectiveness and Quality of Working-Life in the Year 2000*. Peter M. Lang: Zürich/New York.

Széll, G., H. Schlatermundt and U. Széll (eds.) (1993), *Arbeitsorientierte Wissenschaft und Forschung in den Neunziger Jahren in Europa - Labour Oriented Science and Research in Europe in the Nineties*. Secolo: Osnabrück.

Taylor, F.W. (1911), *Principles of Scientific Management*. Harper: New York.

Tchobanian, R. (1992: 37-127), Négociation Collective et Participation dans l'Entreprise en France: vers de nouveaux équilibres?, in: M. Ambrosini, *Participation et Modernisation de l'Entreprise en France*. Franco Angeli, Dcumenti Isvet: Milan.

TCO (Swedish Confederation of Professionnal Employees) (1993), *Förnya arbetslivet genom samverkan fack-forskare*, Stockholm.

The African Charter for Popular Participation in Development (1991), Arusha.

Thorsrud, E. (1981), 'The Changing Structure of Work Organization', in: Kanawaty (ed.), *Managing and Developing New Forms of Work Organization*. Management Development Series No. 16, ILO.

Thuderoz, C. (1993: 41-55), 'Mort ou Résurrection du Cowboy? Quelques considérations sur l'acteur, le modèle et le participatif', in: *CFDT-Aujourd'hui* No. 108. March, Paris.

Trades Union Congress (1968), *Training Shop Stewards*. TUC: London.

Treu, T. (1983: 385), 'L'Accordo del 22 Gennaio: implicazioni e aspetti giuridico-istituzionali', in: *CESOS, Le Relazioni Sindicali in Italia*, Rapporto 1982/83. Lavoro: Rome.

Treu, T. (1986: 395), 'Le Relazioni Industriali nell'Impresa: il protocollo iri', in: *Rivista Italiana di Diritto del Lavoro*.

Treu, T., 'Gruppi di Imprese e Relazioni Industriali: tendenze Europee', in: *Giornale di Diritto del Lavoro e di Relazioni Industriali*, 1988: 641.

Treu, T., 'Cogestione e Participazione', in: *Giornale di Diritto del Lavoro e di Relazioni Industriali*, 1989: 397.

Treu, T., 'Informazione, Consultazione, Partecipazione. Prospettive Comunitaria e Realta Italiana', in: *Quaderni di Diritto del Lavoro e delle Relazioni Industriali*, No. 10. 1991: 57.

Treu, T., 'La Democrazia Economica Tra Associazione e Rappresentanza', in: *Il Progetto*, No. 75/76. 1993: 63.

Treu, T. (ed.), *Participation in Public Policy-Making, the Role of Trade Unions and Employers Associations*. Berlin/New-York, De Gruyter, 1992.

Treu, T. and S. Begrelli, *I Diritti di Informazione nelle'Impresa*. Bologna, Il Mulino, 1985.

Trigilia, C. (1985: 181), La Negolazione Localistica: Economia e politica nelle aree di piccola impresa, in: *Stato e Mercato*, No. 14.

Trist, E.L. (1973), 'A Socio-Technical Critique of Scientific Management', in: D.O. Edge and J.N. Wolfe (eds.), *The Meaning of Control: essays in social aspects of science and technology*. Tavistock: London.

Trist, E.L. and K. Bamforth (1951), 'Some Social and Psychological Consequences of the Longwall Method of Coal-Getting', in: *Human Relations* 4.

Trist, E.L., G. Higgin, H. Murray, and A.B. Pollock (1963), *Organizational Choice: capabilities of groups at the coal face under changing technologies*. Tavistock: London.

United Nations Educational, Scientific and Cultural Organisation (1984: 196-402), 'Industrial Democracy: participation, labour relations and motivation', in: *International Social Science Journal* 36.

Uvalic, M. (1991), The PEPPER Report - Promotion of Employee Participation in Profits and Enterprise Results in the Member States of the European Community. Report for the Commission of the European Communities, in: *Europe Sociale*, Supplement No. 3/91, CCE, DGV: Brussels.

Vanek, J. (1970), *The General Thoery of Labor-Managed Market Economics*. Cornell University Press: Ithaca/New York.

Vanek, J. (1971), *The Participatory Economy. An Evolutionary Hypothesis and a Strategy for Development*. Cornell University Press: Ithaca/New York.

Vanek, J., (ed.) (1975), *Self-Management: economic liberation of man*. Penguin.

Vaughan-Whitehead, D. (1992), *Intéressement, Participation, Actionnariat - Impacts Economiques dans l'Entreprise*, Editions Economica: Paris.

Vaughan-Whitehead, D. (1992), 'Workers' Financial Participation: An east-west comparative perspective' Report submitted to an international symposium in Moscow.

Vaughan-Whitehead, D. (1995), 'Workers' Financial Participation: East-West experiences'. *Labour Management Series*, No. 50, ILO: Geneva.

Vetter, H.O. (ed.) (1975), *Vom Sozialistengesetz zur Mitbestimmung*. Bund: Köln.

Verstegen, R. and J.H..H. Andriessen (1987), Medezeggenschap in Kleine Ondernemingen, Tilburg.

Vilrokx, J. (1993: 205-214), 'Basic Income, Citizenship and Solidarity: towards a dynamic for social renewal', in: H. Coenen and P. Leisink (eds.), *Work and Citizenship in the New Europe*. Edward Elgar: Aldershot.

Vilrokx, J., R. Boogaerts and J. van Leemput (1991: 73-104), 'Sociale Verandering en Conflictgedrag in de Welzijns- en Gezondheidssector', in: P. Gevers (red.), *Collectieve Arbeidsverhoudingen in de Gezondheids- en Welzijnszorg*. Die Keure: Brugge.

Vilrokx, J. and J. van Leemput (1992: 357-392), 'Belgium: a new stability in industrial relations? in: R. Hyman and A. Ferner (eds.), *Industrial Relations in the New Europe*. Basil Blackwell: Oxford.

Visser, J. (1987), *In Search of Inclusive Unionism*. Dissertation, Universiteit van Amsterdam: Amsterdam.

Visser, J. (1992), 'The Netherlands: the end of an era and the end of a system', in: A. Ferner and R. Hyman (eds), *Industrial Relations in the New Europe*. Oxford.

Vos, P.J. (1986), 'Vakbond in een Doe-Het-Zelf Samenleving', in: *Arbeidsmarkt op Drift*. FNV: Amsterdam.

Vulliamy, D. et al (1992), *Trade Unions and Collaborative Research with Universities*.

Wadhwani, S. (1988), 'Profit-Sharing as a Cure for Unemployment: some doubts', in: *International Journal of Industrial Organization*, vol. 6, pp. 59-68, also published as discussion paper no. 86/253, Centre for labour Economics, L.S.E.

Wagenmans, W. (1990), Adjustment, Human-Centered Development and the Role of Trade Unions. Paper, FNV: Amsterdam.

Walton, R.E. and M.E. Gaffney (1991), 'Research, Action and Participation: the merchant shipping case', in: W.F. Whyte, (ed.), *Participatory Action Research*. Sage: Newbury Park.

Webb, S. and B. Webb (1897), *Industrial Democracy Vol. 2*. Longmans, Green and Co.: London.

Weitzman, M.L. (1984), *The Share Economy*. Harvard University Press: Cambridge.

Weitzman, M.L. and D.L. Kruse (1990: 95-139), 'Profit-Sharing and Productivity', in: A.S. Blinder (ed.), *Paying for Productivity - a look at the evidence*, Brookings Institution: Washington D.C.

Williams, J.E. (1954: 113-24), 'An Experiment in Trade Union Education', in: *Adult Education* 27(2).

Wittgenstein, L. (1953), *Philosophical Investigations*. Blackwell: London.

Womack, J.P., D.T. Janes and D. Roos (1990), *The Machine that Changed the World*. Ranson Associates: New York.

Woodworth, W., C. Meek and W.F. Whyte (eds.) (1985), *Industrial Democracy. Strategies for Community Revitalization*. Sage: London & Beverly Hills.

Workers' Educational Association (1953), *Trade Union Education*, A Report from a Working Party set up by the WEA [and chaired by Arthur Creech Jones]. WEA: London.

Workers' Participation Development Center (1981 -1989), Annual Reports. University of Malta: Msida.

WSI-Projektgruppe (1981), 'Mitbestimmung in Unternehmen und Betrieb', in: *Handbuch der Mitbestimmung*. Bund-Verlag: Köln.

Zammit, E.L. (1984), *A Colonial Inheritance - Maltese perceptions of work, power and class structure with reference to the labour movement*. Malta University Press: Msida.

Zammit, E.L. (1989), *Workers' Participation in Malta: options for future policy*. Workers' Participation Development Center and Ministry for Social Policy: Malta.

Zammit, E.L., and G. Baldacchino (1988), Workers on the Board - A sociological comment on recent developments in workers' participation in Malta. Paper presented at the Fifth International Conference on Economics of Self-Management. July, Vienna, Austria.

Zoll, R. (1981), *Partizipation oder Delegation. Gewerkschaftliche Betriebspolitik in Italien und in der BRD*. Frankfurt/M.

Zwerdling, D. (1980), *Workplace Democracy. A Guide to Workplace Ownership, Participation and Self-management Experiments in the United States and Europe*. Harper Colophon Books: New York.

This bibliography was prepared by Raoul Galarraga, Institute of Social Studies, APADEP, The Hague.